European Yearbook of International Economic Law

EYIEL Monographs - Studies in European and International Economic Law

Volume 22

EYIEL Monographs is a subseries of the European Yearbook of International Economic Law (EYIEL). It contains scholarly works in the fields of European and international economic law, in particular WTO law, international investment law, international monetary law, law of regional economic integration, external trade law of the EU and EU internal market law. The series does not include edited volumes. EYIEL Monographs are peer-reviewed by the series editors and external reviewers.

More information about this series at https://link.springer.com/bookseries/8165

Adilbek Tussupov

Corruption and Fraud in Investment Arbitration

Procedural and Substantive Challenges

Springer

Adilbek Tussupov
Frankfurt am Main, Hessen, Germany

ISSN 2364-8392 ISSN 2364-8406 (electronic)
European Yearbook of International Economic Law
ISSN 2524-6658 ISSN 2524-6666 (electronic)
EYIEL Monographs - Studies in European and International Economic Law
ISBN 978-3-030-90605-4 ISBN 978-3-030-90606-1 (eBook)
https://doi.org/10.1007/978-3-030-90606-1

This Springer imprint is published by the registered company Springer Nature Switzerland AG.
The registered company address is: Gewerbestrasse 11, 6330 Cham, Switzerland

In memory of my grandfather, Mutallap Tussupov…

Preface

The issue of corruption and fraud in investor-state disputes has become one of the hottest topics of discussions in the international legal community. This is not surprising as the terms "corruption" and "fraud" are natural triggers of attention, in particular when speaking of multi-million or multi-billion investment scandals. The centrepieces of this discussion are questions that can be framed *inter alia* in the following way:

- Is a State liable for violating its international obligations vis-à-vis an investment that was procured through fraud or corruption?
- Does a State have international obligations vis-à-vis such investments at all?
- How does one prove corruption and fraud in international arbitration?

An attempt to find answers to the above questions and to understand the current status quo of the issues around this topic, as well as to identify possible solutions, has been made in this monograph, which is now presented to you. The amount of case law and literature analysed in the frames of this book is indicative of the fact that the answers to the above listed questions are not entirely straightforward or clearly obvious. The book presents various issues that are being met in investment arbitration when allegations or indicators of corruption and fraud arise. The book also suggests possible solutions to the identified issues.

The monograph was originally submitted as a doctoral dissertation to the Faculty of Law of the University of Saarland under the supervision of Prof. Dr. Marc Bungenberg. Prof. Bungenberg did not only supervise my research, but indeed guided me throughout the whole process. Thank you for your invaluable support and leadership, *Doktorvater*! I am honoured to have had the opportunity to work with you.

Completing this work would also not have been possible without the continued encouragement of my colleagues. I am particularly grateful to Dr. Patricia Nacimiento for motivating, enabling and pushing me towards finishing this monograph. I am truly thankful to Dr. Gani Bitenov, who has become my role model in everything I can think of. Special thanks to Dr. Alessandro Covi and Dr. Bajar

Scharaw for being always available to enter into complex legal discussions over coffee in our kitchen on the 12th. One can only dream of working in such a great team.

I am forever grateful to the person who introduced me to the world of international law—Prof. Dr. Miras Daulenov. Thank you, Professor, for your kind heart and the hard work that you put in educating thousands of Kazakh students.

Many thanks to all of my other colleagues and mentors, who influenced me in many ways in my academic and professional paths: Almat Zhamiyev, Asset Seitkazin, Azamat Kaldybekov, Amankali Sagatov, Daniya Arinova, Prof. Talgat Narikbayev, Prof. Sergey Pen, Prof. Yevgeniya Oralova, Prof. Dr. Abay Abylaiuly, Matthew Kirtland and many others.

Finally and most importantly, I am grateful to my family. My sincerest and foremost appreciation goes to the love of my life, Mirgul, without whom this work would simply not exist. Thank you for being there for me, honey! I am thankful to my mom, Gulbakhyt, for always trusting in me. Last but not least, I am thankful to the most beautiful creatures in my life, my babies, Ayala and Arlan. My angels, you help me understand purpose in everything I do.

Frankfurt am Main, Germany Adilbek Tussupov

Contents

Abbreviations

AED	United Arab Emirates dirham
BIT	Bilateral Investment Treaty
ECT	Energy Charter Treaty
EU	European Union
EUR	Euro
FDI	Foreign Direct Investment
IBA	International Bar Association
ICC	International Chamber of Commerce
ICJ	International Court of Justice
ICSID	International Centre of Settlement of Investment Disputes
IIL	International Investment Law
ISDS	Investor-State Dispute Settlement
LCIA	London Court of International Arbitration
MIC	Multilateral Investment Court
MIT	Multilateral Investment Treaty
NAFTA	North American Free Trade Agreement
OECD	Organisation for Economic Co-operation and Development
PCA	Permanent Court of Arbitration
PCIJ	Permanent Court of International Justice
QC	Queen's Counsel
SCC	Stockholm Chamber of Commerce
UK	United Kingdom
UN	United Nations
UNCAC	United Nations Convention Against Corruption
UNCITRAL	United Nations Commission on International Trade Law
UNCLOS	United Nations Convention on the Law of the Sea
UNDP	United Nations Development Program
US/USA	United States of America
USD	United States Dollar

Chapter 1
Introduction

The World is undergoing constant integration in all spheres of people's lives and States' interactions. A high degree of inter-connection has also taken place in international business community. Businesses are no longer restricted to national borders and they have promising opportunities all around the globe, which is the main reason why foreign direct investments ("**FDIs**") have been on the rise during the last decades.

Together with the growth of the FDIs, it has become necessary for investors and States of their origin to ensure that their investments would not be expropriated or discriminated in the territories of host States. This is an immediate background for the conclusion of various bilateral and multilateral international agreements between States for protection and promotion of foreign investments, which gave rise to the system of law that is now known as International Investment Law.

At the same time and in connection with significant cross border economic developments, arbitration has become a preferred dispute settlement mean for individuals, leading corporations and States. While there is an established rule in public international law providing that under the principle of sovereign equality, a State cannot normally be held responsible by a non-State party, the IIL has evolved in structuring its own dispute settlement mechanism where a foreign investor is entitled to bring a dispute against a sovereign to an international arbitral tribunal for breaches of State's obligations under international investment treaties. This is what is now called International Investment Arbitration or the Investor-State Dispute Settlement mechanism ("**ISDS**"). Although, from the public international law perspective, ISDS might appear to be unconventional, its existence is entirely within the principle of freedom of choice in methods of dispute settlement that was consistently applied by the International Court of Justice ("**ICJ**").[1]

[1] Armed Activities on the Territory of the Congo (Congo v. Rwanda), Jurisdiction of the Court and Admissibility of the Application, 3 February 2006, ICJ Reports 2006, paras. 65–68; Fisheries

A. Tussupov, *Corruption and Fraud in Investment Arbitration*, EYIEL Monographs - Studies in European and International Economic Law 22,
https://doi.org/10.1007/978-3-030-90606-1_1

ISDS is one of several different forms of arbitration. Despite possible differences of various forms of arbitration, they are all based on the same concept and the same idea. It is always the underlining parties' will to submit their disputes to arbitration, and it is always non-public (private) tribunals who decide on the parties' disputes. It is designed that a decision is final and binding upon the parties. And yet again, it is final and binding because parties themselves have agreed that it should be final and legally binding. States usually express their consent through intergovernmental investment treaties. However, lately more and more cases arise under national investment laws and investment codes, in which States entitle foreign investors to initiate investment arbitration against them.[2] Investors' consent is expressed by filling a request for conciliation or arbitration. In some cases, both a State and an investor agree to submit their dispute to international arbitration per dispute resolution clause in an investment contract.[3]

The central idea behind international investment arbitration is that its main objective is to ensure that foreign investments and investors are treated in a proper manner and in accordance with the applicable sources of international investment law, and that States comply with their international obligations towards foreign investors and investments. The description of this central idea is well summarised in the following statement:

> A limited set of jurisdictional and procedural obstacles should allow tribunals to deal with the real (substantive) issues of investment law, i.e. whether and to what extent the standards of investment protection enshrined in bilateral investment treaties (BITs) and investment chapters of international investment agreements (IIAs) have been complied with or not. This would also serve *the primary purpose* of investment arbitration *as protection of foreign investments*.[4]

Some authors are of the opinion that access to an impartial fora in investment treaty arbitration is similarly essential as it is in human rights protection mechanisms, as it ensures realisation of the substantive legal obligations of sovereigns.[5]

One of the goals of this work is to discuss that when pursuing to protect a certain category of persons (in this case—investors with their investments), tribunals are not to forget that there are overriding principles and institutes that are to be closely observed and respected. These are, for instance, the rule of law, justice and good faith.

Jurisdiction (Spain v. Canada), Decision on Preliminary Objection, ICJ Reports 1998, para. 55. *See also,* Waibel (2014), p. 4.

[2]On investment laws, *see,* Paulsson (1995), pp. 232–256; On investment codes, *see* Burgstaller and Waibel (2012).

[3]For instance, Holiday Inns S.A. and others v. Morocco, ICSID Case No ARB/72/1 (for a detailed description of this case, *see,* Lalive (1981), pp. 123–162); World Duty Free Company v. Kenya, ICSID Case No. ARB/00/7; RSM Production Corporation v. Grenada, ICSID Case No. ARB/05/14.

[4]Reinisch (2013), p. 3 [emphasis added].

[5]Schill (2010), pp. 29–50.

From the case law in the last decade, it has become evident that the line between the interests of foreign investors and these overriding principles is particularly blurred in cases where a dispute involves allegations of illicit conduct, such as fraud and corruption. In such situations, arbitral tribunals are met with their own burden to balance the discussed objective of international investment law to protect foreign investments and the raised principles of justice, rule of law and good faith. The difficulty with such cases may be explained with the fact that arbitration in general, as it appears, was not really designed to deliver justice over claims of close-to-criminal nature. As described by a number of scholars, arbitration in its early forms was a relatively informal process of dispute settlement. A classic scholarly example is a dispute between two merchants over a fair price of the good, which they submit to a third merchant, who is well-known and trusted and whose decision both merchants can agree to abide.[6]

In other words, arbitration was to deliver the so-called "private justice". However, a person, in its nature, does not always operate within the boundaries of good faith conduct. To put differently, private or any other matters of the lives of persons do not exclude possible illicit sides and motives. As a result, arbitration may also be shadowed with matters that involve illicit, illegal or even criminal elements that may not only affect parties in dispute but also greater public and moral principles. Therefore, matters that are tainted by illicit elements are at times expected to be addressed by arbitral tribunals in enforceable arbitral awards. This is reflected in the increasing number of cases involving allegations of illegality.[7]

For any legal practitioner (and perhaps indeed for any person) it might be self-explanatory that corruption and fraud are two evils that are being condemned by most (if not all) national and international legal systems. However, investment disputes are usually centred on States' obligations under international investment treaties, which, with the exception of a few,[8] do not normally include any

[6]Blackaby et al. (2015), p. 4; Mustill (2008), p. 1; Paulsson (2013), p. 1.

[7]Under the author's count, more than fifty investment disputes involved examination of "illegality" claims in investment arbitration and almost the same number included claims on fraud, corruption and bribery.

[8]It is to be noted that some modern BITs do include explicit anti-corruption obligations. For instance, *see,* Article 17 of the Morocco-Nigeria BIT: "1) Each Contracting Party shall ensure that measures and efforts are undertaken to prevent and combat corruption regarding matters covered by this Agreement in accordance with its laws and regulations. 2) Investors and their Investments shall not, prior to the establishment of an Investment or afterwards, offer, promise or give any undue pecuniary or other advantage, whether directly or through intermediaries, to a public official of the Host State, or a member of an official's family or business associate or other person in close proximity to an official, for that official or for a third party, in order that the official or third party act or refrain from acting in relation to the performance of official duties, in order to achieve any favour in relation to a proposed investment or any licences, permits, contracts or other rights in relations to an investment. 3) Investors and their Investments shall not be complicit in any act described in Paragraph 1 above, including incitement, aiding and abetting, and conspiracy to commit or authorization of such acts. 4) A breach of this article by an investor or an investment is deemed to constitute a breach of the domestic law of the Host State Party concerning the establishment and operation of an investment. 5) The States Parties to this Agreement, consistent

anti-corruption or anti-fraud obligations in their explicit forms. In other words, when an international investment tribunal hears corruption and fraud claims, there are several procedural as well as substantive matters that it must consider. These are, for instance, (i) whether the allegations of illicit misconduct are to be dealt with at the standpoint of jurisdiction or merits of the case; (ii) who bears the burden of proof and whether it can be shifted or shared; (iii) what standard of proof should be applied; (iv) if corruption and fraud are proven, what it ultimately means for parties and for the tribunal.

In addressing the above questions, the textbook *inter alia* displays the decision making process of various international arbitral tribunals' in cases where allegations of corruption and fraud have been raised. A reader will review the process through the prism of doctrinal opinion and decisions of national and other international tribunals. Considering this analysis, it will be determined whether arbitral tribunals are, in fact, capable of dealing with corruption and fraud allegations in the setting of ISDS. Due regard will be provided to the range of possible procedural and substantive tools that arbitral tribunals have for examining and analysing the illegality allegations and whether these tools are sufficient for such purposes. More importantly, this textbook will attempt to identify any possible challenges and open questions that currently exist for investment tribunals in their "combat" with corruption and fraud. As was mentioned at the outset, the general focus shall be in observing whether arbitral tribunals are efficiently balancing the interests of parties with the rule of law and other essential legal principles.

Corruption and fraud are not the topics that have been chosen spontaneously. These notions have become central subjects of discussion in the international arbitration circles. This is, perhaps, due to two main reasons: (i) both notions are being increasingly mentioned by investment tribunals in their latest decisions, and (ii) both notions are being highly condemned at national and international levels, including via international conventions and guidelines. As was noted by the former United Nations Secretary-General *Mr. Kofi Annan*, corruption "undermines democracy and the rule of law, leads to violations of human rights, distorts markets, erodes the quality of life and allows organized crime, terrorism and other threats to human security to flourish."[9]

As will be noticed, the discussion of corruption and fraud in the framework of international arbitration is not new and has been out in legal literature and arbitral awards for more than half a century. However, as will also be observed, there is still

---

with their applicable law, shall prosecute and where convicted penalize persons that have breached the applicable law implementing this obligation." *See also,* Article 16 of the Cooperation and Facilitation Investment Agreement between the Federative Republic of Brazil and the Republic of Suriname dated 2 May 2018, Article 15 of the Agreement between the Federative Republic of Brazil and the Federal Democratic Republic of Ethiopia on Investment Cooperation and Facilitation dated 11 April 2018, Article 8.24 of the Free Trade Agreement between Argentina and Chile.

[9] Anan, K. (2004), Foreword to the United Nations Convention against Corruption, available at https://www.unodc.org/ropan/en/AntiCorruptionARAC/unodc-and-corruption.html.

no universal consensus among arbitral tribunals and various authors on single uniformed approach to corruption and fraud in ISDS.

In the ICC case No 1110, arbitrated by *Judge Lagergen,* it was found that "a case as this, involving such gross violation of good morals and international public policy, can have no countenance in any court…nor in any arbitral tribunal".[10] In fact, *Judge Lagergen* found that parties "who ally themselves in an enterprise of the present nature must realise that they have forfeited any right to ask for the assistance of the machinery of justice (national courts or arbitral tribunals) in settling their disputes".[11] The beauty of this case is that *Judge Lagergen* decided on the illicit misconduct on his own initiative by witnessing several of the so-called *red flags* of corruption raised during the arbitration. Again, as will be seen in this monograph, despite its application in international arbitration in 1963 and despite its increasing use in anti-trust legislation in various jurisdictions,[12] the notion of *red flags* is still somewhat controversial and there has been a lot of debate over *Judge Lagergen's* approach. In order to better understand what *red flags* are, one could simply define them as "warning signs of possible illicit activity".[13] In other words, various forms of indicia of possible corruption, fraud, money laundering or any other illicit conduct can be termed as *red flags.*[14]

It is reported that the term *red flags,* as well as the particular *red flags* of corruption, originate with the U.S. Foreign Corrupt Practices Act.[15] The monograph is aimed at providing a deeper insight on the meaning of *red flags* in international arbitration. The focus is indeed to see whether *red flags* of corruption and fraud already have (or must have) a special place in international *investment* arbitration due to the existence of public/administrative elements in this type of international dispute settlement mechanism, which will be discussed further in Parts II and III.

As *red flags* do not necessarily constitute actual evidence of illicit activity, but usually only indicate its possible presence, there is an ongoing debate whether it is proper and/or fair to accord evidentiary weight to them.[16] In other words, some may

---

[10]ICC Case No 1110 between Mr. [X] and Company [A], Yearbook Commercial Arbitration XXI (1996), Award, para. 23.

[11]*Id.* Of note, *Kukarni* believes that "[a] paper on corruption in international arbitration is said to be incomplete without making a reference to the very famous and most discussed arbitration award rendered by Judge Gunner Lagergren in 1963 in an ICC Case No. 1110." Kulkarni (2013), p. 2.

[12]*See e.g.,* U.S. Department of Justice, Antitrust Division, Federal Trade Commission (2016), Antitrust Guidance for Human Resource Professionals, Antitrust Red Flags for Employment Practices, available at https://www.justice.gov/atr/file/903511/download.

[13]Low (2019).

[14]Llamzon (2014), para. 9.11.

[15]*See*, Criminal Division of the U.S. Department of Justice and the Enforcement Division of the U.S. Securities and Exchange Commission (2012), A Resource Guide to the U.S. Foreign Corrupt Practices Act, available at https://www.justice.gov/sites/default/files/criminal-fraud/legacy/2015/01/16/guide.pdf, p. 22.

[16]*See*, Gore, N. and Tuninetty, A. (2020), Gazprombank v. Belarus: the value of requiring direct evidence to support illegality allegations, in Global Arbitration Review, available at https://

find it unfair and improper to draw adverse inferences from simple indicators (or *red flags*) or to make a final decision on their basis.

As will be elaborated in detail in this work, ISDS has already formed certain practice in some areas when resolving disputes that involve allegations of illicit acts. The exercise that is to be undertaken in this regard is to evaluate whether the current approach, while being formally correct and legal, lacks the fundamentality of law, i.e. whether the approach serves the purposes of law and protects international "public" interests. It is of great importance for international arbitration, let alone *investment* arbitration, as a dispute settlement mean to be able to address and defeat attempts of being tainted by corrupt and fraudulent acts, so as not to become a safe harbour for the proceeds of crime.[17] Otherwise, there is a risk that arbitration will "no longer be useful for the worldwide business community", and thus will forfeit its position as a leading international dispute settlement mechanism.[18]

Finally, based on the undertaken research and analysis, this textbook is destined to provide several proposals in addressing current challenges and loopholes of the ISDS system in the examination of corruption and fraud allegations.

For these purposes, this textbook is structured in the following way.

The First Part (**I**) is to lay down the current legal framework in international investment arbitration. It shall put the research questions into the context of current international investment arbitration practice and theory. The purpose of the First Part is to provide a basis for the questions that will be analysed in the frames of the case law analysis and outstanding issues/challenges in the subsequent two parts. For this reason, it is to be determined from the outset (i) what is fraud and corruption? (ii) what is "legality" under international investment law? (iii) what are the prescribed procedural rules for determination of law and proof?

The Second Part (**II**) will display highlights of a number of representative decisions of investment tribunals in cases where claims of corruption and/or fraud were put forward. As a result, it is expected to have a reflection of the chronological development of current approach of investment tribunals to the issues of illegality (or indeed its absence). Through the imperative analysis of case law and legal doctrine, Part II of the textbook shall conclude with a chapter that will systematise the approach on particular scopes of questions related to the examination of the

---

globalarbitrationreview.com/article/1228561/gazprombank-v-belarus-the-value-of-requiring-direct-evidence-to-support-illegality-allegations.

[17]When talking of international commercial arbitrations, some authors believe that the trend has already been set on "zero tolerance" towards corruption. *See*, Wolfensohn, J.D. (2005), The Right Wheel: An Agenda for Comprehensive Development, in Voice for the World's Poor: Selected Speeches and Writings of World Bank President James D. Wolfensohn, pp. 138–140; and Malik, D. and Kamat, G. (2018), Corruption in International Commercial Arbitration: Arbitrability, Admissibility & Adjudication, in The Arbitration Brief, December 2018, available at https://paperity.org/p/185990736/corruption-in-international-commercial-arbitration-arbitrability-admissibility, p. 2.

[18]Clouet, L.M. (2018), Arbitrating under the table: the effect of allegations of corruption in relation to the jurisdiction of the arbitral tribunal and the enforcement of foreign arbitral awards, available at https://nyu.academia.edu/LuisMar%C3%ADaClouet.

allegations of fraud and corruption in investment arbitration (e.g. burden and standard of proof, *red flags*, etc.).

The Final Part (**III**) will discuss possible theoretical and practical solutions that may be necessary to extend investment tribunals' ability to address illicit and bad faith actions. This will include concrete suggestions with practical and theoretical analysis and review.

In addition to the above, the textbook is designed to touch upon more general and/or open questions that arise when speaking of corruption and fraud in ISDS cases. One of such questions is the possibility of effecting negative consequences for States in situations of bribery of public officials and the associated possible reform of the international investment arbitration, in particular the suggested introduction of a Multilateral Investment Court.[19]

References

Blackaby N, Partasides C, Redfern A, Hunter M (2015) Redfern and Hunter on international arbitration, 6th edn. Oxford University Press, p 4

Bungenberg M, Reinisch A (2019) From bilateral arbitral tribunals and investment courts to a multilateral investment court - options regarding the institutionalization of investor-state dispute settlement, 2nd edn. Springer Open, available at https://link.springer.com/book/10.1007/978-3-662-59732-3

Burgstaller M, Waibel M (2012) Investment codes. In: Wolfrum R (ed) Max Planck encyclopedia of public international law. Oxford University Press, available at http://opil.ouplaw.com/view/10.1093/law:epil/9780199231690/law-9780199231690-e1532?rskey=bq9HuE&result=2&prd=EPIL

Kaufmann-Kohler G, Potestà M (2017) The composition of a multilateral investment court and of an appeal mechanism for investment awards CIDS supplemental report. Geneva Center for International Dispute Settlement, available at https://www.uncitral.org/pdf/english/workinggroups/wg_3/CIDS_Supplemental_Report.pdf

Kulkarni SA (2013) Enforcing anti-corruption measures through international investment arbitration. Transnatl Dispute Manag 3, available at www.transnational-dispute-management.com/article.asp?key=1957, p 2

Lalive P (1981) The first "world bank" arbitration (Holiday Inns v. Morocco) – some legal problems. Br Yearb Int Law 51:123–162

Llamzon A (2014) Corruption in international investment arbitration. Oxford University Press

Low L (2019) Dealing with allegations of corruption in international arbitration. Am J Int Law Unbound 113

Mustill BM (2008) The history of international commercial arbitration: a sketch. In: Newman, Hill (eds) The leading arbitrators' guide to international arbitration, 2nd edn. Juris Net, p 1

Paulsson J (1995) Arbitration without privity. ICSID Rev – Foreign Invest Law J 10:232–256

[19]For the discussion of a possible introduction of Multilateral Investment Court, *see* Bungenberg and Reinisch (2019) and Kaufmann-Kohler and Potestà (2017).

Paulsson J (2013) The idea of arbitration. Oxford University Press, p 1
Reinisch A (2013) The scope of investor-state dispute settlement in international investment agreements. Asia Pac Law Rev 21:3
Schill S (2010) Private enforcement of international investment law: why we need investor standing in BIT dispute settlement. In: Waibel M et al (eds) The backlash against investment arbitration: perceptions and reality. Kluwer Law International, pp 29–50
Waibel M (2014) Investment arbitration: jurisdiction and admissibility, Legal Studies Research Paper Series, Paper No 9/2014. University of Cambridge, p 4

Part I
Legal Framework

Before going into the analysis of the actual issues and before attempting to see how various arbitral tribunals and scholars tend to deal with fraud and corruption in the frames of international investment arbitration, it is of importance to properly understand the existing legal framework for examination of parties' cases in the ISDS setting. This is important *inter alia* for the identification of possible open questions within the current legal framework and for their further research in the subsequent sections (*see,* case law analysis in Part II and search for solutions in Part III).

At the very outset, while the terms "fraud" and "corruption" are, without doubt, well-known to the readers of this monograph, it is, nevertheless, important to understand what exactly "fraud" and "corruption" mean in the context of international and national law and how they are to be defined for the purposes of the current topic.

Additionally, in this part, certain elements of the existing legal framework that should *inter alia* be useful for disputes involving fraud and corruption in international arbitration are to be analysed, including the following:

- "Legality requirement" for protected investments;
- Determination of applicable law;
- Standard of proof;
- Burden of proof;
- Admissible evidence.

The above questions are analysed in the imperative manner, including analysis of various investment treaties, customary international law norms, principles of law, decisions of international tribunals and legal doctrine.

Chapter 2
Fraud and Corruption

The notions of "fraud" and "corruption" tend to catch a lot of public attention and both trigger serious consequences that are prescribed by national laws of any State whenever they are committed. The familiarity with these notions, their negative connotation and mandatory legal sanction over them in any legal system display that there is a general consensus that both fraud and corruption are to be regarded as serious crimes.

Corruption and fraud as forms of crime or illicit misconduct tend to regularly appear in all jurisdictions and legal systems, including international law. Condemnation of corruption and fraud "is firmly viewed as an aspect of public policy – indeed "transnational public policy" – justifying a denial of enforcement" of an arbitral award that is tainted by such forms of illicit misconduct.[1]

The effects of corruption and fraud on the recognition and enforceability of an award, as was mentioned above by *Bermann,* have also been confirmed by national courts. For instance, the High Court of the Republic of Singapore in its judgement of January 2020 stated the following:

> It was understood that the term "public policy", which was used in the 1958 New York Convention and many other treaties, covered fundamental principles of law and justice in substantive as well as procedural respects. Thus, instances such as corruption, bribery or fraud and similar serious cases would constitute a ground for setting aside.[2]

[1] Bermann, G.A. (2015), Expert Opinion (Part B) dated 20 October 2015, Yukos Universal Limited (Isle of Man) v. The Russian Federation, UNCITRAL, PCA Case No. AA 227: para. 139, available at https://www.italaw.com/sites/default/files/case-documents/italaw4443_1.pdf.

[2] Judgement of the High Court of the Republic of Singapore dated 3 January 2020 in the case between Bloomberry Resorts and Hotels Inc. and Sureste Properties, Inc against Global Gaming Philippines LLC and GGAM Netherlands B.V. with references to PT Asuransi, citing the Commission Report (A/40/17), at para 297. *See also*, the Award in Westacre Investments Inc. v. Jugoimport-SDRP Holdings Co. Ltd and Beogradska Banka, ICC Case No. 7047, para. 36.

A. Tussupov, *Corruption and Fraud in Investment Arbitration*, EYIEL Monographs - Studies in European and International Economic Law 22,
https://doi.org/10.1007/978-3-030-90606-1_2

Fox has opined that practically anyone who is engaged in international business transactions would recognize that corruption and bribery are global problems that "impede performance of commercial agreements".[3]

Besides being criminalised by practically all national legal systems, corruption and fraud are also being condemned at the international level. There is a growing number of international conventions directed at the issues related to fighting fraud, bribery and corruption that are being concluded either at the UN level or regionally. Below, you shall find a brief overview on the way "fraud" and "corruption" are being defined and dealt with in international law and for the purposes of this textbook.

2.1 Fraud

There appears to be no uniform and concrete definition of "fraud" in international legal documents adopted by States. For instance, the Secretariat of the United Nations Commission on International Trade Law ("**UNCITRAL**") explicitly stated that it did not find it appropriate to determine a strict definition of fraud, partly due to the fact that it would not allow sufficient flexibility in determining whether certain acts are fraudulent.[4] However, the UNCITRAL Secretariat provided a descriptive definition that outlines the main elements of commercial fraud with the following indicators:

(1) There is an element of deceit or of providing inaccurate, incomplete or misleading information;
(2) Reliance on the deceit or the information provided or omitted induces the target of the fraud to part with some valuable thing that belongs to the target or to surrender a legal right;
(3) There is a serious economic dimension and scale to the fraud;
(4) The fraud uses or misuses and compromises or distorts commercial systems and their legitimate instruments, potentially creating an international impact; and
(5) There is a resultant loss of value.[5]

It is evident that, at times, the term "fraud" is used inter-changeably with the term "bribery" in the context of discussions around the OECD Convention on Combating Bribery of Foreign Public Officials in International Business Transactions. It is also evident that "bribery" and "fraud" are sometimes used inter-changeably by arbitral

[3]Fox (2009), p. 487, referred in Malik, D. and Kamat, G. (2018), Corruption in International Commercial Arbitration: Arbitrability, Admissibility & Adjudication, in The Arbitration Brief, December 2018, available at https://paperity.org/p/185990736/corruption-in-international-commer cial-arbitration-arbitrability-admissibility.

[4]Recognizing and Preventing Commercial Fraud, Indicators of Commercial Fraud (2013), UNCITRAL Secretariat, United Nations. Available at https://www.uncitral.org/pdf/english/texts/fraud/Recognizing-and-preventing-commercial-fraud-e.pdf.

[5]*Id.*

tribunals and legal commentators, especially by those coming from a common law background.[6]

In continental legal systems the terms "fraud", "corruption" or "bribery" are usually defined differently as they often involve different *actus reus*. Irrespective of the way the crimes are formally categorized and treated in different legal systems, it is quite clear that they have serious negative effect on public interests and morals.

The definition of the term "fraud" is also not uniformed throughout various national legal systems. As mentioned above, this is, in particular, true when comparing definitions provided in common and continental legal systems. From reviewing legislation and legal literature related to the United States, a reasonable assumption can be made that there is no general definition of "fraud" as such. For instance, Chapter 47 of the 18 U.S. Code provides several possible forms of "fraud", e.g. "fraud and related activity in connection with identification documents, authentication features, and information",[7] "fraud and related activity in connection with access devices",[8] "fraud and related activity in connection with computers",[9] "fraud and related activity in connection with obtaining confidential phone records information of a covered entity"[10] and "fraud in connection with major disaster or emergency benefits".[11] Each of the referenced forms would require different types of *actus reus* in order to trigger the definition of "fraud" under individual paragraphs of 18 U.S. Code.

In the United Kingdom, the situation appears to be similar. Under the 2006 U.K. Fraud Act, "[a] person is guilty of fraud if he is in breach of any of the sections listed in subsection (2)".[12] Subsection 2 of the referred provision, in turn, provides the following possible forms of fraud:

- fraud by false representation;[13]
- fraud by failing to disclose information;[14]
- fraud by abuse of position.[15]

Being a Kazakh qualified lawyer, the author feels obliged to provide an example of the definition of "fraud" under Kazakh law. Under article 190 of the Criminal Code of the Republic of Kazakhstan, "fraud" is defined as "theft of another's property or acquisition of the right to another's property by deceit or abuse of

[6] Llamzon and Sinclair (2015), p. 469. *See also,* Betz (2017), p. 48.
[7] Code of Laws of the United States of America, Title 18, para. 1028.
[8] *Id.,* para. 1029.
[9] *Id.,* para. 1030.
[10] *Id.,* para. 1039.
[11] *Id.,* para. 1040.
[12] U.K. Fraud Act 2006, section 1(1).
[13] Dealt with in section 2 of the U.K. Fraud Act 2006.
[14] Dealt with in section 3 of the U.K. Fraud Act 2006.
[15] Dealt with in section 4 of the U.K. Fraud Act 2006.

trust".[16] As can be seen, the notion of fraud is covered by the criminal legislation of Kazakhstan and is being defined more narrowly than in the United States and the United Kingdom.

2.2 Corruption

While it was noted before that the term "corruption" should be well-known to anyone coming from a legal professional background,[17] it might not be entirely evident to lawyers how widespread corruption is geographically. According to the Corruption Perceptions Index of Transparency International for 2018, more than two-thirds of 180 countries score below 50, while the average score is 43.[18] In other words, this displays that corruption is widespread among the majority of governments and their officials. A further study indicates that nearly half of employees across Europe, the Middle East, Africa and India think that bribery and corruption are acceptable ways to survive an economic downturn.[19] This, in turn, evidences that people are used to corruption in their everyday life.

Corruption was reportedly responsible for loss of over USD 1.26 trillion per year for developing countries.[20] This sum is equivalent to economies of Switzerland, South Africa and Belgium combined and could have lifted 1.4 billion people living on less than USD 1.25 a day above this threshold for at least six years.[21] For completeness, it is to be noted that corruption is still quite significant in the developed world. For instance, according to the EU Commissioner for Home Affairs, an estimated EUR 120 billion is lost to corruption annually throughout the twenty-seven EU Member States.[22]

---

[16] Unofficial translation from Russian: "... хищение чужого имущества или приобретение права на чужое имущество путем обмана или злоупотребления доверием...".

[17] For completeness, it is to be noted that some scholars see a "definitional challenge" in ISDS, as there might not be "a universally accepted definition" of corruption (*see*, Low (2019), p. 343). I do not believe that the absence pf a strict universal definition creates many "challenges". Nevertheless, in this chapter, I identify the definition, through which this work is conducted.

[18] 100—highly clean, 0—highly corrupt; *See*, Transparency International (2018), Corruption Perceptions Index, available at https://www.transparency.org/files/content/pages/CPI_2018_Executive_Summary_EN.pdf.

[19] Ernst and Young (2013), Navigating today's complex resources-business risks, in Europe Middle East, India and Africa Fraud Survey 2013, p. 12, available at https://www.ey.com/Publication/vwLUAssets/Navigating_todays_complex_business_risks/$FILE/Navigating_todays_complex_business_risks.pdf.

[20] Transparency International UK, Corruption Statistics, available at https://www.transparency.org.uk/corruption/corruption-statistics/.

[21] *Id.*

[22] Nielsen, N. (2013), €120 billion lost to corruption in EU each year, in EUobserver, available at https://euobserver.com/justice/119300.

With such numbers and perception, it is impossible for corruption not to influence foreign direct investments and international investment relationships. Together with distorting capital markets, corruption also distorts competition, making it impossible for "good faith" foreign investors to compete on fair terms.[23]

Notwithstanding its publicity and eye-catching discussions, it is nevertheless difficult to provide an exact legal definition of corruption that would cover all the possible "corrupt" acts. This is simply because corruption can include all kinds of possible acts and/or omissions. For instance, Transparency International provides the following definition of corruption:

> Corruption is the abuse of entrusted power for private gain. It can be classified as grand, petty and political, depending on the amounts of money lost and the sector where it occurs.[24]

The above definition appears to be quite broad, but at the same time very narrow, because under this definition, one must have (i) powers, which she/he (ii) abuses for (iii) private benefit.

Some legal scholars have differentiated a variety of wrongful acts that would be included under the term "corruption":

> Corrupt practices range from small amounts paid for frequent transactions (petty corruption) to bribes to escape taxes, regulations, or win relatively minor procurement contracts (administrative corruption) to massive and wholesale corruption. Corruption occurs within private corporations (corporate corruption) or, more famously, in the public sector, including the political arena (political corruption). When corruption is prevalent throughout all levels of society it is seen as systemic, and when it involves senior officials, ministers, or heads of State serving the interests of a narrow group of businesspeople, politicians, or criminal elements, it is aptly called grand corruption.[25]

Some other scholars tend to view corruption in the context of so-called "illicit commissions", as well as in the light of circumstances and consequences of such "commissions".[26]

In addition to the above and as was discussed in the introduction to this textbook, there is a growing number of international instruments that are directed at combating corruption at intergovernmental level. Below is a selective list of such documents:

- The Inter-American Convention against Corruption, adopted by the Organization of American States on 29 March 1996;
- The Convention on the Fight against Corruption involving Officials of the European Communities or Officials of Member States of the European Union, adopted by the Council of the European Union on 26 May 1997;

---

[23] *See,* Partasides (2010), pp. 47–48.

[24] Transparency International, official website, available at https://www.transparency.org/what-is-corruption.

[25] Bhargava, V. (2006), Curing the Cancer of Corruption, in Global Issues for Global Citizens: An Introduction to Key Development Challenges, available at http://siteresources.worldbank.org/EXTABOUTUS/Resources/Ch18.pdf. *See also,* Raouf (2009), p. 117.

[26] Llamzon (2014), para. 2.04 with reference to Rossel and Prager (1999), p. 329.

- 1996 OECD Recommendation on the Tax Deductibility of Bribes to Foreign Public Officials;
- The Convention on Combating Bribery of Foreign Public Officials in International Business Transactions, adopted by the OECD on 21 November 1997;
- The Criminal Law Convention on Corruption, adopted by the Committee of Ministers of the Council of Europe on 27 January 1999;
- The Civil Law Convention on Corruption, adopted by the Committee of Ministers of the Council of Europe on 4 November 1999;
- The African Union Convention on Preventing and Combating Corruption, adopted by the Heads of State and Government of the African Union on 12 July 2003;
- The United Nations Convention against Transnational Organized Crime entered into force on 29 September 2003;
- United Nations Convention Against Corruption adopted by the General Assembly resolution No 58/4 of 31 October 2003.

To add to the above, some of the modern BITs have also entered the campaign of combating corruption. For instance, article 17 of the Morocco-Nigeria BIT provides that "each Contracting Party shall ensure that measures and efforts are undertaken to prevent and combat corruption regarding matters covered by this Agreement in accordance with its laws and regulations".[27]

Similarly, some of the free trade agreements have also entered into the campaign of combatting corruption. For instance, the US – Morocco Free Trade Agreement states that both parties are to commit to "eliminate bribery and corruption in international trade and investment".[28] A similar provision can be found in the Argentine – Chile Free Trade Agreement.[29]

Most of the treaties mentioned above do not provide an exact definition of the term "corruption". One of the main international legal instruments that addresses corruption, the OECD Convention on Combating Bribery of Foreign Public Officials in International Business Transactions ("**Anti-Bribery Convention**"), also does not provide a clear answer on what corruption is. Instead, the Anti-Bribery Convention deals with "bribery". The fact that "corruption" includes "bribery" and is at times inter-changeable with the latter is *inter alia* supported by national laws of States. For

[27] *See also*, Article 16 of the Cooperation and Facilitation Investment Agreement between the Federative Republic of Brazil and the Republic of Suriname dated 2 May 2018 and Article 15 of the Agreement between the Federative Republic of Brazil and the Federal Democratic Republic of Ethiopia on Investment Cooperation and Facilitation dated 11 April 2018.

[28] Article 18.5(1) of the United States – Morocco Free Trade Agreement, entered into force on 1 January 2006.

[29] Article 8.25 of the Free Trade Agreement between Argentina and Chile: "For greater certainty, an investor may not submit to arbitration a claim related to investments that have been established or developed [during] their activities through acts of corruption." (Free translation from the Spanish original: "Para mayor certeza, un inversion ista no podrá someter a arbitraje una reclamación relacionada con inversiones que se hayan establecido o desarro llen sus actividades mediante actos de corrupción.")

instance, the Law of the Republic of Kazakhstan on Combating Corruption (No 410-V of 18 November 2015) also primarily deals with "bribery" of public officials.[30] As will be seen in Part II of the present book, arguments on corruption are (almost) always invoked after alleged payments have been made or destined to public officials of host States.[31]

In the context of the present monograph, i.e. dispute settlement between a foreign investor and a State, "bribery" as a form "corruption" would be a primary subject of interest.[32] The Anti-Bribery Convention defines "bribery" as an intentional

> offer, promise or give any undue pecuniary or other advantage, whether directly or through intermediaries, to a foreign public official, for that official or for a third party, in order that the official act or refrain from acting in relation to the performance of official duties, in order to obtain or retain business or other improper advantage in the conduct of international business.[33]

In addition to this, the Anti-Bribery Convention recognizes "complicity in, including incitement, aiding and abetting, or authorisation" of the mentioned acts to be also defined as "bribery".[34]

The approach of the United Nations Convention against Corruption in defining the term "bribery" is very similar.[35]

---

[30] Law of the Republic of Kazakhstan No 410-V of 18 November 2015 on Combating Corruption (Закон Республики Казахстан от 18 ноября 2015 года № 410-V "О противодействии коррупции").

[31] *See,* World Duty Free Company Limited v. the Republic of Kenya at Sect. 6.1 of Part II and Metal Tech v. the Republic of Uzbekistan at Sect. 6.2 of Part II.

[32] *See,* the differentiation of two forms of corruption on (i) bribery and (ii) extortion that is being made in Llamzon (2014), paras. 2.05–2.12.

[33] Article 1(1) of the Anti-Bribery Convention.

[34] "Each Party shall take any measures necessary to establish that complicity in, including incitement, aiding and abetting, or authorization of an act of bribery of a foreign public official shall be a criminal offence. Attempt and conspiracy to bribe a foreign public official shall be criminal offences to the same extent as attempt and conspiracy to bribe a public official of that Party."—Article 1(2) of the OECD Anti-Bribery Convention.

[35] Article 15 of the UN Convention against Corruption: "Each State Party shall adopt such legislative and other measures as may be necessary to establish as criminal offences, when committed intentionally:

(a) The promise, offering or giving, to a public official, directly or indirectly, of an undue advantage, for the official himself or herself or another person or entity, in order that the official act or refrain from acting in the exercise of his or her official duties;

(b) The solicitation or acceptance by a public official, directly or indirectly, of an undue advantage, for the official himself or herself or another person or entity, in order that the official act or refrain from acting in the exercise of his or her official duties.",

As well as Article 16: "1. Each State Party shall adopt such legislative and other measures as may be necessary to establish as a criminal offence, when committed intentionally, the promise, offering or giving to a foreign public official or an official of a public international organization, directly or indirectly, of an undue advantage, for the official himself or herself or another person or entity, in order that the official act or refrain from acting in the exercise of his or her official duties, in order to obtain or retain business or other undue advantage in relation to the conduct of international business.

Therefore, for the purposes of the present monograph, the terms defined by the Anti-Bribery Convention and the UN Convention against Corruption shall be of focus. One shall not, however, disregard the approaches taken by national legislators, as it has become evident, such approaches may be decisive in assessing whether corruption/bribery exists in certain circumstances or not.[36]

References

Betz K (2017) Proving bribery, fraud and money laundering in international arbitration. University of Basel, p 48

Fox W (2009) Adjudicating bribery and corruption issues in international commercial arbitration. J Energy Nat Resour Law 27:487

Llamzon A (2014) Corruption in international investment arbitration. Oxford University Press

Llamzon A, Sinclair A (2015) Investor wrongdoing in investment arbitration: standards governing issues of corruption, fraud, misrepresentation and other investor misconduct. In: van den Berg AJ (ed) Legitimacy: myths, realities, challenges, p 469

Low L (2019) Dealing with allegations of corruption in international arbitration. Am J Int Law Unbound 113:343

Partasides C (2010) Proving corruption in international arbitration: a balanced standard for the real world. ICSID Rev: Foreign Invest Law J 25(1):47–48

Raouf M (2009) How should international arbitrators tackle corruption issues? ICSID Rev: Foreign Invest Law J 24(1):117

Rossel J, Prager H (1999) Illicit commissions and international arbitration: the questions of proof. J Int Arbitr 15:329

2. Each State Party shall consider adopting such legislative and other measures as may be necessary to establish as a criminal offence, when committed intentionally, the solicitation or acceptance by a foreign public official or an official of a public international organization, directly or indirectly, of an undue advantage, for the official himself or herself or another person or entity, in order that the official act or refrain from acting in the exercise of his or her official duties."

[36] *See,* Kim et al. v. the Republic of Uzbekistan at Sect. 7.4 of Part II.

Chapter 3
Legality Requirement as a Safeguard to Abuse

When speaking of corruption and fraud it is not unexpected that arbitral tribunals have to analyse whether a certain investment was made "in accordance with the law", or in other words whether that investment was incorporated lawfully.

The wording "in accordance with the law" is often used in international investment treaties. Usually, this or equivalent terms[1] can be found in provisions that define a foreign "investment" in the applicable legal instrument. The determination of the exact definition of "investment" is necessary and crucially important in order to delineate the scope of a host State's consent to investor-state arbitration, which is usually expressed in dispute settlement provisions of bilateral or multilateral investment treaties.[2]

The inclusion of the clause "in accordance with the law" in an international investment agreement is designed to sanction unlawful and illicit acts and any possible resulting effect that may come to the attention of an arbitral tribunal, by excluding them from the scope of international protection.[3] In an attempt to provide explanation to this type of clauses, *Schill* opined that "these clauses do not target any breach of domestic law, but are limited to investments in illegal businesses, to assets that are prohibited by domestic law, and to investments that are per se legal, but have been acquired by illegal conduct".[4] Therefore, the presence of the requirement for an investment to be made in accordance with the law may imply that only such investments can be protected through the system of international investment law and ISDS.

The discussed notion has been called differently by various authors, the most popular terms are the "legality requirement" and the "compliance clause". In legal

[1] For various possible equivalent terms *see*, Schill (2012), pp. 281–323.

[2] Yeginsu and Knoebel (2018), p. 1.

[3] Inceysa v. El Salvador, ICSID Case No. ARB/03/26, Award, 2 August 2006, paras. 215–247.

[4] Schill, S.W. (2012), Illegal Investments in International Arbitration, available at https://papers.ssrn.com/sol3/papers.cfm?abstract_id=1979734.

A. Tussupov, *Corruption and Fraud in Investment Arbitration*, EYIEL Monographs - Studies in European and International Economic Law 22,
https://doi.org/10.1007/978-3-030-90606-1_3

literature and various investor-state arbitral awards (as will be seen in Part II), the former appears to be used more frequently than the latter.

The legality requirement is a filter of international investment law that is designed to preclude illicit investments from the international dispute resolution mechanisms. It is a "threshold filter"[5] against investments that are not in conformity with the law.[6] In other words, the legality (lawfulness) of an investment may become a serious requirement for the conferral of adjudicative powers, i.e. the jurisdiction of an arbitral tribunal. Otherwise, if an investment in question was made illegally, it is open for argument that an arbitral tribunal should have no jurisdiction to hear a case concerning an illegal (unlawful) foreign investment, because the arbitral tribunal would have no "power. . . to entertain an action, petition or other proceeding" in such a setting.[7]

It is argued that the legality requirement is directly connected to the general principles of law, such as good faith and clean hands.[8] The arbitral tribunal in the Gustav Hamester case in very particular terms stated that

> [a]n [i]nvestment will not be protected if it has been created in violation of national or international principles of good faith; by way of corruption, fraud, or deceitful conduct; or if its creation itself constitutes a misuse of the system of international investment protection [. . .] [i]t will also not be protected if it is made in violation of the host State's law ....[9]

The main idea behind the legality requirement can be associated with the desire of preservation of the respect to the integrity of the international investment law system and due consideration to sovereign State's internal legislation.[10]

The end-result of the legality requirement is preventing international investment treaties from "protecting investments that should not be protected, particularly because they would be illegal".[11] The general point that foreign investments that have been illicitly made shall not be protected by law is widely argued by parties in investment arbitration and is often supported by arbitral tribunals. As was noted above, this is true in disputes that involve the allegations of corruption and fraud.

Moreover, with the risk of stating the obvious, it is noted that the legality requirement, in the form and scope that is discussed in the present monograph, is

---

[5] Aquas del Tunari S.A. v. Bolivia, ICSID Case No. ARB/02/3, Decision on Respondent's Objections to Jurisdiction, 21 October 2005, para. 153.

[6] Diel-Gligor and Nennecke (2015), p. 566.

[7] Waibel (2014), p. 2 with reference to Burke (1977), p. 1034; Garner (1999); Douglas (2009), para. 293.

[8] *See,* Gustav F W Hamester GmbH & Co KG v. Republic of Ghana, ICSID Case No. ARB/07/24, Award, 18 June 2010, para. 123.

[9] *Id.*

[10] *Id. also see,* Fraport AG Frankfurt Airport Services Worldwide v. Republic of the Philippines, ICSID Case No ARB/03/25, Award, 16 August 2007, para. 402: "Respect for the integrity of the law of the host state is also a critical part of development and a concern of international investment law. That said, the Tribunal's decision in this matter does not rest on policy. It is the language of the BIT which is dispositive and it is unequivocal in this matter."

[11] Diel-Gligor and Nennecke (2015), p. 566.

only to be met in investor-state cases (possibly including state-to-state investment disputes[12]) and not to be seen (in the discussed form and scope) in other types of arbitration disputes.

This chapter is designed to provide an overview of the current approaches in evaluating and analysing the presence and application of the legality requirement. In particular, for the purposes of the present monograph it is useful to understand the necessary standards to be applied in determining a possible breach of the legality requirement, the necessary procedural setting for such determination and the attribution of illicit conduct to one of the parties in a dispute.

3.1 Legality Requirement Assessment

Besides being an ordinary provision of a considerable number of investment treaties, it appears that the legality requirement has evolved in the way it is currently interpreted based on the findings in several investor-state arbitration cases that are discussed below. If one to simplify the meaning of the legality requirement, then it could be generally said that an investment is not to be protected by international investment law if it was made in violation of the laws (either national or international),[13] because such an investment would not be recognized as meeting the requirements under the prescribed and/or implied definition of "investment".

However, it would be fair to say that dismissing investors' claims over any possible violation of national law would be an over-reaction and would not serve the true purpose of international investment law. It is perhaps for these reasons that certain prerequisites were established through practice by various arbitral tribunals and crystalized in academic writings. In this regard it is seen that two particular characteristics shall be assessed and evaluated by an investment tribunal when examining allegations of illegality of a foreign investment in arbitration, i.e. *severity* and *chronology*. Both are discussed in sub-sections below.

3.1.1 Severity

A criterion for the determination of the breach of the legality requirement is the severity of an established violation, providing for a differentiation between minor[14]

[12] For details on particulars of state-to-state investment arbitration, *see* Hazarika, A. (2020), State-to-State Arbitration based on International Investment Agreements – Scope, Utility and Potential.

[13] Depending on the text of the relevant BIT and/or circumstances of the case (i.e. the degree of the unlawful act).

[14] Case law granting investment protection in case of insignificant deviations from host State law: Metalpar S.A. and Buen Aire S.A. v. Argentine, ICSID Case No. ARB/03/5, Decision on Jurisdiction, 21 April 2006, para. 84; Mytilineos Holdings SA v. Serbia & Montenegro, UNCITRAL,

and major[15] irregularities.[16] It has been established by both scholars and arbitral tribunals that only in situations when there is a serious violation of law, an investment shall be regarded as in breach of the legality requirement.[17] This guarantees protection to foreign investors who have committed minor and inconsiderable violations or errors.

In other words, if an investor failed to submit mandatory paperwork in appropriate manner or missed certain obligatory deadlines, this in itself (under ordinary conditions) would not pull the brakes to the entire plea of investment protection. For instance, the arbitral tribunal in the Tokios Tokeles v. Ukraine case found that simple and technical errors cannot constitute illegality of an entire investment:

> Even if we were able to confirm the Respondent's allegations, which would require a searching examination of minute details of administrative procedures in Ukrainian law, to exclude an investment on the basis of such minor errors would be inconsistent with the object and purpose of the Treaty.[18]

As a result, the Tokios Tokeles tribunal confirmed that the breach of the law at the time of the establishment of the investment must be of a serious nature. The reasoning of the Tokios Tokeles tribunal is of particular interest, as it invoked the "object and purpose of the Treaty" in assessing whether minor errors could deprive the investment of its protection.[19] This approach is consistent with the findings of arbitral tribunals in the LESI, SpA and Astaldi, SpA v. People's Democratic Republic of Algeria case and Rumeli Telekom AS and Telsim Mobil telekomunikasyon Hizmetleri AS v. Republic of Kazakhstan.[20]

Partial Award, Jurisdiction, 8 September 2006, para. 151; Tokios Tokeles v. Ukraine, ICSID Case No. ARB/02/18, Award, 26 July 2007, para. 97; Inmaris Perestroika Sailing Maritime Services GmbH and others v. Ukraine ICSID Case No. ARB/08/8, Decision on Jurisdiction, 8 March 2010, para. 145; Alpha Projektholding GmbH v. Ukraine, ICSID Case No. ARB/07/16, Award, 8 November 2010, para. 297.

[15] Case law assuming a fundamental violation of host State law (and thus denying investment protection): Inceysa v. El Salvador, ICSID Case No. ARB/03/26, Award, 2 August 2006, para. 202 (fraud); World Duty Free Company Limited v. The Republic of Kenya, ICSID Case No. ARB/00/7, Award, 4 October 2006, para. 157 (corruption); Fraport AG Frankfurt Airport Worldwide v. the Republic of the Philippines, ICSID Case No. ARB/03/25, Award, 16 August 2007, para. 398 (circumvention of host State law); Plama Consortium Limited v. Republic of Bulgaria, ICSID Case No. ARB/03/24, Award, 27 August 2008, paras. 135–137, 143 (fraudulent misrepresentation).

[16] Diel-Gligor and Nennecke (2015), p. 572.

[17] *See*, Summerfield (2009); Kulick and Wendler (2010), p. 98; Kulkarni (2013), p. 25.

[18] Tokios Tokeles v. Ukraine, ICSID Case No ARB/02/18, Decision on Jurisdiction, 29 April 2004, para. 82

[19] The arbitral tribunal in the Tokios Tokeles case appeared to follow the reasoning in the case Salini Costruttori S.p.A. and Italstrade S.p.A. v. Kingdom of Morocco [I], ICSID Case No. ARB/00/4, Decision on Jurisdiction, 31 July 2001, para. 46.

[20] *See also*, Desert Line Projects LLC v. The Republic of Yemen, ICSID Case No. ARB/05/17, Award, 6 February 2008.

3.1.2 *The Timing of the Alleged Illegal Act*

The general approach is that the legality requirement is breached if (1) an illegal act took place during the acquisition of such investment and (2) the illegal act contributed to the acquisition of the investment.[21] In other words, there must be a causal link between the alleged illegal conduct and the establishment of the investment.

Normally, the violations post factum do not lead to the breach of the legality requirement, however, this does not mean that there would be no other obstacle to access international protection for such an investment. From the analysis of case law and growing scholar opinions, it is evident that the principle of "good faith" and the "clean hands" doctrine may play a major role in declining protection over certain investments regardless of an (explicit or implicit)[22] application of the legality requirement.[23]

3.2 Implied Application: Good Faith & Clean Hands

There is a considerable degree of support directing at the idea that the notion of a protected "investment" is to include the legality requirement irrespective of its explicit presence or absence in the text of a relevant investment treaty.[24] In other words, there is room for discussion whether an investment must be established "in accordance with the law of the host State" in order to qualify for international protection without the relevant international investment instrument explicitly saying that it should.

The most straightforward opinion in support of the implicit application of the legality requirement was provided by the arbitral tribunal in the case Phoenix Action, Ltd. v. the Czech Republic:

> In the Tribunal's view, States *cannot be deemed to offer access* to the ICSID dispute settlement mechanism to investments made in violation of their laws. [...] These are illegal investments according to the national law of the host State and cannot be protected through an ICSID arbitral process. And it is the Tribunal's view that this condition – *the conformity*

[21] Diel-Gligor and Nennecke (2015), p. 575 with reference to Fraport AG Frankfurt Airport Services Worldwide v. The Republic of the Philippines, ICSID Case No. ARB/03/25, Award, 16 August 2007, para. 345 and Gustav F W Hamester GmbH & Co KG v. Republic of Ghana, ICSID Case No. ARB/07/24, Award, 18 June 2010, para 127.

[22] To be discussed in the following chapter.

[23] Lotz and Busch (2015), p. 583; Dumberry (2016), p. 231: "...the imposition by tribunals of such a legality requirement (**whether or not the treaty actually contains an explicit clause to that effect**) is in fact a manifestation of the clean hands doctrine. Thus, the different Latin maxims which are often used by tribunals to determine issues of jurisdiction/admissibility in this context are expressions of the broader doctrine of clean hands." [emphasis added]

[24] Lotz and Busch (2015), p. 583.

> *of the establishment of the investment with the national laws – is implicit even when not expressly stated in the relevant BIT.*[25]

The Phoenix tribunal makes two very important statements in its analysis: (1) there should be no assumption that States offer access to the ISDS mechanism to illegal investments, and (2) the legality requirement is to be applied irrespective of the fact whether it was enshrined in the text of the applicable investment treaty.

Some other tribunals have expressed similar opinions but with different terms and reasons. For example, in Inceysa v. El Salvador the arbitral tribunal found that the scope of consent to arbitration did include the requirement for an investment to be made in accordance with the law based on the BIT's *travaux preparatoires* and the general principles of good faith.[26] On the latter, the tribunal provided that "[g]ood faith is a supreme principle, which governs legal relations in all of their aspects and content."[27]

The good faith principle has been widely relied upon by arbitral tribunals and legal scholars when determining the question of implied applicability of the legality requirement. In particular,

> it has been suggested to interpret the consent to arbitration given in the BIT by the host State, in accordance with the principle of good faith treaty interpretation stated in Article 31(1) of the Vienna Convention on the Law of Treaties, to be under the implied condition of lawful conduct of the investor; if then, due to investor's corrupt behaviour, this condition is not met, the arbitral tribunal should consequently deny jurisdiction for lack of consent of the respondent host State.[28]

Similarly, many argue that an illicit investor may also be well estopped from running a claim against a host State under the doctrine of "clean hands", which in the author's opinion is again a direct product of the principle of good faith. In this regard, *Tanzi* has opined in the following way:

> The notion that a claim (actio) cannot arise from a wrongdoing (causa turpi) is a straightforward application of the principle of good faith. Likewise, it stands to reason that a right cannot arise from a wrongdoing, let alone from fraudulent behavior. . . . *Good faith appears as a hermeneutic tool which allows the tribunal to find justice* in any specific case and identify the instances of wrongdoing that warrant a denial of protection.[29]

---

[25] Phoenix Action, Ltd. v. The Czech Republic, ICSID Case No. ARB/06/5, Award, 15 April 2009, para. 101 [emphasis added].

[26] Inceysa v. El Salvador, ICSID Case No. ARB/03/26, Award, 2 August 2006, paras. 191–207. *See also*, Saluka Investments BV v. Czech Republic, UNCITRAL, Partial Award, 17 March 2006, para. 204.

[27] Inceysa v. El Salvador, ICSID Case No. ARB/03/26, Award, 2 August 2006, para. 230.

[28] Lotz and Busch (2015), p. 584; This point of view can also be supported by the United Nation's General Assembly's position that is reflected in the Document A/5100 ADD1 1962: ". . .foreign investment agreements freely entered into by or between sovereign States shall be observed in **good faith**." [emphasis added]

[29] Tanzi (2018), pp. 193 and 202 [emphasis added].

There are also views that the legality requirement is, in fact, the very manifestation and imposition of the doctrine of "clean hands" and the principle of good faith.[30] For the avoidance of doubt, it is to be noted that the doctrine of "clean hands", as well as the principle of good faith, would have far broader application rather than the legality requirement. While the latter would normally be only applicable to the events that took place during the making of the investment, "clean hands" and good faith could be applied to any possible conduct of a party to a dispute.[31]

The arbitral tribunal in the Gustav Hamester GmbH & Co KG v. Ghana case has differentiated the applicable legal norms to the determination of the illicit conduct:

> An investment will not be protected if it has been created *in violation of national or international principles of good faith*; by way of corruption, fraud, or deceitful conduct; or if its creation itself constitutes a misuse of the system of international investment protection under the ICSID Convention. *It will also not be protected if it is made in violation of the host State's law.*[32]

This is mainly because of the nature of the principle of good faith and the doctrine of "clean hands" that both have their roots in the very basis of the understanding of justice and have their reflection in essentially any legal system.[33] This has been recognized already some sixty years ago by *Sir Fitzmaurice* who, when discussing state-to-state disputes in The Hague, stated:

> 'He who comes to equity for relief must come with clean hands.' Thus a State which is guilty of illegal conduct may be deprived of the necessary locus standi in judicio for complaining of corresponding illegalities on the part of other States, especially if these were consequential on or were embarked upon in order to counter its own illegality – in short were provoked by it.[34]

Furthermore, and in addition to the above, the Energy Charter Treaty ("**ECT**") also does not contain the relevant wording that could have explicitly required an investment to be made in accordance with the law. Nevertheless, the arbitral tribunal in the Plama Consortium case found that irrespective of this fact, it should not mean

---

[30] Dumberry (2016), p. 231: "…the imposition by tribunals of such a legality requirement (**whether or not the treaty actually contains an explicit clause to that effect**) is in fact a manifestation of the clean hands doctrine. Thus, the different Latin maxims which are often used by tribunals to determine issues of jurisdiction/admissibility in this context are expressions of the broader doctrine of clean hands." [emphasis added]. *See also,* Lamm et al. (2010), pp. 723–726.

[31] While this view is supported by some arbitral tribunals in their decisions (e.g. Niko Resources (Bangladesh) Ltd. v. Bangladesh Petroleum Exploration & Production Company Limited and Bangladesh Oil Gas and Mineral Corporation, ICSID Case No. ARB/10/18, Decision on Corruption Claim, 25 February 2019), it was not supported by the arbitral tribunal in the Yukos Universal Limited (Isle of Man) v. The Russian Federation, UNCITRAL, PCA Case No. 2005-04/AA227.

[32] Gustav F W Hamester GmbH & Co KG v. Republic of Ghana, ICSID Case No. ARB/07/24, Award, 18 June 2010, para. 123 [emphasis added].

[33] The principle of "clean hands" is associated with the Roman maxims, such as *ex delicto non orituractio* ("an unlawful act cannot serve as the basis of an action at law") and *ex turpicausa non oritur* ("an action cannot arise from a dishonorable cause"). *See,* Llamzon (2015).

[34] Fitzmaurice (1958), p. 119. *See also,* Kreindler (2010), pp. 309 and 316–317.

"that the protections provided for by the ECT cover all kinds of investments, including those contrary to domestic or international law".[35] After making a finding that the claimant's investment was "obtained by deceitful conduct", the arbitral tribunal stated that granting the ECT's protections to Plama's investment would be contrary to the principles of good faith and *nemo auditor propriam turpitudinem allegans* and "the basic notion of international public policy – that a contract obtained by wrongful means (fraudulent misrepresentation) should not be enforced by a tribunal".[36] While the Plama tribunal had previously decided that it had jurisdiction to hear the case,[37] it subsequently found the claims of the foreign investor to be inadmissible due to the reasons provided above.

The same finding on the implied application of the legality requirement within the ECT has been made by the arbitral tribunal in the Yukos Universal Limited (Isle of Man) v. The Russian Federation case, where it stated:

> An investor who has obtained an investment in the host State only by acting in bad faith or in violation of the laws of the host state, has brought itself within the scope of application of the ECT through wrongful acts. Such an investor should not be allowed to benefit from the Treaty.[38]

In other words, the Plama and the Yukos tribunals' decisions are based on the implied (non-existent in the text of the ECT) legality requirement or simply on the principle of good faith. Similar decisions, with somewhat different language, had been made in other investment arbitration cases[39] and international state-to-state disputes.[40]

---

[35] Plama Consortium Limited v. Republic of Bulgaria, ICSID Case No. ARB/03/24, Award, 27 August 2008, para. 138.

[36] Dumberry (2016), p. 236 with reference to Plama Consortium Limited v. Republic of Bulgaria, ICSID Case No. ARB/03/24, Award, 27 August 2008, para. 143.

[37] Plama Consortium Limited v. Republic of Bulgaria, ICSID Case No. ARB/03/24, Decision on Jurisdiction, 8 February 2005.

[38] Yukos Universal Limited (Isle of Man) v. The Russian Federation, UNCITRAL, PCA Case No. 2005-04/AA227, Final Award, para. 1352.

[39] Hulley Enterprises (Cyprus) Limited v. Russia, UNCITRAL, PCA Case No AA 226, Final Award, 18 July 2014; Cementownia "Nowa Huta" S.A. v. Republic of Turkey, ICSID Case No. ARB(AF)/06/2, Award, 17 September 2009, para. 153: "Parties to an arbitration proceeding must conduct themselves in good faith. This duty, as the Methanex tribunal found, is owed to both the other disputing party and to the Tribunal."; Malicorp Limited v. The Arab Republic of Egypt, ICSID Case No. ARB/08/18, Award, 7 February 2011, para. 116: "It is indisputable, and this Arbitral Tribunal can do no more than confirm it, that the safeguarding of good faith is one of the fundamental principles of international law and the law of investments."; Sanum Investments Limited v. Lao People's Democratic Republic, UNCITRAL, PCA Case No. 2013-13, Award, 6 August 2019, para. 171; Cortec Mining Kenya Limited, Cortec (Pty) Limited and Stirling Capital Limited v. Republic of Kenya, ICSID Case No. ARB/15/29, Award, 22 October 2018, paras. 303–308; Glencore International A.G. and C.I. Prodeco S.A. v. Republic of Colombia, ICSID Case No. ARB/16/6, Award, 27 August 2019, paras. 748, 826, 844, 855, 859, 1534–1537.

[40] Legal Consequences for States of the Continued Presence of South Africa in Namibia (South West Africa) notwithstanding Security Council Resolution 276 (1970), Advisory Opinion, International Court of Justice Reports 1971, p. 16, para. 94; Military and Paramilitary Activities in and

The main difference that is observed in approaches to the legality assessment in disputes where the applicable investment treaty contains an explicit "in accordance with the law" term and in disputes where no such term is being met, is that in the latter situation arbitral tribunals tend to examine the illegality allegations at the merits stage, while at the former there are pressing reasons for arguments and respective decisions made at the jurisdictional phase of a dispute.

For completeness, it is to be noted that while the doctrine of "clean hands" has been applied in a considerable number of ISDS cases by arbitral tribunals, the position on its application is not entirely uniformed. Nevertheless, it may be accepted that some basic elements and understanding of the doctrine can be and are being applied at the discretion of an arbitral tribunal.[41]

At the same time, there is an alternative point of view stating that if the legality requirement was not explicitly incorporated in an applicable treaty, then it should be understood that the respective State-parties to the treaty extended their consent to the jurisdiction of arbitral tribunals *inter alia* over investments that have been made in violation of national and/or international laws.[42]

3.3 Procedural Setting of Legality Examination

It has become evident (and will be observed in more detail in Part II) that sometimes differences in approach of the assessment of the legality requirement arise when discussing the timing and the outset of arbitral tribunals' decisions over illegality arguments. The approach that is often taken by arbitral tribunals is that the legality requirement gives rise to considerations of the existence of an arbitral tribunal's jurisdiction (the "**jurisdictional stage approach**").[43] Under this approach, an arbitral tribunal is to make a decision on lawfulness of the investment already before parties can plead on the merits of their cases.

In other instances, tribunals took a different approach and assessed illegality allegations together with the merits of the case (the "**merits stage approach**"). For example, in the Malicorp Limited v. the Arab Republic of Egypt case, the arbitral tribunal undertook a detailed assessment of the legality requirement and its procedural and material stance. On the latter, the Malicorp tribunal noted that "[it] can do no more than confirm it, that the safeguarding of good faith is one of the fundamental

---

against Nicaragua (Nicaragua v. United States of America) (Merits), 1986 ICJ 259, 391, Dissenting Opinion of Judge Schwebel; Gabčikovo-Nagymaros Project (Hungary v. Slovakia), 1997 ICJ 7, 76, para. 133.

[41] Pomson (2017), pp. 712, 726: "Whereas certain forms of the clean hands doctrine have relatively well established recognition in the jurisprudence of international courts and tribunals, this is not the case for all forms of the clean hands doctrine."

[42] Liman Caspian Oil BV and NCL Dutch Investment BV v. Republic of Kazakhstan, ICSID Case No ARB/07/14, Award, 22 June 2010, para. 187.

[43] Diel-Gligor and Nennecke (2015), p. 570.

principles of international law and the law of investments."[44] On the procedural side of the assessment, the tribunal acknowledged that there existed two approaches on how to deal with the illegality claims in international arbitration:

- The issues of illegality of an investment (as a requirement for protection) must be dealt from the standpoint of jurisdiction;
- The issues of illegality of an investment are to be examined from the standpoint of the merits of the case.[45]

Both approaches and the reasoning behind them are displayed in the paragraphs below.

3.3.1 *Jurisdictional Stage Approach*

Some tribunals and authors have considered the legality requirement to be a jurisdictional condition under relevant BITs, holding that it constituted a limit to a host State's consent to arbitration (i.e. a requirement to jurisdiction *ratione voluntatis*).[46] As has been laid down by the ICJ in the Corfu Channel case, consent is a cornerstone for the powers of any international tribunal.[47] In investment arbitration consent is

[44] Malicorp Limited v. the Arab Republic of Egypt, ICSID Case No ARB/08/18, Award, 7 February 2011, para. 116.

[45] "Some have addressed the issue at the outset of the case, from the standpoint of jurisdiction. In order for the jurisdiction of an ICSID arbitral tribunal to be established, the State against which proceedings are brought must have validly given its consent. In such proceedings this presupposes that the party bringing the claim has made an investment that meets the requirements the State may have laid down, as well as the general conditions of validity (Saba Fakes v. Turkey, ICSID Case No. ARB/07/20, Award of 14 July 2010, paragraph 108; denying however that good faith constitutes a precondition for jurisdiction, see paragraph 112). That is why questions of the possible application of the principle of good faith are approached from the standpoint of Article 25 of the ICSID Convention, as part of the examination of jurisdiction (in particular, Phoenix Action v. Czech Republic, op. cit.). Other tribunals have examined the issue at the second stage, from the standpoint of the merits, in relation to the validity of the investment. In order for an ICSID arbitral tribunal to be able to render an award against a State for breach of obligations concerning the protection of an investment, such investment must be valid. That is why the issue of the possible application of the principle of good faith is then considered as part of the issues on the merits.", Malicorp Limited v. the Arab Republic of Egypt, ICSID Case No ARB/08/18, Award, 7 February 2011, para. 117.

[46] Diel-Gligor and Nennecke (2015), p. 570 with references to Inceysa v. El Salvador, ICSID Case No. ARB/03/26, Award, 2 August 2006, paras. 142–161; Fraport AG Frankfurt Airport Worldwide v. Philippines ICSID Case No. ARB/03/25, Award, 16 August 2007, paras. 300, 306–307, 319, 323, 332, 335, 350, 383, 385, 396–398, 401–404; Alasdair Ross Anderson and others v. Costa Rica, ICSID Case No. ARB(AF)/07/3, Award, 19 May 2010, para. 59; Saba Fakes v. Turkey, ICSID Case No. ARB/07/20, Award, 14 July 2010, paras. 112–114, 121.

[47] Waibel (2014), p. 2 with reference to Corfu Channel case (United Kingdom of Great Britain and Northern Ireland v. Albania), Preliminary Objections, ICJ Rep. 194815. *See also*, Waibel (2010), pp. 792–797.

usually enshrined in an applicable international investment treaty, which could be (explicitly) conditional on certain criteria (e.g. the legality requirement).

A demonstrative analysis took place in the Salini Costruttori S.p.A. and Italstrade S.p.A. v. the Kingdom of Morocco case, in which the arbitral tribunal found that the purpose of the legality requirement within the applicable treaty was "to prevent the Bilateral Treaty from protecting investments that should not be protected, particularly because they would be illegal", which makes the assessment of legality a jurisdictional obstacle *per se.*[48]

Another indicative example of the jurisdictional stage approach to assessment of investment legality can be witnessed in the decision in the Inceysa Vallisoletana S.L. v. Republic of El Salvador case[49] where the arbitral tribunal was convinced that the investor's illicit conduct made the foreign investment "unprotectable" under international investment law, which is why no jurisdiction could have existed in the first place:

> El Salvador gave its consent to the jurisdiction of the Centre, presupposing good faith behavior on the part of future investors. El Salvador did not have any basis to suppose that Inceysa would submit false information and would commit fraudulent acts for the purpose of establishing a legal relationship with MARN, which was embodied in the Contract that gives rise to this dispute.
>
> By falsifying the facts, Inceysa violated the principle of good faith from the time it made its investment and, therefore, it did not make it in accordance with Salvadoran law. Faced with this situation, this Tribunal can only declare its incompetence to hear Inceysa's complaint, since its investment cannot benefit from the protection of the BIT, as established by the parties during the negotiations and the execution of the agreement.[50]

Utilising similar approaches, many other arbitral tribunals in various cases concluded that the legality of an investment is an unconditional prerequisite for protection under international investment instruments and, therefore, for jurisdiction of international arbitral tribunals.[51]

Clearly, in order to make such an important and serious decision at such an early stage of proceedings, a tribunal must be satisfied that it has enough evidence of the alleged unlawfulness of a foreign investment, which could prove to be difficult as will be observed further below in this textbook. Any possible doubt of the existence of the breach of the legality requirement could therefore provide basis for tribunal's inference that no breach exists and an arbitral tribunal should have jurisdiction to

---

[48] Salini Costruttori S.p.A. and Italstrade S.p.A. v. Kingdom of Morocco, Case No ARB/00/4, Decision on Jurisdiction, 23 July 2001, para. 46. *See also,* Tokios Tokeles v. Ukraine, ICSID Case No ARB/02/18, Decision on Jurisdiction, 29 April 2004.

[49] Inceysa Vallisoletana S.L. v. Republic of El Salvador, ICSID Case No. ARB/03/26, Award, 2 August 2006.

[50] *Id.*, paras. 238–239.

[51] *See e.g.*, Phoenix v. Czech Republic, ICSID Case No. ARB/06/5, Award, 15 April 2009; Fraport AG Frankfurt Airport Worldwide v. Philippines ICSID Case No. ARB/03/25, Award, 16 August 2007; Alasdair Ross Anderson and others v. Costa Rica, ICSID Case No. ARB(AF)/07/3, Award, 19 May 2010; Saba Fakes v. Turkey, ICSID Case No. ARB/07/20, Award, 14 July 2010.

examine the matter further. Notably, the arbitral tribunal itself is the main judge of its own competence under the doctrine of *Kompetenz-Kompetenz*.[52] This is generally the case with tribunals and courts in wider public international law dispute settlement mechanisms.[53]

3.3.2 Merits Stage Approach

Some authors argue that tribunals should first accept jurisdiction and then examine illegality claims on their merits.[54] It is argued that to do otherwise might be premature and, possibly, prejudicial towards a defending party.

In addition to such doctrinal views, there are examples where arbitral tribunals had undertaken such an approach in investor-state cases. One of such examples is the ICSID case between TSA Spectrum de Argentina S.A. and the Argentine Republic.[55] Argentine put forward a massive defence against the jurisdiction of the arbitral tribunal based on several arguments, one of them being an allegation of corruption and illegality on the part of the investor.[56] The investor (TSA) on the other hand, submitted "that the legality of an investment is a question for the merits".[57] Although the tribunal decided that it does not have to make findings on those matters since the jurisdiction had already been denied based on other grounds, it nevertheless stated that "if there had been no other jurisdictional obstacle in the present case, the tribunal would have decided to join the fourth jurisdictional objection to the merits of the case".[58] In other words, the tribunal's understanding was that it would be more appropriate to review and decide on the allegations of corruption at the stage of the merits.

Similar understanding was reached by the arbitral tribunal in the previously discussed Malicorp case, where the tribunal first went on to recognise the existence of two different approaches:

> The distinction between the two approaches is not of merely theoretical significance, if only because of the remedies available against the decision. Undoubtedly there are good reasons

---

[52] Weiler (1999), pp. 286–323; Brown (2007), pp. 61–63; Levy (2005).

[53] *See*, Crawford (2010), discussing the *Betsey case* (1797) that was decided by a British–United States Commission formed under the Treaty of Amity, Commerce and Navigation, between His Britannic Majesty and The United States of America of 1794.

[54] Fathallah (2010), pp. 40–41 and 65–70 referenced in Clouet, L.M. (2018), Arbitrating under the table: the effect of allegations of corruption in relation to the jurisdiction of the arbitral tribunal and the enforcement of foreign arbitral awards, available at https://nyu.academia.edu/LuisMar%C3%ADaClouet.

[55] TSA Spectrum de Argentina S.A. v. Argentine Republic, ICSID Case No. ARB/05/5, Award, 19 December 2008.

[56] *Id.*, para. 173.

[57] *Id.*

[58] *Id.*, para. 176.

for choosing one or the other approach, and it is possible that the circumstances in which the issue arises can justify different solutions.[59]

The key element of the quote above is the appreciation of the "circumstances" of the case, in which the dispute arises, which is why the tribunal did not seek to provide a universal answer to the question.[60] However, for "the present case" the Malicorp tribunal found that it should examine allegations of illicit misconduct from the standpoint of the merits of the dispute. In support to its finding, the tribunal invoked "the principle of autonomy of the arbitration agreement". It also noted the difficulty "to determine whether the ground derives from an act contrary to good faith" that therefore "requires an in-depth examination, which is difficult to separate out as the facts may be closely interwove".[61]

The point that deserves separate attention in the Malicorp arbitral tribunal's reasoning is the reference and weight that was accorded to "the principle of autonomy of the arbitration agreement", or the so-called principle of separability. This principle is usually applied in commercial arbitration, where parties practically conclude two agreements: an agreement to arbitrate and an agreement for commercial transaction. Although, as it follows from the arbitral tribunal's reasoning in the Malicorp case, "the principle of autonomy of the arbitration agreement" was not the sole basis for its decision to examine those allegations at the outset of the merits, it was still applied because in Malicorp tribunal's opinion this "principle [is] so fundamental" and "has its place in investment arbitration" too.

The position taken by the tribunal in the Malicorp case can be (partly) explained by the practical necessity of examination of the allegations of unlawfulness at a certain evidentiary standard level. Notwithstanding the general practice established by several arbitral tribunals, there is indeed room for the argument that in certain cases the examination of the factual background of foreign investment's acquisition may and shall be done at the merits stage of the dispute.

Notably, investment tribunals are not the first ones to meet and actually assess the dilemma of determining the proper stage of examination of the preliminary objections that often question the jurisdiction of the adjudicator. In 1933, the Permanent Court of International Justice in the case of Prince von Pless Administration stated the following:

> At the present stage of the proceedings a decision cannot be taken either as to the preliminary character of the objections or on the question whether they are well founded; any such decision would raise questions of fact and law in regard to which the Parties are in several respect in disagreement and which are too closely linked to the merits for the Court to adjudicate upon them at the present stage;
>
> . . .if it were now to pass upon these objections, the Court would run the risk of adjudicating on questions which appertain to the merits of the case or of prejudging the solutions;

[59] Malicorp Limited v. the Arab Republic of Egypt, ICSID Case No ARB/08/18, Award, 7 February 2011, para. 117.

[60] *Id.*: "It is not the intention of this Arbitral Tribunal to provide a general answer to the question. . ."

[61] *Id.*, para. 119.

> Whereas the Court may order the joinder of preliminary objections to the merits whenever the interest of the good administration of Justice require it.[62]

As was noted by the arbitral tribunal in the EDF Services Limited v. Romania case, illicit conduct (in that dispute—*corruption*) is by default conducted in strict secrecy and, therefore, it is ostensibly difficult to prove.[63] The same concern has been expressed in doctrinal studies.[64] Subsequently, it is not wrong to assume that in some cases the examination of illicit conduct can only be completed after full and frank disclosure and detailed witness and/or expert examination, which is usually more practical to undertake at the merits stage.

Based on this, it may be seen that pragmatic considerations in light of complexity of factual circumstances of a dispute may require that an arbitral tribunal assumes jurisdiction and examines questions of illegality with more procedural "resources". For a proper assessment of the correct approach in a case, it appears that one would have to put two items of equal importance on scales:

- Non-entertainment of claims concerning illicit investments;
- The autonomy of arbitral tribunals to decide on its jurisdiction and the admissibility of claims.

The first item above is best described by a Roman maxim—*nemo auditor propiam turpitudinem allegans.* The maxim has also been cited in investment arbitral awards denying jurisdiction over investments that had not been made in accordance with the host State's law[65] and its best English equivalent would be "the courts will not recognise a benefit accruing to a criminal from his crime".[66]

In addition to this and completely independent from the difficulty to prove illicit misconduct by the alleging party, there are also views in support of the examination of alleged illegality at the merits stage from the procedural fairness point of view. A

[62] Administration of the Prince Von Pless, Germany v. Poland, 1933 P.C.I.J., Series A/B, No. 52 quoted in Kulkarni (2013), p. 29 with reference to Lalive (2002), p. 129.

[63] "In any case, however, corruption must be proven and is notoriously difficult to prove since, typically, there is little or no physical evidence. The seriousness of the accusations of corruption in the present case, considering that it involves officials at the highest level of the Romanian Government at the time, demands clear and convincing evidence."—EDF Services Limited v. Romania, ICSID Case No ARB/05/13, Award, 8 October 2009, para. 221.

[64] "Certainly the corrupt party will make every effort to obscure or disguise the corrupt conduct. And often the party victim of such corruption ... will have been denied access to the evidence necessary to establish it and/or, worse, prohibited from presenting what evidence they may have by the very officials who benefited. [...] It is clear that, like most crimes and intentional misconduct, and perhaps more so, acts of corruption and collusion are specifically designed not to be able to be identified or detected."—Mills, K. (2003), Corruption and Other Illegality in the Formation and Performance of Contracts and in the Conduct of Arbitrations Relating Thereto, in ICCA Congress Series No. 11, p. 295. *See also*, Partasides (2010); Martin (2004), p. 1; Raouf (2009), pp. 116–136; Gaillard (2019), p. 4.

[65] Fraport AG Frankfurt Airport Services Worldwide v. Republic of the Philippines, ICSID Case No ARB/03/25, Award, 16 August 2007.

[66] *Id.*, para. 123.

concern has been expressed that in complex investment relationships, misconduct may also be mutual.[67] Such an opinion, for instance, was raised in the dissenting opinion in the Fraport v. Philippines case:

> If the legality of the Claimant's conduct is a jurisdictional issue, and the legality of the Respondent's conduct a merits issue, then the Respondent Host State is placed in a powerful position. In the Biblical phrase, the Tribunal must first examine the speck in the eye of the investor and defer, and maybe never address, a beam in the eye of the Host State. Such an approach does not respect fundamental principles of procedure.[68]

Perhaps because of the appreciation of the possible misbalance as indicated above, arbitral tribunals may also wish to give a defending party a benefit of a doubt and grant an opportunity to address the illegality claims and to undertake a detailed examination of the issues together with the merits of the case. Some say that not giving such an opportunity may place "legal certainty into serious jeopardy".[69] It is noted that in some cases the standard of proof that was applied for alleged criminal misconduct was so high that it did not only require a careful look at the issues, but indeed proper investigation.[70]

Additionally, the difference in approach can be met in situations when an applicable investment treaty is silent on the legality requirement for a protected investment. This is *inter alia* because an arbitral tribunal would have no "hard" basis to limit its jurisdiction *ratione materia* or *ratione voluntatis*. Therefore, where an applicable investment treaty does not include an explicit legality requirement, arbitral tribunals generally tend to treat the question of legality as an issue for debates on merits.[71]

Moreover, in the arbitral award in the Sanum Investments Limited v. the Lao People's Democratic Republic case, the tribunal stated that it understood the respondent's illegality claims and requests to dismiss the investors' claims due to illegality not as "an objection to the Tribunal's jurisdiction, but an affirmation of the Tribunal's jurisdiction to consider the claims on their merits, which the Government says, ought to be dismissed because of the Claimants' illegal conduct."[72] This is yet

---

[67] Newcombe, A. (2010), Investor misconduct and investment treaty arbitration: mapping the terrain, in Kluwer Arbitration Blog, available at: http://arbitrationblog.kluwerarbitration.com/2010/01/25/investor-misconduct-and-investment-treaty-arbitration-mapping-the-terrain/.

[68] Fraport AG Frankfurt Airport Services Worldwide v. The Republic of the Philippines, ICSID Case No. ARB/03/25, Dissenting Opinion of Mr. Bernardo M. Cremades, para. 37.

[69] Kulick and Wendler (2010), pp. 61–85.

[70] The applicable standard of proof is discussed in the following chapters.

[71] Diel-Gligor and Nennecke (2015), p. 571 with references to Fraport AG Frankfurt Airport Worldwide v. Philippines, ICSID Case No. ARB/03/25, Award, 16 August 2007, para. 300; Alasdair Ross Anderson and others v. Costa Rica, ICSID Case No. ARB(AF)/07/3, Award, 19 May 2010, para. 59; Saba Fakes v. Turkey, ICSID Case No. ARB/07/20, Award, 14 July 2010, paras. 112–114.

[72] Sanum Investments Limited v. the Lao People's Democratic Republic, PCA Case No 2013-13, Award of Jurisdiction, 13 December 2013, para. 87.

another approach, which once again evidences that there is no universal formula for addressing illegality in investment arbitration.

Some authors opined that accepting jurisdiction, while reserving the right to refuse it at a later stage, creates a legal fiction, which would be "tantamount to an exercise of the tribunal's power ex aequo et bono".[73] According to *Schreuer,* exercise *ex aequo et bono* by an arbitral tribunal requires parties' consent, in the absence of which the tribunal may risk to act in excess of powers.[74] However, for the purposes of the present monograph, this is only imaginable in a situation where one party alleges illegality, while the other party denies it. It would be difficult to imagine the losing (corrupt/fraudulent) party, who denied illegality and, therefore, triggered the postponement of the illegality examination to the merits stage, to actually blame the arbitrators for acting in excess of powers, simply because this would have been caused by their own (continued) misconduct. In common law jurisdictions, this might be regarded as unequitable and, therefore, unworthy of legal or equitable protection.

Finally, when speaking of investment disputes that find their basis in international investment contracts rather than investment treaties, the situation can also be different. Precisely based on this difference, the tribunal in Niko Resources v. Bangladesh case found that the breach of the principle of "good faith" would not automatically and necessarily lead to denial of jurisdiction:

> ...[I]n the present case jurisdiction is not based on such a[n investment] treaty but on two agreements. The arbitration clause in these agreements is not merely an offer subject to conditions which may or may not be accepted. Rather it contains a firm agreement binding both parties to submit their disputes to ICSID arbitration [...] The question whether the investment was made in good faith or not and, if not, what consequences would have to be drawn from it, are matters which must be resolved in the agreed manner. In a contractual dispute as the present one, alleged or established lack of good faith in the investment does not justify the denial of jurisdiction but must be considered as part of the merits of the dispute.[75]

3.4 Concluding Remarks

As a threshold remark, it is to be noted that there is a general consensus that international investment law and arbitral tribunals shall not entertain claims based on the products of illicit misconduct. There is also an overall agreement that corruption and fraud are public "enemies" of the societies and are contrary to

[73] Losco (2014), pp. 37–52, available at https://scholarship.law.duke.edu/cgi/viewcontent.cgi?referer=&httpsredir=1&article=1004&context=dlj_online, p. 49.

[74] Schreuer (1996), p. 37.

[75] Niko Resources (Bangladesh) Ltd. v. Bangladesh Petroleum Exploration & Production Company Limited and Bangladesh Oil Gas and Mineral Corporation, ICSID Case No. ARB/10/18, Decision on Jurisdiction, paras. 470–471.

international public policy.[76] The definition of public policy as provided by the Singapore High Court has been previously discussed,[77] and it is generally similar to the definitions provided by legal scholars and other national courts.[78] In some way, or another, both corruption and fraud shall meet strong opposition in the frames of international investment arbitration.

It has also been observed that not every illegal act would deprive an investment of its protection under international investment law. A due consideration must be given to the level of severity of an unlawful conduct. Not every minor legal or paperwork "mistake" shall lead to the dismissal of claims of an investor, as this would be regarded as being against the object and purpose of the system of international protection of foreign investments. Also, it is generally believed that the timing of the alleged unlawful act is of importance, i.e. when the relevant illicit act took place.

From the analysis of arbitral tribunals' decisions and doctrinal views, it has been established that there are pressing grounds to believe that the legality of a foreign investment is an implied prerequisite for it to be protected under international investment treaties and, more broadly, within the framework of the ISDS mechanism. However, at the same time, opposing views have also been witnessed.[79]

Additionally, it is found that there are two possible approaches to the examination of the legality requirement, i.e. (i) at the jurisdictional phase of the dispute, and (ii) together with the merits of the dispute. Many authors believe that the former is the correct approach.[80] Several arbitral tribunals have come to a similar

---

[76] *See*, World Duty Free Company Limited v. The Republic of Kenya, ICSID Case No. ARB/00/7, Award, 4 October 2006, para. 157: "In light of domestic laws and international conventions relating to corruption, and in light of the decisions taken in this matter by courts and arbitral tribunals, this Tribunal is convinced that bribery is contrary to the international public policy of most, if not all, States or, to use another formula, to transnational public policy."

[77] Judgement of the High Court of the Republic of Singapore dated 3 January 2020 in the case between Bloomberry Resorts and Hotels Inc. and Sureste Properties, Inc against Global Gaming Philippines LLC and GGAM Netherlands B.V. with references to PT Asuransi, citing the Commission Report (A/40/17), at para 297. *See also,* the Award in Westacre Investments Inc. v. Jugoirriport-SDPR Holdings Co. Ltd and Beogradska Banka, ICC Case No. 7047, para. 36.

[78] Egerton v. Lord Brownlow, [1853] 4 H.L. 1, p. 196, referring to public policy as a "principle of law which holds that no subject can lawfully do that which has a tendency to be injurious to the public or public good." *See also*, Lew, J.D.M., Mistelis, L.A. and Kröll, S. (2003), Comparative International Commercial Arbitration, p. 209.

[79] *See,* Liman Caspian Oil BV and NCL Dutch Investment BV v. Republic of Kazakhstan, ICSID Case No ARB/07/14, Award, 22 June 2010, para. 187.

[80] Dumberry (2016), p. 233. *See also,* Douglas (2004), p. 155; Newcombe (2011), p. 198; Dissenting opinion of Keith Highet in Waste Management, Inc v. Mexico, ICSID Case No ARB(AF)/00/3, 30 April 2004, paras 57–58: "International decisions are replete with fine distinctions between jurisdiction and admissibility. For the purpose of the present proceedings it will suffice to observe that lack of jurisdiction refers to the jurisdiction of the Tribunal and inadmissibility refers to the admissibility of the case. . . . Jurisdiction is the power of the tribunal to hear the case; admissibility is whether the case itself is defective–whether it is appropriate for the tribunal to hear it. If there is no title of jurisdiction, then the tribunal cannot act".

conclusion.[81] On this point, it is to be noted that the line between jurisdiction and admissibility, which is usually examined at the merits, is particularly "fluid".[82] The delimitation between the two concepts is not straightforward and the terms are at times used interchangeably.[83] However, irrespective of this difficulty, it is very important to have a clear distinction. It is being said that the boundaries between the two lay in a "twilight zone".[84]

For the purposes of the present textbook, guidance on the concept of admissibility may be drawn from the approach of the ICJ in the Oil Platforms case, where it was found that

> [o]bjections to admissibility normally take the form of an assertion that, even if the Court has jurisdiction and the facts stated by the applicant State are assumed to be correct, nonetheless there are reasons why the Court should not proceed to an examination of the merits.[85]

Similar view had been expressed by *Fitzmaurice* who explained that

> an objection to the substantive admissibility of the claim is plea that the tribunal should rule the claim inadmissible on some ground other than its ultimate merit; an objection to the jurisdiction of the tribunal is a plea that the tribunal itself is incompetent to give any ruling at all whether as to the merits or as to the admissibility of the claim.[86]

To conclude on this question, it is important to bear in mind that discretion of deciding the appropriate stage for illegality examination lays exclusively with an arbitral tribunal and shall provide for a certain degree of appreciation of the possible unique circumstances of each case. In other words, arbitral tribunals are (currently) free to choose the merits stage for their examination of the illegality allegations (be it in the frames of the question of admissibility or not) and there are sufficient examples for this. At the same time, arbitral tribunals can, on its own initiative, re-examine, at any stage of the proceeding, whether the dispute or any claim is within its jurisdiction and/or competence.[87]

---

[81] Alasdair Ross Anderson et al v. Costa Rica, ICSID Case No ARB(AF)/07/3, Award, 19 May 2010; Metal-Tech Ltd v. Uzbekistan, ICSID Case No ARB/10/3, Award, 4 October 2013.

[82] Waibel (2014), p. 3.

[83] Douglas (2009), para. 295. *See also*, Salini Costruttori S.p.A. and Italstrade S.p.A. v. Jordan, ICSID Case No. ARB/02/13, Decision on Jurisdiction, 31 July 2001, para. 131.

[84] Paulsson (2005), pp. 601–617. The importance of the delimitation between admissibility and jurisdiction was also noted by the arbitral tribunal in Methanex Corporation v. USA, UNCITRAL (NAFTA), Partial Award on Jurisdiction and Admissibility, 7 August 2002, para. 139.

[85] Oil Platforms (Iran v. USA), Judgment, ICJ Rep. 2003, 161, para. 29. *See also*, South West Africa Cases (Ethiopia v. South Africa; Liberia v. South Africa), First Phase, ICJ Reports 1962, p. 319 and South West Africa Cases (Ethiopia v. South Africa; Liberia v. South Africa), Second Phase, ICJ Reports 1966, p. 6.

[86] Laird (2005), pp. 201–222. *See also*, Waste Management, Inc v. Mexico, ICSID Case No ARB (AF)/00/3, Dissenting opinion of Ms Keith Highet, 30 April 2004, para. 58: "[j]urisdiction is the power of the tribunal to hear the case; admissibility is whether the case itself is defective – whether it is appropriate for the tribunal to hear it."

[87] Douglas (2009), para. 141; Schreuer et al. (2009), paras. 43. 52 and 498; Waibel (2014), p. 68.

In light of the above analysis, it is clear that whatever the stage of examination of the legality requirement may be and whatever procedural decision an arbitral tribunal may take, the final consequence for an illegal investment shall be the same, i.e. denial of protection under the system of international investment law and its ISDS mechanism, either through refusal of jurisdiction or admissibility of claims.

References

Brown C (2007) A common law of international adjudication. Oxford University Press, pp 61–63
Burke J (1977) Jowitt's dictionary of English law. In: Sweet, Maxwell (eds), vol 1, p 1034
Crawford J (2010) Continuity and discontinuity in international dispute settlement: an inaugural lecture. J Int Dispute Settlement 1
Diel-Gligor K, Nennecke R (2015) Investment in accordance with the law. In: Bungenberg M et al (eds) A handbook: international investment law
Douglas Z (2004) The plea of illegality in investment treaty arbitration. ICSID Rev: Foreign Invest Law J 29(1):155
Douglas Z (2009) The international law of investment claims. Cambridge University Press
Dumberry P (2016) State of confusion: the doctrine of 'clean hands' in investment arbitration after the Yukos award. J World Invest Trade 17
Fathallah R (2010) Corruption in international commercial and investment arbitration: recent trends and prospects for Arab countries. Int J Arab Arbitr 2(3):40–41 and 65–70
Fitzmaurice G (1958) The general principles of international law considered from the standpoint of the rule of law. RdC 92:119
Gaillard E (2019) The emergence of transnational responses to corruption in international arbitration. J Int Arbitr 35(1):4
Garner BA (1999) Black's law dictionary. West
Kreindler R (2010) Corruption in international investment arbitration: jurisdiction and the unclean hands doctrine. In: Hobér K et al (eds) Between East and West: essays in honour of Ulf Franke, pp 309 and 316–317
Kulick A, Wendler C (2010) A corrupt way to handle corruption? Thoughts on the recent ICISD case law on corruption. In: Legal issues of economic integration. Kluwer Law International, vol 37(1)
Kulkarni SA (2013) Enforcing anti-corruption measures through international investment arbitration. Transnatl Dispute Manag 3, available at www.transnational-dispute-management.com/article.asp?key=1957
Laird I (2005) A distinction without a difference? An examination of the concepts of admissibility and jurisdiction in Salini v. Jordan and Methanex v. USA. In: Weiler T (ed) International investment law and arbitration: leading cases from the ICSID, NAFTA, bilateral treaties and customary international law, pp 201–222
Lalive P (2002) Some objections to jurisdiction in investor-state arbitration. In: Publié dans les Procèsverbaux de l'ICCA, p 129
Lamm CB, Pham HT, Moloo R (2010) Fraud and corruption in international arbitration. In: Fernandez-Ballesteros, Arias (eds) Liber Amicorum Bernardo Cremades. Kluwer, pp 723–726
Levy L (2005) Anti-suit injunctions issued by arbitrators. In: Gaillard E (ed) Anti-suit injunctions in international arbitration. Juris
Llamzon AP (2015) Yukos Universal Limited (Isle of Man) v. The Russian Federation: the state of the "unclean hands" doctrine in international investment law: Yukos as both omega and alpha. ICSID Rev 30
Losco MA (2014) Charting a new course: Metal-Tech v. Uzbekistan and the treatment of corruption in investment arbitration. Duke Law J Online 64:37–52

Lotz RA, Busch M (2015) Investment in accordance with the law – specifically corruption. In: Bungenberg M et al (eds) A handbook: international investment law, p 583

Martin A (2004) International arbitration and corruption: an evolving standard. Transnatl Dispute Manag J:1

Newcombe A (2011) Investor misconduct: jurisdiction, admissibility, or merits? In: Brown C, Miles K (eds) Evolution in investment treaty law and arbitration. Cambridge University Press, p 198

Partasides C (2010) Proving corruption in international arbitration: a balanced standard for the real world. ICSID Rev: Foreign Invest Law J 25(1)

Paulsson J (2005) Jurisdiction and admissibility. In: Aksen G et al (eds) Global reflections on international law, commerce and dispute resolution, Liber Amicorum in honour of Robert Briner. ICC Publishing, pp 601–617

Pomson O (2017) The clean hands doctrine in the Yukos awards: a response to Patrick Dumberry. J World Invest Trade 18:712, 726

Raouf M (2009) How should international arbitrators tackle corruption issues? ICSID Rev: Foreign Invest Law J 24(1):116–136

Schill SW (2012) Illegal investments in investment treaty arbitration. Law Pract Int Courts Tribunals 11:281–323

Schreuer C (1996) Decisions Ex Aequo et Bono under the ICSID Convention. ICSID Rev 11:37

Schreuer C, Malintoppi L, Reinisch A, Sinclair A (2009) The ICSID Convention. Cambridge University Press

Summerfield JN (2009) The corruption defense in investment disputes: a discussion of the imbalance between international discourse and arbitral decisions. Transnatl Dispute Manag 6(1)

Tanzi A (2018) The relevance of the foreign investor's good faith. In: Gattini A et al (eds) General principles of law and international investment arbitration, pp 193 and 202

Waibel M (2010) Corfu channel case. In: Rüdiger W (ed) Max Planck encyclopedia of public international law, vol II. Oxford University Press, pp 792–797

Waibel M (2014) Investment arbitration: jurisdiction and admissibility. In: Legal Studies Research Paper Series, Paper No 9/2014. University of Cambridge

Weiler JHH (1999) The autonomy of the community legal order: through the looking glass. In: Weiler JHH (ed) The Constitution of Europe 'Do the new clothes have an emperor?' and other essays on European Integration. Oxford University Press, pp 286–323

Yeginsu C, Knoebel C (2018) Covered investment. In: Legum B (ed) The investment treaty arbitration review, 3rd edn, p 1

Chapter 4
Applicable Law for the Examination of Illicit Conduct

The determination of the applicable law in international arbitration may be seen as an uncomplicated question. It is usually indeed a very straightforward matter, provided that the parties to the dispute agreed on applicable law at some point of time. The modern laws of arbitration are consistent in its approach to grant the disputing parties as much freedom to decide on the applicable law as possible.[1] However, if parties have not made its choice of applicable law, then it is for arbitral tribunals to decide upon it.

The issue is of direct relevance for the purposes of the present book. The allegations of fraud and corruption are to be examined under the norms of law. The question that arises is what law shall be applied by arbitral tribunals in their examination of acts that are alleged to be illicit.

The complexity of this question, especially in investment arbitration, is that in most of the cases investments treaties (either of bilateral or multilateral character) do not contain a choice of law clause within its provisions. For instance, none of the 47 bilateral investment treaties concluded or drafted on behalf of the United States contained a provision with a choice of applicable law.[2]

---

[1] Blackaby et al. (2015), p. 156.

[2] *See,* the collection of the BITs entered by the United State at http://investmentpolicyhub.unctad.org/IIA/CountryBits/223. *See also,* Banifatemi, Y. (2010), The Law Applicable in Investment Treaty Arbitration, available at https://www.shearman.com/~/media/Files/NewsInsights/Publications/2010/06/The-Law-Applicable-in-Investment-Treaty-Arbitrat__/Files/View-full-article-The-Law-Applicable-in-Investme__/FileAttachment/IA061010TheLawApplicableinInvestmentTreatyArbitr__.pdf.

A. Tussupov, *Corruption and Fraud in Investment Arbitration*, EYIEL Monographs - Studies in European and International Economic Law 22,
https://doi.org/10.1007/978-3-030-90606-1_4

4.1 Choice of Law in Investment Treaties

International investment arbitration, just as any other type of arbitration, provides considerable respect to the parties' will, including in the context of the choice of law. As a rule, if the applicable law was duly chosen and agreed by parties, arbitral tribunals are under the duty to respect such a choice and apply that law. It is only when parties fail to make such a choice that the tribunals have discretion to decide on that matter. The same is anticipated in major international arbitration instruments.

For instance, the first sentence of Article 42(1) of the ICSID Convention provides the following:

> The Tribunal shall decide a dispute in accordance with such *rules of law* as may be agreed by the parties. [emphasis added]

A similar clause can be met in the ICC Arbitration Rules (Article 21(1), first sentence), which reads as follows:

> The parties shall be free to agree upon the *rules of law* to be applied by the arbitral tribunal to the merits of the dispute. [emphasis added]

By way of comparison, the UNCITRAL Arbitration Rules provide a different angle to the question of the parties' autonomy in connection to the choice of applicable law. Article 33(1) of the UNCITRAL Rules:

> The Arbitral Tribunal shall apply *the law* designated by the parties as applicable to the substance of the dispute. [emphasis added]

Moreover, the Arbitration Rules of the Stockholm Chamber of Commerce ("**SCC**") represent a type of a combination of what is seen in the ICSID and UNCITRAL instruments. Article 22(1) of the SCC Rules states the following:

> The Arbitral Tribunal shall decide the merits of the dispute on the basis of *the law or rules of law* agreed upon by the parties. [emphasis added]

As can be noticed, the difference between the rules is in the specific language of the provisions, i.e. the term "rules of law" or the term "law" are either used separately, individually, or together. Whereas, theoretically, both could mean the same, in practice the term "rules of law" could provide an opportunity to selectively refer to some particular rules of law within one legal system for assessment of some matters, and to refer to other rules of law from another legal system in relation to different matters. For instance, parties may agree to use international law for the determination of general questions and host State's law for interpretation of some operating contracts in case of a dispute.[3] In addition to that, parties may refer to general principles of law or principles of public international law, as well as specific commercial standards such as the *Incoterms*.[4]

---

[3]Such a practice is known to be called as a "*depeçage* technique".

[4]Incoterms are a standard set of terminology created by the International Chamber of Commerce, which are used universally for the definition of the terms of the freight forwarding.

At the same time, nothing stops parties to refer all questions to the law of a host State. Something to keep in mind is that arbitral tribunals are not actually bound by established practices and/or interpretation normally given to such national laws by respective national courts. It is often that an arbitral tribunal with an international composition would come to conclusions that are different from those that would have been expected from a national court applying the same law.[5] As was stated by *Spiermann*,

> [a]rbitral tribunals do not necessarily confine legal analysis to the particular system of national law over which the host State reigns supreme and which normally, together with choice of laws principles, forms the proper law of contract with foreign investors; time and again, disputes have been resolved on a more "international" basis, supplementing national law as seen fit with elements from outside the legal system in question.[6]

In the scenario where there is proper and undisputed choice of law, it would normally be left for arbitral tribunals to only identify such choice, determine its scope and apply the law that was agreed upon.

There is also an alternative (exceptional) approach to this matter. In some investment disputes, notwithstanding the existence of the choice of law clause in investment treaties, parties went through heated debates over the content and scope of the applicable law provisions. For instance, in the CME Czech Republic B.V. v. the Czech Republic case the arbitral tribunal seated under the auspices of the SCC had to hear extensive submissions on the question of the applicable law.[7] The disagreement on the issue arose on the basis of Article 8(6) of the Czech Republic—Netherlands BIT, which states the following:

> 6) The arbitral tribunal shall decide on the basis of the law, *taking into account* in particular though *not exclusively:*
> - the law in force of the Contracting Party concerned;
> - the provisions of this Agreement, and other relevant Agreements between the Contracting Parties;
> - the provisions of special agreements relating to the investment;
> - the general principles of international law. [emphasis added]

The Respondent in the CME dispute argued that the host State's law should take precedence over other rules of law for the determination whether the Czech Republic violated its treaty obligations. Whereas, the claimant argued the opposite.

As the CME tribunal noted, the provision did not contain any numbering of the enlisted rules and principles and it was, therefore, impossible to tell whether the drafters were intending to provide some sort of hierarchy in the scope of that provision. After difficult deliberations the majority of the tribunal found that the provision was quite broad and contains a self-explanatory confirmation of the duty of

---

[5] Spiermann (2015), p. 1374.

[6] *Id.*

[7] CME Czech Republic B.V. (The Netherlands) v. The Czech Republic, UNCITRAL Arbitration Proceedings, Final Award, 14 March 2003.

the tribunal "to decide on the basis of the law" rather than *ex aequo et bono*.[8] It then found that the enlisted items of Article 8(6) of the BIT were to be "taken into account" only and not to be bindingly guided by.[9] Finally, the tribunal decided that it had full discretion to make a ruling on the applicable law by itself. One of the arbitrators dissented in his findings.[10]

4.2 Tribunal's Determination of the Applicable Law

It was previously established that arbitral tribunals enjoy discretion in determining the applicable law, where no choice of law was made by parties. Such discretion is enshrined in the rules of major arbitration institutions. The texts and the language of such legal instruments may differ considerably.

For instance, under the second sentence of Article 42(1) of the ICSID Convention the rule is the following:

> In the absence of such agreement, the *Tribunal shall apply the law of the Contracting State party to the dispute* (including its rules on the conflict of laws) and such rules of international law as may be applicable. [emphasis added]

The ICC Arbitration Rules state the following in the relevant parts of Article 21:

> (1) ...In the absence of any such agreement, the arbitral tribunal shall apply the rules of law *which it determines to be appropriate.*
> (2) The arbitral tribunal shall *take account* of the provisions of the *contract*, if any, between the parties and of any *relevant trade usages.* [emphasis added]

The UNCITRAL Arbitration Rules, in Article 35(1), take a much broader approach, providing the tribunals with more discretion to select the law that is to be applied to the disputed matters:

> The arbitral tribunal shall apply the rules of law designated by the parties as applicable to the substance of the dispute. Failing such designation by the parties, the arbitral tribunal shall apply the law *which it determines to be appropriate.* [emphasis added]

The Arbitration Rules of the SCC provide for a similar approach:

> The Arbitral Tribunal shall decide the merits of the dispute on the basis of the law(s) or rules of law agreed upon by the parties. In the absence of such agreement, the Arbitral Tribunal shall apply the law or rules of law *that it considers most appropriate.* [emphasis added]

The procedure and practice under the ICC, UNCITRAL and SCC Rules deem to be self-explanatory. They focus on the arbitral tribunals' discretion to establish the

[8] *Id.*, para. 403.

[9] CME Czech Republic B.V. (The Netherlands) v. The Czech Republic, UNCITRAL Arbitration Proceedings, Separate Opinion of Ian Brownlie, C.B.E., Q.C., 14 March 2003.

[10] CME Czech Republic B.V. (The Netherlands) v. The Czech Republic, UNCITRAL Arbitration Proceedings, Dissenting Opinion of JUDr Jaroslav Handl, 11 September 2001.

relevant applicable law for the disputed matters. Understandably, such discretion is not without limits. In the situation of the ICC Arbitration Rules, the limit is set in clause 21(2), which says that "the arbitral tribunal shall take account of the provisions of the contract, if any, between the parties and of any relevant trade usages."[11] However, in respect of the various arbitral tribunals operating under other sets of arbitration rules, no other explicit limits seem to exist. Nevertheless, arbitral tribunals in the ISDS disputes must keep in mind the specific nature of questions in international investment arbitration and extend the due regard to the circumstances of each case.[12]

Notably, the approach of the ICSID tribunals for the determination of the applicable law was not always consistent. It has been developing throughout time and practice. This might be due to relatively complex language in Article 42 of the ICSID Convention, which mentions both "the law of the Contracting State party to the dispute" and the "rules of international law". From the analysis of different publications and case law, it seems that the initial position was that the ICSID tribunals should normally apply the law of the Contracting State party first and that the result of the application of that law should then be tested against international law to detect any unfair outcomes.[13] Subsequently, an arbitral tribunal could have substituted the "unfair" parts of the host State legislation to the particular parts of international law, or refer entirely to international law.

As can be seen from the known case law, the position on the approach on the determination of the applicable law must have slightly changed after the decision of the *ad hoc* committee in the Wena Hotels v. Egypt case, where the committee attempted to interpret the text of Article 42(1) of the ICSID Convention.[14] The *ad hoc* committee made two conclusions:

- It was found that international law should be considered for application equally with national law;
- It was decided that different rules of law of different systems could be used for different scopes of questions of a dispute (for example, public international law for interpretation of contracts, host State's law for the determination of the "delict", general principles of law for the analysis of the "good faith" of the parties).[15]

Through this approach, the *ad hoc* committee decided to use international law for the purposes of quantum only. For other questions, the committee found it

[11] Article 21(2) of the ICC Arbitration Rules.

[12] *See,* Di Pietro (2005).

[13] *Id.* with references to Broches (1993), p. 627.

[14] Wena Hotels Limited v. the Arab Republic of Egypt, ICSID Case No ARB/98/4, Award, 8 December 2000.

[15] Wena Hotels Limited v. the Arab Republic of Egypt, ICSID Case No ARB/98/4, Decision on the Application by the Arab Republic of Egypt for Annulment of the Arbitral Award, 28 January 2002, paras. 37–53.

appropriate to use the law of the host State. The law of the host State was not applied for the evaluation of damages since under the committee's analysis the Egyptian law could not provide for reasonable level of protection, unlike international law.[16]

The Wena v. Egypt annulment committee's decision opened an evident interpretation of the second sentence of Article 42(1) of the ICSID Convention:

> In the absence of such agreement, the Tribunal shall apply the law of the Contracting State party to the dispute (including its rules on the conflict of laws) *and* such rules of international law as may be applicable. [emphasis added]

Indeed, the language of the provision does not oblige to first use national law and only then public international law. In fact, the second sentence of Article 42(1) is quite precise that national law "and" international law are applicable to the disputes. Therefore, the choice between the two is at the discretion of the tribunal. In the perfect scenario and as was suggested by the *ad hoc* committee in the Wena v. Egypt case, the rule should create an interplay of international law and the law of the concerned contracting State.[17]

Based on the above and from the drawn analysis of other arbitral awards,[18] it is to be concluded that in a situation when no choice of law has been made, the ICSID tribunals have discretion to apply international and national law without immediate preference of one law over another.

4.3 Concluding Remarks

It has been identified that most investment treaties do not contain a choice of law provision. This is explained by the fact that in contrast to commercial agreements, parties to investment treaties are not entirely the same as potential parties to international investment disputes.[19] In international commercial transactions, parties to an arbitration agreement anticipate a possible dispute between themselves, its scope and possible risks, which is why it is reasonable for them to determine applicable law. In investment arbitration, parties to international investment treaties are always States and they usually do not have a prospective vision of a possible investor-state dispute.

In relation to the selection of applicable law by an arbitral tribunal, it is to be noted that although tribunals enjoy a wide discretion in this question, they are

[16] *Id.*, para. 53.

[17] *Id.*, para. 941.

[18] *See,* GMS Gas Transmission Company v. The Republic of Argentina, ICSID Case No ARB/01/8, Award, 12 May 2005 and Middle East Cement Shipping and Handling Co. S.A. v. the Arab Republic of Egypt, ICSID Case No ARB/99/6, Decision on Jurisdiction, 28 November 2000.

[19] Safe for rare examples of the State-to-State investment disputes, *e.g.* Italian Republic v. Republic of Cuba, Ad hoc Arbitration, Final Award, 1 November 2008 and Mexico v. United States (US Trucking Case), Ad hoc Arbitration, Final Report, 6 February 2001.

usually expected to apply the law, which has the closest connection to issues in dispute.[20] It has also been established that notwithstanding the nature of the disputed subjects in international investment arbitration, public international law has a central role in investment disputes. Nevertheless, national law, at least in some ISDS cases, "forms part and parcel of the tribunal's applicable law".[21] The *sui generis* nature of the ISDS, at times, makes the determination of the applicable law for certain questions very nuanced.[22]

Clearly, the determination of the correct applicable law is very important for the potential outcome of any dispute. It can even be decisive in some situations, as a certain event under different legal regimes can have opposite legal outcomes. This is the reason why an objective failure to determine and apply relevant applicable law can potentially amount to an excess of power, which could lead to the annulment of an arbitral award under Article 52 of the ICSID Convention.[23]

As was stated by the *ad hoc* committee in the Maritime International v. the Government of Guinea, "a tribunal's disregard of the agreed rules of law would constitute a derogation from the terms of reference within which the tribunal has been authorized to function."[24] This, however, must not be confused with the incorrect application of the correct applicable law. In support of this, the decision in the Azurix Corp. v. the Argentine Republic case can be recalled, where the arbitral tribunal found that

> ...while non-application by the tribunal of the law applicable under Article 42 [of the ICSID Convention] may be a ground for annulment, the incorrect application by the tribunal of the applicable law is not.[25]

References

Blackaby N, Partasides QC, Redfern A, Hunter M (2015) Redfern and hunter on international arbitration, 6th edn. Oxford University Press, p 156

---

[20] *See,* Di Pietro (2005); *see also,* Spiermann (2015).

[21] Waibel (2014), p. 11.

[22] Douglas (2003), pp. 194–213.

[23] Article 52 (1)b of the ICSID Convention: "Either party may request annulment of the award by an application in writing addressed to the Secretary-General on one or more of the following grounds:... (b) that the Tribunal has manifestly exceeded its powers...".

[24] Maritime International Nominees Establishment v. the Government of Guinea, ICSID Case No. ARB/84/4, Decision on the Application by Guinea for Partial Annulment of the Arbitral Award dated 6 January 1988 rendered by the Ad Hoc Committee, 14 December 1989, para. 5.03; *See also,* Enron Creditors Recovery Corp. Ponderosa Assets, L.P. v. The Argentine Republic, ICSID Case No. ARB/01/3, Decision on the Application for Annulment of the Argentine Republic, 30 July 2010, paras. 216–292.

[25] Azurix Corp. v. The Argentine Republic, ICSID Case No. ARB/01/12, Decision on the Application for Annulment of the Argentine Republic, 1 September 2009, para. 137.

Broches A (1993) Convention on the settlement of investment disputes between states and nationals of other states of 1965 explanatory notes and survey of its application? Yearb Commer Arbitr XVIII:627

Di Pietro D (2005) Applicable law Under Article 42 of the ICSID. In: Weiler (ed) International investment law and arbitration: leading cases from the ICSID, NAFTA, bilateral treaties and customary international law. Available at: https://blogs.law.nyu.edu/transnational/2011/10/applicable-law-under-article-42-of-the-icsid-convention/

Douglas Z (2003) The hybrid foundations of investment treaty arbitration. Br Yearb Int Law 74: 194–213

Spiermann O (2015) Investment arbitration: applicable law. In: Bungenberg M et al (eds) A handbook: international investment law. C.H. Beck/Hart/Nomos, p 1374

Waibel M (2014) Investment arbitration: jurisdiction and admissibility. In: Legal studies research paper series, Paper No 9/2014. University of Cambridge, p 11

Chapter 5
Evidence and Proof

Evidence plays an important role for the outcome of any dispute that is being settled either in municipal courtrooms or before arbitral tribunals. It is reported that around 60–70% of international arbitration cases turn on facts, rather than law.[1] This is especially true in the context of the present topic when the claims of illegality (i.e. corruption, fraud or bribery) may have very serious legal consequences.

In common law jurisdictions the questions of taking of evidence is usually regulated by the designated rules on evidence, as well as common law and practice directions. In continental legal system the questions of evidence and proof are often dealt with in civil, administrative and criminal procedural codes, rules and guidelines. However, in contrast to the national systems, international investment arbitration does not typically contain any mandatory evidentiary rules; if these aspects are not addressed in the arbitration clause they are remitted to the discretion of the tribunal in their entirety.[2]

The question of evidence and proof in investment arbitration proceedings does not seem to be over-researched. This might be because of the belief that the approach to evidence and proof is not much different from the way these matters are approached in commercial arbitration. This may be true to a certain extent. However, when talking about untypical elements in investment arbitration, such as fraud and corruption, these questions become of central interest, partly because investment arbitration has public law elements unlike commercial arbitration.

The public law elements in international investment arbitration are present due to several factors, such as:

- the presence of a sovereign as a party to the arbitration,
- the conduct complained of is usually the conduct of a State in exercise of a governmental function, and

[1] Blackaby et al. (2015), p. 375.

[2] Sasson (2015), p. 1305. *See also*, Pietrowski (2006), pp. 373, 374.

A. Tussupov, *Corruption and Fraud in Investment Arbitration*, EYIEL Monographs - Studies in European and International Economic Law 22,
https://doi.org/10.1007/978-3-030-90606-1_5

- the dispute settlement mechanism arises out of a public international law instrument, i.e. BITs or multilateral investment treaties (e.g. ECT).

For these reasons, it is believed that the questions of evidence and proof in ISDS system are to be re-examined in light of such public law factors.[3] However, at this stage it would be helpful to first introduce the current approaches to evidence and proof in international (including investment) arbitration with emphasis on situations where allegations of illegality are being pursued.

5.1 Evidence in International Arbitration

Parties to arbitration are free to agree on application of certain evidentiary rules for the respective arbitration proceedings. This freedom is included in the essential principle of parties' autonomy, which is supported by institutional agreements, arbitration rules and national laws.[4]

In the absence of such agreement, an arbitral tribunal is free to exercise its discretion and either to provide guidance on evidentiary questions itself or to refer to a concrete set of rules. Although, arbitral tribunals do not have an obligation to apply strict evidentiary rules, they are also not restricted from doing so.[5] In practice, arbitral tribunals often tend to apply the International Bar Association's Rules on the Taking of Evidence in International Arbitration ("**IBA Rules**").[6]

To stop for a moment on the IBA Rules, it may be recalled that the initial version of the rules had been built upon the less successful Supplementary Rules Governing the Presentation and Reception of Evidence in International Commercial Arbitration dated 1983.[7] In contrast to its predecessor, the 1999 project, as well as the revised (or updated) 2010 version of the IBA Rules received much wider recognition and application.[8]

In the rules, the International Bar Association has attempted "to supplement the legal provisions and the institutional, ad hoc or other rules that apply to the conduct of the arbitration."[9] In other words, as *Tawil* and *Gill QC* noted in the Foreword of the IBA Rules, they are merely "designed to be used *in conjunction with*, and adopted together with, institutional, ad hoc or other rules or procedures governing

[3] The particular effect of the public elements in ISDS is to be discussed further in Part III below.

[4] *See*, Article 43 of the ICSID Convention and Rules 34, 35 and 36 of the ICSID Rules of Procedure for Arbitration Proceedings, as well as Section 34 of the English Arbitration Act of 1996.

[5] Dugan et al. (2011), p. 161. *See also*, Malik and Kamat (2018), p. 14.

[6] International Bar Association Rules on the Taking of Evidence in International Arbitration, adopted by a resolution of the IBA Council on 29 May 2010, available at https://www.ibanet.org. *See*, Schreuer et al. (2009), p. 642; *see also*, Kubalczyk (2015), pp. 85–109.

[7] Blackaby et al. (2015), p. 381.

[8] *Id.*

[9] IBA Rules, Preamble, para. 1.

international arbitrations."[10] This means that parties are still to select rules of relevant institutions (e.g., ICC, LCIA, ICSID, etc.) or to opt for ad hoc rules.[11] In that sense, while still being overly recognized and utilised, the IBA Rules remain to be a soft instrument on the taking of evidence that explicitly refuses "to limit the flexibility" of arbitral tribunals and parties to adapt other approaches on the questions of taking of evidence.[12] Whether this is a positive characteristic for the purposes of combating corruption and fraud in ISDS, or whether the system requires rather more binding instruments for that purpose, will be discussed further in Part III of the present textbook. One thing is certain, however—the IBA Rules have a central place in investment treaty arbitration. As was observed by *Antuna*, it has become very common that Procedural Order No.1 issued by almost all tribunals makes an explicit reference to these rules.[13]

Furthermore, when turning to provisions on taking of evidence that are enshrined in arbitration rules, the ICSID Arbitration Rules are of particular relevance. Thus, Article 34 of the ICSID Arbitration Rules has a central role in the adducing of evidence in the ICSID arbitration proceedings. Paragraph 1 of Article 34 provides arbitral tribunals with considerable freedom on deciding on the admissibility of evidence:

> The Tribunal shall be the judge of the admissibility of any evidence adduced and of its probative value.

By way of comparison, the same is provided in the IBA Rules under clause 9(1), although in broader terms:

> The Arbitral Tribunal shall determine the admissibility, relevance, materiality and weight of evidence.

The tribunal's discretion on the questions of evidence and proof is confirmed by the UNCITRAL Model Law on International Commercial Arbitration (i.e. Article 19)[14] and by some national laws on arbitration (e.g. see Section 34 of the English Arbitration Act of 1996).[15] This view is also reportedly consistent with the domestic

---

[10] IBA Rules, Foreword by Tawil, G.S. and Gill QC, J. [emphasis added].

[11] Commentary on the revised text of the 2010 IBA Rules on the Taking of Evidence in International Arbitration, 1999 IBA Working Party & 2010 IBA Rules of Evidence Review Subcommittee, available at https://www.ibanet.org/Document/Default.aspx?DocumentUid=DD240932-0E08-40D4-9866-309A635487C0, p. 3.

[12] IBA Rules, Preamble, para. 2.

[13] Antuna (2020), para. 12.

[14] Article 19 of the UNCITRAL Model Law on International Commercial Arbitration: "(1) Subject to the provisions of this Law, the Parties are free to agree on the procedure to be followed by the arbitral tribunal in conducting the proceedings. (2) Failing such agreement, the arbitral tribunal may, subject to the provision of this Law, conduct the arbitration in such manner as it considers appropriate. The power conferred upon the arbitral tribunal includes the power to determine the admissibility, relevance, materiality, and weight of any evidence."

[15] Section 34 (1) and (2) of the 1996 English Arbitration Act: "(1) It shall be for the tribunal to decide all procedural and evidential matters, subject to the right of the parties to agree any matter.

courts' practice when reviewing arbitral awards.[16] In particular, the questions of admissibility, relevance and value of evidence are all, normally, guided and answered by an arbitral tribunal by its own account. As to the first two questions (admissibility and relevance), while arbitral tribunals do enjoy a wide discretion in dismissing any kind of evidence on various grounds,[17] they are usually reluctant to formally dismiss evidence so as not to make an impression that certain questions have been prejudged and to avoid any possible motions to set-aside or annul the arbitral award on that basis after it is issued.[18]

In the frames of the present topic, it is to be reasonably assumed that in many cases, a party asserting fraud or corruption would face difficulty of providing direct evidence of possible illicit acts of an opposing party. Often, in such situations an alleging party is building its case on indirect and circumstantial evidence.[19] Circumstantial evidence may also be in the form of indicators, or as was previously defined—*red flags*. In other words, the circumstances of a case, such as for instance, "excessive commissions to third-party agents or consultants", "unreasonably large discounts to third-party distributors" or "third-party consulting agreement that include only vaguely described services", may raise *red flags* of the existence of illicit activity, such as corruption.[20] There are no binding exhaustive lists of *red flags* of exact crimes. However, there are a number of "soft" documents that provide high level examples of possible *red flags* of particular offences.[21] Evidently, *red flags* do

(2) Procedural and evidential matters include - ... (f) whether to apply strict rules of evidence (or any other rules) as to the admissibility, relevance or weight of any material (oral, written or other) sought to be tendered on any matters of fact or opinion, and the time, manner and form in which such material should be exchanged and presented; [...]."

[16] Wiebecke (2018), p. 95 with reference to Born (2014), p. 2308.

[17] *See,* Article 8(2) of the IBA Rules of Evidence: "... The Arbitral Tribunal may limit or exclude any questions to, answer by or appearance of a witness, if it considers such question, answer or appearance to be irrelevant, immaterial, unreasonably burdensome, duplicative or otherwise covered by a reason for objection..."

[18] Born (2014), p. 2311.

[19] *See,* Sistem v. Uzbekistan (Chapter 2.1 of Part II), Siag v. Egypt (Chapter 2.3 of Part II), Metal Tech v. Uzbekistan (Chapter 1.2 of Part II), Churchill v. Indonesia (Chapter 1.3 of Part II), Spentex v. Uzbekistan (Chapter 1.4 of Part II), Kim v. Uzbekistan (Chapter 2.4 of Part II).

[20] Criminal Division of the U.S. Department of Justice and the Enforcement Division of the U.S. Securities and Exchange Commission (2012), A Resource Guide to the U.S. Foreign Corrupt Practices Act, available at https://www.justice.gov/sites/default/files/criminal-fraud/legacy/2015/01/16/guide.pdf, p. 22.

[21] *See for instance*, Woolf Committee Report on Business Ethics, Global Companies and the Defence Industry: Ethical Business Conduct in Bae Systems Plc 25–26 (2008), prepared at the request of the Board of Directors of Bae Systems Plc; Competence Center on Arbitration and Crime, Basel Institute on Governance (2019), Corruption and Money Laundering in International Arbitration: A Toolkit for Arbitrators, available at https://www.baselgovernance.org/sites/default/files/2019-05/a_toolkit_for_arbitrators_29_05_2019_single_pages.pdf; UK Government (2017), 'Flag It Up', available at https://flagitup.campaign.gov.uk/.

have a place in international arbitration.[22] Their practical value will be separately analysed in Part II further below.

It is also established that when, due to objective reasons, direct evidence of certain alleged facts does not exist, an arbitral tribunal may, in principle,

> rely on presumptions or inferences and consider facts proven on the basis of other proven facts or factual knowledge, a series of facts linked together or accepted factual knowledge, such as in the Corfu Channel case of the International Court of Justice.[23]

Such inferences may also be drawn from the conduct of parties, when, for instance, a party is unreasonably uncooperative or it is not producing a document or a witness that it has a proven access to.[24]

Generally, and for the purposes of identifying the currently applicable legal framework on evidentiary questions in international investment arbitration, it can be easily concluded that the main actor in deciding on all aspects of evidence in investment arbitration is the arbitral tribunal itself.

5.2 Burden of Proof

The general practice applied by arbitral tribunals is that the burden of proof rests with the claimant or with the party that alleges a certain fact.[25] At the same time, however, it is argued that the burden of proof may shift to the other side under certain circumstances, for example when a party proves a certain fact on a *prima facie* basis.[26]

The burden of proof in investment arbitration may narrow or widen depending on the alleged facts and the stage of the proceedings, i.e. the jurisdictional stage or

---

[22] *See for instance,* Llamzon (2014); Betz (2017); Partasides (2010); Branson and Manon (2020).

[23] Wiebecke (2018), p. 97 with reference to Corfu Channel case, 1949, ICJ Rep 4,18; *see also*, Scherrer (2002), pp. 34–35.

[24] *See,* Article 9 (5), (6) and (7) of the IBA Rules on Evidence: "(5) If a Party fails without satisfactory explanation to produce any Document requested in a Request to Produce to which it has not objected in due time or fails to produce any Document ordered to be produced by the Arbitral Tribunal, the Arbitral Tribunal may infer that such document would be adverse to the interests of that Party. (6) If a Party fails without satisfactory explanation to make available any other relevant evidence, including testimony, sought by one Party to which the Party to whom the request was addressed has not objected in due time or fails to make available any evidence, including testimony, ordered by the Arbitral Tribunal to be produced, the Arbitral Tribunal may infer that such evidence would be adverse to the interests of that Party. (7) If the Arbitral Tribunal determines that a Party has failed to conduct itself in good faith in the taking of evidence, the Arbitral Tribunal may, in addition to any other measures available under these Rules, take such failure into account in its assignment of the costs of the arbitration, including costs arising out of or in connection with the taking of evidence."

[25] Sasson (2015), p. 1359.

[26] Schreuer et al. (2009), p. 669; *See also*, Fathallah (2010), p. 73.

merits. In particular, the arbitral tribunal in the Phoenix v. the Czech Republic case stated that

> [i]f the alleged facts are facts that, if proven, would constitute a violation of the relevant BIT, they have indeed to be accepted as such at the jurisdictional stage, until their existence is ascertained or not at the merits level.[27]

In other words, according to this tribunal, an asserting party (or, mainly, a claimant in the jurisdictional stage) does not necessarily have to bear the burden of proving the accuracy of alleged facts.[28] It has been found to be sufficient for a claimant to prove that the alleged facts, if true, would lead to a violation of international investment law in order to decide on jurisdiction. This logic, however, has to work the other way around as well, i.e. if jurisdiction depends on the existence of certain facts (rather than their accuracy), they must be proven at the jurisdictional stage before the case is examined on its merits.[29]

Moreover, and as mentioned above, some could argue that, in cases of corruption and fraud, a party only needs to establish a *prima facie* case, which would trigger the shift of the burden of proof to the other party, who would ultimately have to prove the absence of fraud and corruption.[30] This, however, would result in the other party having to prove the negative case, which might not be easy to do, particularly in the case of corruption.[31]

5.3 Standard of Proof

Similarly to the burden of proof, findings on the applicable standard of proof are usually determinative for the outcome of a case. This question is important for parties and arbitral tribunals. As with evidentiary and burden of proof questions, an arbitral tribunal normally enjoys wide discretion on the determination of the applicable standard of proof.

From the current case law, it is evident that the most common standard in international arbitration practice (both commercial and investment) is the so-called "balance of probabilities" standard. In other words, a tribunal is to see whether a certain fact is more probable to be true than not. There is an ongoing discussion whether the same standard of proof (i.e. "balance of probabilities") is to be applied

---

[27] Phoenix Action, Ltd. V. Czech Republic, ICSID Case No. ARB/06/5, Award, 15 April 2009, para. 61.

[28] A certain level of proportionality and reasonableness is, of course, to be observed.

[29] Phoenix Action, Ltd. V. Czech Republic, ICSID Case No. ARB/06/5, Award, 15 April 2009, para. 61.

[30] Clouet (2018), p. 12; Partasides (2010).

[31] Wiebecke (2018), p. 99.

for the allegations of fraud and corruption, or whether this standard must be higher (e.g. "clear and convincing evidence").[32] The latter triggers two further questions:

- Is it reasonably feasible for an alleging party to clear a standard of proof that is as high as "clear and convincing evidence" when dealing with illicit actions that are usually being conducted in deep secrecy?
- Would the application of the usual standard of proof ("balance of probabilities") be insufficient to decide on such serious allegations as fraud and corruption?

As it is also generally evident from the scholarly writings, there is no uniformed approach to the above questions,[33] and the aim will be to further examine them in light of the case law and doctrine analysis in Parts II and III.

5.4 Concluding Remarks

In this chapter, the way the questions of evidence and proof are being dealt with in international investment arbitration have been identified. It has been observed that investment tribunals generally enjoy wide discretion in deciding on the evidentiary questions, unless these questions have been pre-regulated by parties to various international investment treaties and disputes. Parties are generally free to agree on certain evidentiary rules. The most referenced rules are the IBA Rules. The applicable law can play a major role in the application of certain procedures and standards towards evidence and proof.

Additionally, it has been noted that there is no specific written norm as to the regulation of the burden of proof. However, as customary in almost any dispute-settlement mechanism, the burden of proof usually lays with the asserting party.

All findings in this chapter, as well as generally in Part I, will be used as background material for the analysis of the existing case law on corruption and fraud allegations in investment arbitration in the following chapters. The legal framework will further be utilized in the analysis of practical challenges of this topic and formulation of the author's proposals in Part III of this textbook.

---

[32]Betz (2017), p. 277. *See also*, Llamzon (2014); Wiebecke (2018), p. 99 and the Dissenting Opinion of Professor Francesco Orrego Vicuna in Waguih Elie George Siag and Clorinda Vecchi v. the Arab Republic of Egypt, ICSID Case No ARB/05/15, discussed in Chapter 2.3 of Part II.

[33]*See for instance,* Catti (2013), pp. 36–38; Crivellaro (2003), p. 109; and Clouet, L.M. (2018), Arbitrating under the table: the effect of allegations of corruption in relation to the jurisdiction of the arbitral tribunal and the enforcement of foreign arbitral awards, available at https://nyu.academia.edu/LuisMar%C3%ADaClouet.

References

Antuna AF (2020) Evidence in Investor-State Arbitration. Jus Mundi, Available at https://jusmundi.com/en/document/wiki/en-evidence-in-investor-state-arbitration

Betz K (2017) Proving bribery, fraud and money laundering in international arbitration. University of Basel, Cambridge University Press

Blackaby N, Partasides QC, Redfern A, Hunter M (2015) Redfern and hunter on international arbitration, 6th edn, Oxford University Press, p 375

Born G (2014) International commercial arbitration, vol. II, 2nd edn. Kluwer Law International, Hague, p 2308

Branson J, Manon R (2020) Why tribunals should not ignore "red flags" of corruption. Global Arbitr Rev. Available at https://globalarbitrationreview.com/article/1229354/why-tribunals-should-not-ignore-%E2%80%9Cred-flags%E2%80%9D-of-corruption

Catti C (2013) The arbitrability of corruption claims. Young Arbitration Review, 8th edn, pp 36–38

Clouet LM (2018) Arbitrating under the table: the effect of allegations of corruption in relation to the jurisdiction of the arbitral tribunal and the enforcement of foreign arbitral awards, p 12. https://nyu.academia.edu/LuisMar%C3%ADaClouet

Crivellaro A (2003) Arbitration case law on bribery: issues of arbitrability, contract validity, merits and evidence. In: Karsten K, Berkeley A (eds) Arbitration, money laundering, corruption and fraud. Dossiers - ICC Institute of World Business Law, p 109

Dugan C, Wallace D, Rubins N, Sabahi B (2011) Investor-State Arbitration. Oxford University Press, p 161

Fathallah R (2010) Corruption in international commercial and investment arbitration: recent trends and prospects for Arab countries. Int J Arab Arbitr 2(3):73

Kubalczyk AM (2015) Evidentiary rules in international arbitration: a comparative analysis of approaches and the need for regulation. Groningen J Int Law 3:85–109

Llamzon A (2014) Corruption in international investment arbitration. Oxford University Press

Malik D, Kamat G (2018) Corruption in international commercial arbitration: arbitrability, admissibility & adjudication. The Arbitration Brief, Available at https://paperity.org/p/185990736/corruption-in-international-commercial-arbitration-arbitrability-admissibility, p 14

Partasides C (2010) Proving corruption in international arbitration: a balanced standard for the real world. ICSID Rev Foreign Invest Law J 25(1)

Pietrowski R (2006) Evidence in international arbitration. J Int Arbitr 22(3):373, 374

Sasson M (2015) Investment arbitration: procedure. In: Bungenberg M et al (eds) A handbook: international investment law, p 1305

Scherrer M (2002) Circumstantial evidence in corruption cases before international arbitral tribunals. Int Arbitr Law Rev 5(2):34–35

Schreuer C, Malintoppi L, Reinisch A, Sinclair A (2009) The ICSID convention: a commentary. Cambridge University Press, p 642

Wiebecke M (2018) Evidence and proof. In: Barton Legum, the investment treaty arbitration review, 3rd edn, p 95

Part II
Current Arbitral Practice in the Context of Corruption and Fraud

Over fifty-five years ago, *Judge Lagergren* issued his landmark award in the confidential ICC Case No. 1110 between Mr. X and Company A. It is *Judge Lagergren* who has not shied away from taking the initiative of investigating the sham constructions that were put in front of him and self-examined the jurisdiction of the tribunal. "[I]n the presence of a contract in dispute of the nature set out hereafter, condemned by public decency and morality, I cannot in the interest of due administration of justice avoid examining the question of jurisdiction on my own motion" stated *Judge Lagergren*.[1] Back then (and up until these days) his self-initiative was heavily discussed, criticised and at the same time praised.[2]

The claims of illegality that are put before international arbitral tribunals are not so rare anymore. States and investors tend to use the allegations of corruption and fraud as "swords"[3] and "shields".[4] In this Part, the author will try to systematise the findings of arbitral tribunals on corruption and fraud allegations and draw a chronological chain on how the approach of dealing with such allegations has, so far, developed.

Dozens of arbitral awards that include a plea of illegality in their reasoning were identified and thoroughly reviewed. The astonishing fact is that notwithstanding the previous experience of other arbitral tribunals, the approach to dealing with arguments of illicit conduct is often very different. Despite a growing number of tribunals' decisions over allegations of fraud and corruption, tribunals' opinions still differ in many matters, which might be regarded as untypical for the practice of investment tribunals. In contrast to commercial arbitration, the ISDS tribunals tend to follow the legal conclusions made in other previous awards, especially if they touch upon similar subject matters. As was opined by *Bungenberg* and *Titi,* "[d]espite the absence of a formal doctrine of binding precedent, investment tribunals

[1] Sayed (2004), p. 61.

[2] *Id.*, p. 66.

[3] *i.e.*, arguments used to establish liability.

[4] *i.e.*, arguments used as defense.

generally rely on earlier awards to buttress their legal reasoning, often treating them as determinative or authoritative statements of applicable rules or principles of law".[5] At the same time, both *Bungenberg* and *Titi* note that this does not suggest that arbitral tribunals (or other third parties) are somehow bound by earlier arbitral awards.[6]

This Part will identify how arbitral tribunals have so far dealt with arguments on illicit misconduct. For these reasons, ten arbitral awards that provide a certain degree of guidance on arbitral tribunals' practice with illegality examination have been selected. The ten selected arbitral awards have been divided into two categories: **1.** where the allegations of fraud or corruption were outcome determinative, and **2.** where the allegations of fraud or corruption were not upheld.

Factual and legal arguments of the parties are analysed together with the arbitral tribunals' findings on them. The review and analysis of each "landmark" case will mostly be conducted in the following order:

1. Factual and procedural background;
2. Findings of the arbitral tribunal/dissenting opinions over the allegations of corruption or fraud;
3. Analysis of the arbitral tribunal's decision.

The last chapter of this Part, which is titled as "Lessons Learned" will be dedicated to the overall analysis of current trends, approaches and inconsistencies that are evident from the ten selected arbitral decisions and doctrinal views on the respective issues.

References

Bungenberg M, Titi C (2015) Precedents in international investment law. In: Bungenberg M et al (eds) A handbook: international investment law, p 1508

Sayed A (2004) Corruption in international trade and commercial arbitration. Kluwer Law International, p 61

[5] Bungenberg and Titi (2015), p. 1508.

[6] *Id.*

Chapter 6
Arbitral Tribunals Upholding Corruption and Fraud Arguments

Below are summaries of five disputes in which arbitral tribunals upheld the allegations of fraud or corruption. These cases have been chosen due to the analysis and findings made by tribunals on questions of direct relevance to the topic of the present monograph.

6.1 World Duty Free v. Kenya

> Big money, big names, and a mega scandal. The story of the World Duty Free complex must rank as one of the most extraordinary trade disputes in Kenya's history.[1]

It is to be noted from the very outset that the dispute discussed in this chapter is not "treaty based". The ICSID arbitration clause was included into the 1989 contract between the predecessor of World Duty Free Company Limited ("**Duty Free**") and the Republic of Kenya ("**Kenya**"). Due to crucial analysis and statements that were made during these arbitral proceedings, it is believed that this case must be dully reviewed and analysed for the purposes of the present research, together with analysing other scholarly writings that were dedicated to this case.[2]

Remarkably, the World Duty Free case is the first ICSID case where it was found that "claims based on contracts of corruption or on contracts obtained by corruption cannot be upheld".[3]

---

[1] Odumosu (2011), p. 88 referring to Africa News, "Kenya: Genesis of an Extraordinary Case", the East African Standard, 3 April 2005.

[2] *See for instance*, Odumosu (2011); Lamm et al. (2014); Nappert (2013); Betz (2017), Chapter 5.1.1.

[3] Clouet (2018), p. 29.

A. Tussupov, *Corruption and Fraud in Investment Arbitration*, EYIEL Monographs - Studies in European and International Economic Law 22,
https://doi.org/10.1007/978-3-030-90606-1_6

6.1.1 Factual and Procedural Background

The dispute concerns a contract between the claimant and the respondent on the construction and operation of the so-called *Duty Free shops* in two international airports of Kenya (in Nairobi and Mombasa). While presenting the factual background to the tribunal, the claimant submitted that "in order to be able to do business with the Government of Kenya, [the Claimant] was required in March 1989 to make a "personal donation" to Mr. Daniel arap Moi, then President of the Republic of Kenya".[4] The claimant added that the amount of such donation equalled to USD 2 million and was paid as part for consideration in obtaining the contract in dispute.

Additionally, the claimant put forward that his company was made to become a part of the massive multi-million fraud scheme. It was asserted that more than USD 483 million was laundered by the people close to the Government by faking financial documents that included *inter alia* the claimants' company. The funds were allegedly used for President Moi's political campaign.

6.1.2 Findings and Analysis of the Tribunal

The essential question before the arbitral tribunal was whether bribery, as contested by Kenya, indeed took place and what the ultimate consequence of such a finding should be for the parties. The World Duty Free tribunal's job in determining whether the payment of USD 2 million to the then President of Kenya indeed took place was not very difficult. In fact, the claimant himself provided details of such payment in his testimony:

> I felt uncomfortable with the idea of handing over this "personal donation" which appeared to me to be a bribe. However, this was the President, and I was given to understand that it was lawful and that I didn't have a choice if I wanted the investment contract.[5]

Therefore, both parties agreed that the payment of USD 2 million did take place, although Kenya asserted that the State was not aware of the payment at that time. The other issues, which were in contest by both parties and therefore submitted to the tribunal to decide was whether the payment to President Moi constituted a bribe and was therefore illegal. The subsequent question was whether a bribe as such is against the international public policy and should be outcome determinative for the arbitral proceedings.

The claimant argued that he did not know and could not have known that the payment of USD 2 million was a bribe to a state official. Contrary to that, the claimant's position was that the payment was required under the political protocol in

---

[4]World Duty Free Company Limited v. The Republic of Kenya, ICSID Case No. ARB/00/7, Award, 4 October 2006, para. 66.

[5]*Id.*, para.19.

Kenya.[6] Additionally, the Duty Free submitted that even if the payment was to be treated as a bribe to a governmental official, "bribery is not a strict liability offence, mens rea is relevant".[7] The respondent's position was the opposite.[8]

6.1.2.1 Local Tradition or Bribery?

One of the fundamental questions before the tribunal was whether the payment to the then-President of Kenya constituted a bribe or whether it was indeed a legitimate donation paid under the local customary traditions (the so-called "*Harambees*"). The tribunal's position in this regard was straightforward and it is best recapitulated with its own words:

> ...the Tribunal has no doubt that the concealed payments [...] could not be considered as a personal donation for public purposes. Those payments were made not only in order to obtain an audience with President Moi (as submitted by the Claimant), but above all to obtain during that audience the agreement of the President on the contemplated investment. The Tribunal considers that those payments must be regarded as a bribe made in order to obtain the conclusion of the 1989 Agreement.[9]

Additionally, the tribunal referred to the report on *Harambee* tradition that was submitted to it and conducted a certain due diligence of Kenyan cultural aspects in that regard. Based *inter alia* on this report, the tribunal concluded that the payment of USD 2 million did not constitute a legitimate donation.[10]

---

[6] *Id.*, para. 110: "Mr. Ali made a payment to President Moi that he believed lawful. At that time, it was routine practice to make such donations in advance of doing business in Kenya; said practice had cultural roots and was buttressed by the "Harambee" system, one which mobilized resources through private donations for public purposes."

[7] *Id.*

[8] *Id.*, paras. 105–107. In that application, the Respondent states that "it is the Claimant's case that the Contract upon which its claims in these proceedings are based was procured by paying a bribe of US $2 million to the then President of Kenya, Daniel arap Moi... The Respondent further submits that "Bribery of the type that the Claimant has now affirmed is contrary to international public policy."

[9] *Id.*, para. 136.

[10] *Id.*, para. 134. It has also noted the report of the Task Force on Public Collections or "Harambees" presented in December 2003 to the Minister of Justice of Kenya. According to this report "the concept of Harambee had its root in the African culture where societies made collective contribution toward individual or communal activities" and this practice became popularised by President Kenyatta just after Kenyan independence. However, the report adds that "over the years, the spirit of Harambee has undergone a metamorphosis which has resulted in gross abuses. It has been linked to the emergence of oppressive and extortionist practices and entrenchment of corruption and abuse of office."

6.1.2.2 Consequence of Bribery

On the submission of Kenya, the tribunal had to determine whether the bribe, which was found to be paid in consideration of awarding the contract to the claimant, was contrary to the international public policy. In that case the State argued that it should "not have force of law" in the arbitration or else-where.[11]

The tribunal first recapitulated what public policy, *public ordre* and *bona mores* are and what is their stance in international legal systems. The arbitral tribunal then stated that in order to find a particular act or conduct to be contrary to public policy, it has to analyse whether there is common ground on that in international conventions, comparative law and previous international arbitral decisions.[12]

Coming to the analysis of "bribery" in the light of public policy considerations, the tribunal first noted that bribery is contrary to Kenyan law, as well as of many other States (if not all of them). Furthermore, the arbitrators brought their attention to various international conventions on combating corruption and bribery, to some of which Kenya was also a party.[13] As a result, the tribunal had no doubt that there was a formed consensus in the legal world that bribery should not be tolerated.

The tribunal was also of the opinion that bribery is not to be tolerated even if it is widespread in the relevant countries. In other words, while the arbitral tribunal acknowledged that corruption and bribery may be typical for business operations in some States, such practices (or the results of such illicit practices) nevertheless should not enjoy international legal protection.

Finally, the arbitral tribunal stated that "claims based on contracts of corruption or on contracts obtained by corruption cannot be upheld by this Arbitral Tribunal",[14] and that the claimant "is not legally entitled to maintain any of its pleaded claims in these proceedings on the ground of ex turpi causa non oritur actio."[15]

---

[11] *Id.*, para. 138.

[12] *Id.*, para. 141.

[13] The Tribunal made note of the following international instruments: Inter-American Convention against Corruption of 29 March 1996, Convention on Combating Bribery of Foreign Officials in International Business Transactions of 21 November 1997, Criminal Convention on Corruption of 27 January 1999, African Union Convention on Preventing and Combating Corruption of 11 July 2003, United Nations Declaration against Corruption and Bribery in International Commercial Transactions of 16 December 1996, United Nations Convention against Corruption of 31 October 2003, etc.

[14] World Duty Free Company Limited v. The Republic of Kenya, ICSID Case No. ARB/00/7, Award, 4 October 2006, para. 157.

[15] *Id.*, para. 179.

6.1.3 *Analysis of the Award*

Since the claimant himself informed the tribunal and the respondent of the USD 2 million payment to the former President of Kenya, the tribunal did not have to deal with the questions of standard of proof and evidence, but it rather took that position for granted. However, it did come to very important conclusions when looking at corruption through the prism of (i) validity of the investment contract, and (ii) public policy considerations. These conclusions have led some international law scholars to a determinative finding that corruption, within the frames of arbitration, is "more odious than theft".[16]

6.1.3.1 Corruption v. Contract

The determination of the genuine link between the payment to the then President of Kenya and the acquisition of the contract was quite brief but nevertheless important. It is difficult to disagree with the tribunal's analysis finding that there may be no separateness between the bribe and the contract, as it was the bribe that procured the contract itself. In other words, in order for corruption to be decisive for the outcome of the case there must be a link between a bribe and an investment.

An outstanding question in connection to this is what approach should be undertaken in identifying the genuine link in the situations where parties are not so sincere about their conduct such as in this case. This is in particular relevant where there have been several different payments made with some being used for public or semi-public purposes, or if there have been years between the acquisition of the investment and the alleged bribe.[17]

6.1.3.2 Corruption v. Public Policy

The significance of this case may also be seen in the approach that the tribunal took in assessing bribery in the context of public policy. The arbitral tribunal "paid tribute" to notions that were used by tribunals in other cases (i.e. ordre public, international public policy, transnational public policy, truly international public policy, good morals, *bonas mores*, ethics of international trade, etc.) and grouped them together under one "public policy" heading.

[16] Nappert (2013).

[17] These particular issues will be further analysed in details on the basis of the findings of an Arbitral Tribunal in Sistem v. Kyrgyz Republic case.

It was then noted that domestic courts usually base their decision on public policy that is applicable to their particular jurisdiction rather than transnationally.[18] In that regard, the tribunal felt obliged to look beyond domestic law and to

> very carefully check the objective existence of a particular transnational public policy rule in identifying it through international conventions, comparative law and arbitral awards.[19]

This is generally consistent with the views expressed in academic writings.[20]

It may also be concluded that in determining the scope of public policy it is important to look at international practice too. The exercise is not particularly complex with regards to corruption. It is clear from the outcome of this case, as well as from scientific publications, that there is an overall agreement to forbid and combat corruption as one of the main evils of the present days.[21]

Notably, in this case the combat against corruption had stopped short on "penalizing" the investor and not taking any recourse against the State. Some authors have expressed concerns that the Duty Free tribunal did not set a precedent by expressly criticizing Kenya's involvement in (in fact—solicitation of) corruption.[22] The tribunal also did not create any legal consequences steaming from the fact that the State did not actively prosecute or did not investigate the act of corruption, which some authors believe to be a requirement for a State to be able to successfully raise a corruption defence in arbitration.[23]

6.2 Metal-Tech v. Uzbekistan

This investment arbitration case is significant for the topic of the present monograph, as it is the first ICSID case where the tribunal had denied jurisdiction over a BIT claim[24] due to corruption.[25] Apart from this rather symbolic reason, it is also of particular interest due to a variety of questions that were put before the arbitral

---

[18] World Duty Free Company Limited v. The Republic of Kenya, ICSID Case No. ARB/00/7, Award, 4 October 2006, para. 140.

[19] *Id.*, para. 141.

[20] *See*, Hwang, M. S.C. and Lim, K., Corruption in Arbitration — Law and Reality, available at https://www.arbitration-icca.org/media/4/97929640279647/media013261720320840corruption_in_arbitration_paper_draft_248.pdf; Kreindler (2002), p. 253.

[21] *See,* Odumosu (2011), Lamm et al. (2014); Nappert (2013).

[22] Kulkarni (2013), available at www.transnational-dispute-management.com/article.asp?key=1957, p. 19.

[23] *See*, Llamzon (2008), p. 81; Kulkarni (2013), available at www.transnational-dispute-management.com/article.asp?key=1957, p. 26.

[24] In the World Duty Free case, the arbitral tribunal dealt with claims arising out of an investment contract.

[25] Lamm et al. (2014), p. 329. *See also*, Losco (2014a), pp. 37–52, available at https://scholarship.law.duke.edu/cgi/viewcontent.cgi?referer=&httpsredir=1&article=1004&context=dlj_online, p. 38.

tribunal and due to the findings that were subsequently made.[26] The arbitral tribunal in the Metal-Tech v. Uzbekistan case considered such questions as (i) the scope of the legality requirement, (ii) its application in subject and in time, (iii) attribution of conduct, (iv) bribery in light of public policy, as well as (v) consequences for States for tolerating corruption.

6.2.1 Factual and Procedural Background

Metal-Tech Ltd. ("**Metal-Tech**") is a company incorporated under the laws of Israel. In 1998–1999, Metal-Tech and the Republic of Uzbekistan ("**Uzbekistan**") negotiated a creation of a joint venture called "Uzmetal", the purpose of which was "to build and operate a modern plant for the production of molybdenum products".[27] On 26 January 2010, Metal-Tech submitted a request for arbitration to the ICSID Centre under the Israel-Uzbekistan BIT. The Metal-Tech's claims were partially based on the initiated criminal proceedings against its managers in Uzbekistan.[28]

In its defence the respondent *inter alia* alleged that the claimant's investment in Uzbekistan was procured by corruption and was, therefore, outside of the scope of protection guaranteed under the Israel-Uzbekistan BIT. The respondent invited the attention of the arbitral tribunal to the allegedly sham consulting contracts that were concluded by the claimant. It was submitted that in the period of 2000 to 2005 the claimant entered into several consulting contracts with different legal entities and natural persons.[29]

Whereas the fact of the existence of such contracts was not disputed, the parties argued about their scope, purpose and effects on the Israel-Uzbekistan BIT protection. In fact, the claimant's Chairman and CEO conceded to the facts that the consulting agreements were concluded and the subsequent sums were paid:

Q.	How much money have you paid these gentlemen, and over what period of time?
A.	We paid about $4 million in the span from 2001 until 2007.
	[. . .]
PRESIDENT KAUFMANN-KOHLER:	You mentioned, if I took my notes correctly, that you paid them 4 million

[26] For this reason, the case had been analyzed by other scholars previously, such as *Betz, Llamzon, Lamm, Greenwald* and *Young. See,* Betz (2017); Llamzon (2014); Lamm et al. (2014).

[27] Metal-Tech Ltd. v. The Republic of Uzbekistan, ICSID Case No. ARB/10/3, Award, 4 December 2013, para. 7.

[28] *Id.*, para. 37.

[29] *Id.*, para. 29.

from 2001 to 2007. Is that correct? Can you confirm that?

THE WITNESS: Yes, I can confirm that.[30]

This testimony contradicted to the previous submissions of the claimant who *inter alia* stated that the consultants were engaged "for assistance with Uzmetal's day-to-day operations".[31] The respondent claimed that the above-mentioned "consulting contracts" were nothing more than sham contracts designed to extend bribes to politically exposed people in Uzbekistan.

6.2.2 *Findings and Analysis of the Tribunal*

As was mentioned above, in its analysis of the bribery allegations the arbitral tribunal made significant and relevant (for the present research) findings. The tribunal had a task to evaluate whether the contracts at questions could be regarded as legitimate agreements or whether they were products of corruption. The most important question before the arbitral tribunal was the determination of legal consequences for both parties in the event such findings were to be made.

6.2.2.1 Burden of Proof

While assessing the arguments of the parties, the tribunal made note of the fact that the responsibility of a party asserting the facts to prove them is widely recognized by international tribunals and national courts.[32] However, the tribunal also noted that since the facts of possible bribery became evident only during the hearing and that such facts raised reasonable suspicions of the tribunal, it did not have to go into the discussion of the burden of proof.[33] The tribunal felt that it had "a duty to inquire" for additional explanation and witness examination because of the raised suspicions.[34] As a result, the arbitral tribunal invited the parties to present additional submissions and ordered further disclosure of evidence on the issues of corruption.[35]

Effectively, the arbitral tribunal shared the burden of proving illegality between both parties. The possibility of sharing and/or shifting the burden of proof (or its

[30] *Id.*, para. 197.

[31] Perry (2013).

[32] Metal-Tech Ltd. v. The Republic of Uzbekistan, ICSID Case No. ARB/10/3, Award, 4 December 2013, para. 237.

[33] *Id.*, para.239.

[34] Metal-Tech Ltd. v. The Republic of Uzbekistan, ICSID Case No. ARB/10/3, Award, 4 December 2013, para. 241.

[35] Losco (2014a), pp. 37–52, available at https://scholarship.law.duke.edu/cgi/viewcontent.cgi?referer=&httpsredir=1&article=1004&context=dlj_online, p. 41.

part) has been somewhat discussed in scholarly writings with some authors coming to conclusions that are aligned with the findings of the tribunal in Metal-Tech.[36]

6.2.2.2 Standard of Proof

While the Metal-Tech tribunal went into the discussion of the applicable standard of proof, it nevertheless did not make an explicit decision thereof. Despite other ICSID tribunals applying stricter standards of proof for allegations of corruption,[37] the arbitral tribunal seemed to have agreed with the analysis that was conducted in the World Duty Free v. Kenya case and opined that corruption must be established "with reasonable certainty" and that because of the difficulty to prove corruption it is "generally admitted that it can be shown through circumstantial evidence."[38]

6.2.2.3 Red Flags

The Metal-Tech tribunal in its analysis of the evidence on corruption presented by the respondent made explicit reference to *red flags* and their role in "the prohibition of corruption".[39] The tribunal decided to seek guidance from the so-called Woolf Report,[40] which included a list of "Key Red flags", i.e.:

- an adviser has a lack of experience in the sector;
- non-residence of an adviser in the country where the customer or the project is located;
- no significant business presence of the adviser within the country;
- an adviser requests 'urgent' payments or unusually high commissions;
- an adviser requests payments in cash, use of a corporate vehicle such as equity, or be paid in a third country, to a numbered bank account, or to some other person or entity;

---

[36] *See for instance,* Fathallah (2010), p. 73; Clouet (2018). *Mills* and *Born* also discussed the possibility of drawing adverse inferences if a party refuses to produce specific evidence – *see,* Mills (2003), p. 295; and Born (2014), p. 2311.

[37] Losco (2014a), pp. 37–52, available at https://scholarship.law.duke.edu/cgi/viewcontent.cgi?referer=&httpsredir=1&article=1004&context=dlj_online, p. 46.

[38] Alekhin and Shmatenko (2018), p. 161.

[39] Metal-Tech Ltd. v. The Republic of Uzbekistan, ICSID Case No. ARB/10/3, Award, 4 December 2013, para. 293.

[40] Woolf Committee Report on Business Ethics, Global Companies and the Defence Industry: Ethical Business Conduct in Bae Systems Plc 25–26 (2008), prepared at the request of the Board of Directors of Bae Systems Plc. The Woolf Committee was chaired by the Rt Hon Lord Woolf, former Lord Chief Justice of England and Wales.

- an adviser has a close personal/professional relationship to the government or customers that could improperly influence the customer's decision.[41]

The arbitral tribunal established that "many of these red flags are present here."[42] Evidently, the Metal-Tech tribunal also reviewed and analysed other "red flag lists", as it stated that "the international community has established lists of indicators, sometimes called red flags and that "although worded differently, [they] have essentially the same content."[43] Conclusively, the tribunal did recognize the possible lack of direct evidence, but nevertheless found that the "unexplained circumstances were such that they led to the conclusion that bribery had actually been committed."[44]

6.2.2.4 Finding on Corruption

At the outset of the bribery allegation (which was submitted as a jurisdictional objection by Uzbekistan) the tribunal decided that the legality requirement as enshrined in the Israel-Uzbekistan BIT was only applicable to the period of establishment of a foreign investment.[45] In other words, it was decided that in order to breach the legality requirement, the Uzbek law had to be violated at the time when Metal-Tech made its investment rather than during its operation. Considering this finding, the arbitral tribunal decided that it did not have to look into the events that took place after the investment had been made and the joint venture became operative.

In its assessment of the facts relating to the acquisition of the investment, the arbitral tribunal went into the details of the contracts and payments that were made to the alleged consultants. While the sums that were paid as "bonuses" to the consultants sometimes equalled to no more than USD 5.000, the arbitral tribunal, nevertheless, looked at that amount in the context of the economic situation in Uzbekistan. In its analysis, the arbitral tribunal paid close attention to the economic realities of Uzbekistan at that time, pointing out the fact that the monthly salary of a top manager in a similar Uzbek company equalled to 50 times less than that amount.[46] In other words, the arbitral tribunal was not blinded by *considerably* non-significant sums

[41] Metal-Tech Ltd. v. The Republic of Uzbekistan, ICSID Case No. ARB/10/3, Award, 4 December 2013, para. 293 with reference to Woolf Committee Report on Business Ethics, Global Companies and the Defence Industry: Ethical Business Conduct in Bae Systems Plc 25-26 (2008).

[42] *Id.*, para. 293.

[43] *Id.*

[44] Malik and Kamat (2018), December 2018, available at https://paperity.org/p/185990736/corruption-in-international-commercial-arbitration-arbitrability-admissibility, p. 18.

[45] Metal-Tech Ltd. v. The Republic of Uzbekistan, ICSID Case No. ARB/10/3, Award, 4 December 2013, para. 193.

[46] *Id.*, paras. 199–203.

and assessed the facts of the alleged bribery in perspective of the environment surrounding the Metal-Tech's investment.[47]

Additionally, the Metal-Tech tribunal was not satisfied with the suggested explanations in relation to the questions whether the consultants possessed necessary qualifications to offer consulting services and whether there existed any proof of rendered services under the contracts.[48] The arbitral tribunal also took note of the fact that there was a link between the consultants and the Uzbek government officials in charge of the claimant's investment[49] and that the payments were made in an unreasonably shadowed way through intermediary companies registered in "tax heaven" jurisdictions.[50]

Finally (and summarily), in light of all the findings made above, the Metal-Tech tribunal did find that the "consulting agreement" was nothing more than a sham contract designed to conceal the true nature and purpose.[51]

6.2.2.5 Violations of Uzbek Law

Having made its findings in relation to the key facts surrounding the arguments of bribery, the tribunal looked at Uzbek law to see whether sham contracts and corruption are contrary to the laws of the host State. It is to be mentioned that since the tribunal found that the legality requirement only extended to the time of the acquisition of the investment (and not its operation), the tribunal had to evaluate the Uzbek law retrospectively and only in light of the evidence that related to 1998–1999.[52] In its assessment, the arbitral tribunal came to the conclusion that corruption had been established to the extent sufficient to violate Uzbekistan law. As a consequence, the investment has not been "implemented in accordance with the laws and regulations of the Contracting Party in whose territory the investment is made" as required by Article 1(1) of the Israel-Uzbekistan BIT.[53]

Subsequently, the arbitral tribunal further noted that Uzbekistan's consent to ICSID arbitration, as expressed in Article 8(1) of the Israel-Uzbekistan BIT, was restricted only to disputes "concerning an investment" as defined in Article 1(1) of the BIT. Since the definition of "investment" was to mean only investments that had been implemented in compliance with the local laws, the arbitral tribunal found that the present dispute did not come within the reach of Article 8(1) and was not covered

[47] *See,* Karkey v. Pakistan case, where the tribunal had a different approach in assessing similar facts under similar allegations.

[48] Metal-Tech Ltd. v. The Republic of Uzbekistan, ICSID Case No. ARB/10/3, Award, 4 December 2013, paras. 208–212.

[49] *Id.*, paras. 225–227.

[50] *Id.*, paras. 219–224.

[51] *Id.*, para. 218.

[52] *Id.*, paras. 278–371.

[53] *Id.*, para. 372.

by Uzbekistan's consent to arbitrate.[54] Therefore, in the tribunal's analysis, the current dispute did not meet the consent requirement that was set in Article 25(1) of the ICSID Convention, which is why the tribunal found that it lacked jurisdiction over this dispute.[55]

6.2.2.6 Impact of Corruption Findings on Costs Allocation

The tribunal was asked by the claimant to decide that Uzbekistan should be paying the costs of the arbitral proceedings, while the respondent requested the opposite. When assessing this question, the tribunal found it appropriate to look at it in light of its findings on corruption. The arbitral tribunal stated that there was a general consensus that an investment tainted by corruption could not seek international treaty protection.[56] On the other hand, the tribunal noted that it did not mean that the State did not have a role in creating the environment for corruption. Due to the latter, it was found appropriate to order the parties to share the costs of arbitration.[57]

6.2.3 Analysis of the Award

The views expressed by some scholars are that the Metal-Tech decision reflects some customary rules and practices.[58] There are several major take-aways that this arbitration case has to offer in the frames of the present research:

6.2.3.1 Legality Requirement Application

The arbitral tribunal found that the legality requirement is an essential pre-requisite of the tribunal's jurisdiction and that States usually give consent to arbitrate disputes only in relation to investments that have been made in accordance with local laws. As was opined by *Clouet,* the tribunal here "determined that it lacked jurisdiction to

---

[54] *Id.*, para. 373.

[55] It has been argued that the ICSID jurisdiction has 'outer limits', and that the parties cannot engage ICSID jurisdiction without sufficient regard for the objective core of its subject matter jurisdiction. *See*, Waibel (2014), p. 50, and Broches (1972), pp. 331–410.

[56] Metal-Tech Ltd. v. The Republic of Uzbekistan, ICSID Case No. ARB/10/3, Award, 4 December 2013, para. 165.

[57] *Id.*, para. 422.

[58] Losco (2014a), pp. 37–52, available at https://scholarship.law.duke.edu/cgi/viewcontent.cgi?referer=&httpsredir=1&article=1004&context=dlj_online, p. 51.

adjudicate the matter due to corruption".[59] The Metal-Tech v. Uzbekistan case once again reminds that the legality requirement is applicable to the period of the acquisition of a foreign investment.

6.2.3.2 Surrounding Circumstances

While analysing the main facts of alleged corruption the tribunal reviewed the evidence in the context of the case and jurisdictions involved. In other words, it was noted that illicit misconduct should be seen and evaluated in light of the surrounding circumstances rather than in general (*common sense*) terms. Thus, the tribunal's analysis was consistent with the analysis of some authors in relation to circumstantial evidence and its value.[60]

6.2.3.3 Ex-officio Examination of Corruption

As the Metal-Tech tribunal examined the facts of corruption on its own initiative, it is fair to say that the arbitral tribunal's ability to examine potential illicit acts *ex-officio* is re-confirmed through its arbitral award. After identifying certain *red flags* of illicit conduct, the arbitral tribunal can assess the possible illegality of the investment on its own initiative.

6.2.3.4 Burden and Standard of Proof

Consistently with some views expressed in legal doctrine,[61] the Metal-Tech tribunal had effectively shared the burden of proof among the parties. Interestingly, the reasoning behind this step was the fact that the tribunal itself initiated examination of these questions, without the claimants explicitly raising the corruption allegations.

Notwithstanding the fact that in this case the arbitral tribunal did not make a determinative decision on the applicable standard of proof, it nevertheless contributed to the discussion that a lowered standard of proof should apply to the allegations of corruption, bribery and fraud. This was reasoned with the fact that corruption is,

---

[59] Clouet (2018), p. 29.

[60] *See*, Wiebecke (2018), p. 97 and Scherrer (2002), pp. 34–35.

[61] *See*, Schreuer et al. (2009), p. 669. *See also*, Fathallah (2010), p. 73; Clouet (2018).

by its essence, difficult to establish, which is why it should be allowed to display it through circumstantial evidence.[62]

6.2.3.5 Red Flags

The Metal-Tech tribunal appeared to accept the notion of *red flags* and their evidentiary power in international dispute settlement. It appears that in coming to its conclusions, the tribunal analysed a number of soft-law instruments on *red flags* and took guidance from the so-called Woolf Report.[63]

6.2.3.6 Effects of Corruption on Quantum

It is clear from the Metal-Tech v. Uzbekistan award that the findings of corruption (or any other illicit misconduct for this purpose) may have an impact on quantum, in particular on the decision of allocation of costs. The tribunal made note that corruption always involves both parties, which is why it was found appropriate to order each party to pay their own costs. Notably, it seems like that the decision on quantum was the only legal consequence for Uzbekistan in connection with the corrupt activities, as no charges seem to have been brought towards anyone involved in corruption, except for the joint venture officers.[64]

In other words, the Metal-Tech award signalled the "perceived inequity in the result", which was attempted to be remedied by the distribution of costs.[65] Some commentators went as far as labelling such decision as "game over" for States that tolerate bribery of public officials.[66] However, without particularly agreeing with the "game over" label, it is nevertheless clear that the tribunal's decision on quantum is a certain reflection of the "zero tolerance" approach towards corruption in international arbitration.[67]

---

[62] The role and weight of the circumstantial evidence has been studied by Scherrer and Partasides. *See*, Scherrer (2002); and Partasides (2010).

[63] Metal-Tech Ltd. v. The Republic of Uzbekistan, ICSID Case No. ARB/10/3, Award, 4 December 2013, para. 293.

[64] Lund-Turner (2015), p. 5.

[65] Losco (2014a), pp. 37–52, available at https://scholarship.law.duke.edu/cgi/viewcontent.cgi?referer=&httpsredir=1&article=1004&context=dlj_online, p. 48.

[66] Meshel (2013b).

[67] On "zero tolerance" approach, *see*, Crivellaro (2003), p. 21. Interestingly, *Torres-Fowler* opined that by punishing only the investors, "zero tolerance" may actually trigger the rise of corruption, as the state agents would remain without consequences – Torres-Fowler (2012), available at https://papers.ssrn.com/sol3/papers.cfm?abstract_id=2322129.

6.3 Churchill and Planet v. Indonesia

Churchill Mining PLC and Planet Mining Pty Ltd. v. Indonesia case is one of the rare examples where the allegations of fraud were made and became outcome decisive. It is an interesting case from the scientific point of view as the arbitral tribunal made a finding on the legality of the investment based on an omission to duly investigate the *red flags* of illicit conduct, rather than based on the illicit conduct itself.

6.3.1 *Factual and Procedural Background*

Churchill Mining PLC ("**Churchill**") and Planet Mining Pty Ltd. ("**Planet**") (collectively - claimants) are companies that made investments into the coal mining business in Indonesia. One of the companies through which the claimants made their investments was a company called Ridlatama ("**Company**").

After several years of operating and maintaining investments in the mining sector in Indonesia, on 22 May 2012 Churchill filed the Request for Arbitration to ICSID pursuant to the UK-Indonesia BIT.[68] On 26 November 2012, Planet filed its Request for Arbitration with ICSID pursuant to the Australia-Indonesia BIT.[69] It was decided that the two requests from Churchill and from Planet would be heard in a consolidated case, and it was further decided that there would be one consolidated award, which is analysed in the scope of this chapter.

In this case, Indonesia faced claims of expropriation of the claimants' investment. Indonesia, in turn, alleged that several essential documents of the Company were forged. In particular, the respondent presented a list of at least 34 documents that were claimed to be tainted by fake signatures.[70] Subsequently, the State claimed that since the allegedly false documents formed the basis of the claimants' operation in Indonesia, their claims were to be declared inadmissible.

The claimants denied any possible involvement in the alleged forgery. Furthermore, the claimants confirmed that there were certain *red flags* relating to the suspicious appearance of the documents of the Company before, but those had been addressed and all the queries had been lifted. Additionally, the claimants denied that they had known or should have had knowledge of the alleged forgery and,

---

[68] "The Contracting Party in the territory of which a national or company of the other Contracting Party makes or intends to make an investment shall assent to any request on the part of such national or company to submit. For conciliation or arbitration, to the Centre established by the Convention on the Settlement of Investment Disputes between States and Nationals of Other States opened for signature at Washington on 18 March 1965 any dispute that may arise in connection with the investment.", Article 7 of the UK-Indonesia BIT.

[69] Churchill Mining PLC and Planet Mining Pty Ltd v. Republic of Indonesia, ICSID Case No. ARB/12/14 and 12/40, Award, 6 December 2016, para. 5.

[70] *Id.*, para. 108.

therefore, they could not have been found liable/responsible for the alleged acts of fraud.

6.3.2 *Findings and Analysis of the Tribunal*

The catching feature of the award in the present case is that unlike in many other cases, the Churchill tribunal's approach in determining the procedural and substantive matters was truly "academic". The arbitral tribunal allocated its attention to each procedural point including the determination of the applicable law, which has been very rarely undertaken in other cases that have been analysed in the frames of this textbook.

6.3.2.1 Applicable Law

The arbitral tribunal's determination of the applicable law was made in accordance with Article 42(1) of the ICSID Convention.[71] Under the rule of that provision, in a situation when the parties have not agreed on the applicable law, the arbitral tribunal is free to apply the law of the Contracting State party to the dispute and rules of international law that may be applicable. Since the claimants and the respondent did not come to the consensus on this matter, the tribunal chose to apply Indonesian law, the BITs and international law, where appropriate.[72] Moreover, the tribunal noted that in light of the principle "iura nova curia", or better "iura novit arbiter", it was not bound by the arguments and legal sources that were put forward by the parties and instead was free to form its own opinion on the meaning of the law.[73] In this sense, the position of the Churchill tribunal is not different from the views expressed by some scholars, who, at times, even step a bit further by saying that the

> the tribunal may be entitled to conclude that event if the agreed substantive law is the law of that single country, it will disregard that governing law if applying it would contravene international public policy.[74]

[71] "The Tribunal shall decide a dispute in accordance with such rules of law as may be agreed by the parties. In the absence of such agreement, the Tribunal shall apply the law of the Contracting State party to the dispute (including its rules on the conflict of laws) and such rules of international law as may be applicable", Article 42(1) of the ICSID Convention.

[72] Churchill Mining PLC and Planet Mining Pty Ltd v. Republic of Indonesia, ICSID Case No. ARB/12/14 and 12/40, Award, 6 December 2016, para. 235.

[73] *Id.*, para. 236.

[74] Kreindler (2002), p. 253. *See also,* Michael Hwang and Lim (2012).

6.3.2.2 Burden and Standard of Proof

In determining the party carrying the burden of proof, the tribunal applied the rule of international law *actori incumbit onus probandi.*[75] In other words, consistently with many academic publications,[76] the tribunal found that each party bears the burden of proving the facts which it alleges.

As to the standard of proof for the allegations of fraud, the arbitral tribunal was faced with two different positions that were suggested by the parties. The respondent's position was that the appropriate standard of proof would be the "balance of probabilities",[77] whereas the claimants pursued the argument that due to the seriousness of allegations, the applicable standard of proof should be "clear and convincing evidence".[78]

Similarly to the opinions expressed by *Catti* and *Clouet,*[79] the Churchill tribunal also recognized that there was no universal answer to the question as to which standard of proof should be applicable to the allegations of illicit acts. It was, however, noted that in some cases tribunals applied the "clear and convincing evidence" standard to allegations of fraud due to the seriousness of the allegation and the consequences of such acts. On the other hand, the arbitral tribunal also recalled that some tribunals applied a more flexible standard of proof, such as "balance of probabilities" or its civil law counterpart—the "intime conviction".[80]

In the present case the arbitral tribunal decided to apply a more flexible standard, such as "balance of probabilities" (or alternatively the tribunal named it as "intime conviction"). The tribunal believed that this standard was enough to assess the allegations of forgery and fraud in the setting of a dispute resolution of a commercial nature. Nevertheless, the arbitral tribunal also decided that it would require more persuasive evidence for clearly implausible facts.[81]

[75] Churchill Mining PLC and Planet Mining Pty Ltd v. Republic of Indonesia, ICSID Case No. ARB/12/14 and 12/40, Award, 6 December 2016, para. 238.

[76] *See,* Haugeneder (2009), pp. 323–339; Lamm et al. (2010), pp. 699–731; Rosell and Prager (1999), pp. 329–348; Alekhin and Shmatenko (2018), pp. 157–158; Hunter (1992), pp. 204–211.

[77] The same approach is advocated by some legal scholars. *See,* Partasides (2010).

[78] Churchill Mining PLC and Planet Mining Pty Ltd v. Republic of Indonesia, ICSID Case No. ARB/12/14 and 12/40, Award, 6 December 2016, para. 237.

[79] *See,* Catti (2013), pp. 36–38; and Clouet (2018).

[80] Churchill Mining PLC and Planet Mining Pty Ltd v. Republic of Indonesia, ICSID Case No. ARB/12/14 and 12/40, Award, 6 December 2016, para. 240.

[81] *Id.*, para. 244.

6.3.2.3 Findings on Fraud

The arbitral tribunal engaged itself in extensive review of the parties' submissions and evidence, which were reflected on more than 100 pages in the award. The result of its analysis was that it would have been more probable than not that the authorisation on the documents in question was forged. However, the arbitral tribunal found that it did not have sufficient evidence to make the finding that the claimants themselves were directly responsible for forgery. Instead, the tribunal chose not to make such an assessment and left the question unanswered.

After making the factual findings, the arbitral tribunal evaluated the legal consequences of the determined fraud in this case. The Churchill tribunal made note of the fact that neither the ICSID Convention, nor the applicable BITs contained any substantive provision that could have provided guidance as to the consequences of fraudulent conduct for the purposes of investment protection.[82] Having found no answers in the treaties underlining the arbitration, the arbitral tribunal turned to the principles of public international law to determine what legal consequences should fraud and forgery trigger.

For these purpose, the decisions in several other arbitrations with similar allegations were assessed. In particular, it was noted that some tribunals found that all systems of law, including the international legal system, contain concepts that had been designed to prevent the abuse of law.[83] Moreover, in the arbitrators' view, the tribunal had to make sure that it was not furthering an abuse of the system of international investment protection.[84] This approach is generally consistent with a number of scholarly writings.[85]

While the Churchill tribunal acknowledged the fact that the legal assessment of fraudulent acts is to be conducted based on the circumstances and on individual basis, it also concluded that there exists a "general principle that one does not benefit from treaty protection when underlying conduct is deemed improper."[86]

In this regard, it appears that that the tribunal made a couple of important findings. First, the tribunal confirmed the place and application of the principle of good faith in

[82] *Id.*, para. 488.

[83] *Id.*, para. 489, with reference to Venezuela Holdings B.V. and others v. Bolivarian Republic of Venezuela, ICSID Case No. ARB/07/27, Decision on Jurisdiction, 10 June 2010, para. 167.

[84] *Id.*, with reference to Phoenix Action, Ltd. v. Czech Republic, ICSID Case No. ARB/06/5, Award, 15 April 2009, para. 144.

[85] *See,* Born (2014), p. 2705: "Inherent in the legally binding resolution of a dispute and the making of a legally binding award is the duty to consider and resolve public-policy issues and other mandatory legal objections." *See also*, Clouet (2018).

[86] Churchill Mining PLC and Planet Mining Pty Ltd v. Republic of Indonesia, ICSID Case No. ARB/12/14 and 12/40, Award, 6 December 2016, para. 492 with reference to Renée Rose Levy and Gremcitel S.A. v. Republic of Peru, ICSID Case No. ARB/11/17, Award, 9 January 2015, paras. 194–195 and Philip Morris Asia Limited v. Commonwealth of Australia, PCA Case No. 2012-12, Award on Jurisdiction and Admissibility, 17 December 2015, para. 585.

international investment law. Second, the Churchill tribunal made the finding that investors could not benefit from treaty protection in a situation when their general underlying conduct with respect to their investment was improper or in bad faith. However, it must be noted that the latter is not a clear-cut finding and could be subjected to different interpretation.[87]

Furthermore, the tribunal recognized that there exists a difference in approaching the allegations of fraud in different arbitration cases. Some tribunals chose to decide on such allegations as a matter of jurisdiction, while others examined the allegations of illegality at the merits stage.[88] As was explained by the Churchill tribunal, the existing difference was due to individual circumstances of each case. For the purposes of the present dispute, because the forged documents, as represented by the respondent, constituted the basis of claimants' investment, the tribunal decided that the legal consequence of the finding of fraud would impact the admissibility of the claims.

At the same time, while making the factual findings on fraud and understanding its general legal consequence, the arbitral tribunal still had to undertake one further step—to evaluate whether the act of fraud could be attributable to the conduct of the claimants. In this respect, the Churchill tribunal undertook a twofold analysis—it determined the seriousness of the fraud,[89] and assessed the claimants' diligence in respect of it.[90] In relation to the first point, the tribunal found that

> the acts of forgery brought to light in these proceedings are of a particularly serious nature in light of the number and nature of forged documents and of the aim pursued, namely to orchestrate, legitimize and perpetuate a fraudulent scheme to gain access to valuable mining rights.[91]

As to the assessment of the claimants' diligence, the tribunal decided that no due diligence of the raised *red flags* had been undertaken before the commencement of the arbitration proceedings by the claimants, which is why the claimants could, in principle, be found responsible for any consequences of such fraud and forgery. In other words, the claimants' investment was found to be tainted by the fraudulent conduct.

As a result, the arbitral tribunal found that all the claims of Churchill and Planet were to be declared as inadmissible.[92]

---

[87] *Id.*, the idea is derived from the tribunal's following statement: "That theory is another manifestation of the general principle that one does not benefit from treaty protection when underlying conduct is deemed improper."

[88] *Id.*, para. 494 with reference to Gustav F W Hamester GmbH & Co KG v. Republic of Ghana, ICSID Case No. ARB/07/24, Award, 18 June 2010, paras. 127, 129 (Exh. RLA-058); Quiborax S. A., Non Metallic Minerals S.A. and Allan Fosk Kaplún v. Plurinational State of Bolivia, ICSID Case No. ARB/06/2, Decision on Jurisdiction, 27 September 2012, paras. 192, 266, 271.

[89] *Id.*, paras. 510–515.

[90] *Id.*, paras. 516–527.

[91] *Id.*, para. 515.

[92] *Id.*, para. 532.

6.3.3 Analysis of the Award

As was discussed in the beginning of this chapter, the Churchill & Planet v. Indonesia case provides a few important take away-s for further analysis and research. The tribunal made a number of findings of procedural and substantive character, that are summarised below.

6.3.3.1 Applicable Law

In procedural matters, the Churchill tribunal analysed the questions of applicable law and decided that the law of the host State was the most relevant law to be applied for the assessment of the illegality allegations. A related finding in this regard is that the tribunal stated that it was not bound by the suggested interpretation of the host State's law and instead found it appropriate to decide on its scope and meaning by itself based on the principle of "iura nova curia – or better, iura novit arbiter".[93]

Even though, the tribunal's analysis of national law did not seem to go against the parties' legal interpretation, the end effect of this was that the tribunal addressed the general position that arbitral tribunals enjoy discretion on interpretation of domestic law, which also finds its support in legal literature.[94]

6.3.3.2 Burden of Proof

The question of the burden of proof in this case was quite straightforward. The arbitral tribunal decided that each party is to carry its own burden of proving the facts which it asserted. The arbitral tribunal did not explore the possibility of shifting or sharing the burden of proof, which might be due to the fact that it was not entirely necessary in this case because the relevant facts of the case were more obvious than in other discussed cases.

6.3.3.3 Standard of Proof

As to the question of the applicable standard of proof, the idea of applying a lowered standard of proof, such as the "balance of probabilities" or "intime conviction", was supported by the arbitral tribunal. However, while seeking to balance the standard in relation to the allegations that were implausible, the tribunal found that it may heighten the standard of proof to "clear and convincing evidence". In other words,

[93] *Id.*, para. 236.

[94] *See for instance,* Kreindler (2002), p. 253; Hwang, M. S.C. and Lim, K., Corruption in Arbitration — Law and Reality, available at https://www.arbitration-icca.org/media/4/97929640279647/media013261720320840corruption_in_arbitration_paper_draft_248.pdf.

if the parties alleged something, which was *prima facie* not convincing, the tribunal could have required that parties provide "clear and convincing" in order to prove their cases.

6.3.3.4 Consequences of Fraud

On the substantive matters, the Churchill tribunal found that an investment that was based on fraud could not benefit from international protection. This was found to be true even if the act of fraud in question was not committed directly by the investors themselves. A foreign investment is not to be protected in a situation when an investor fails to exercise reasonable diligence in investigating possible compliance issues. In other words, the tribunal found that in a situation when an investor is turning "a blind eye" on obvious *red flags*, it cannot request protection from an international tribunal provided that the act of fraud indeed took place. Additionally, the tribunal opined on the principle of good faith in ISDS.

As it is evident from the provided analysis, the Churchill & Planet v. Indonesia award reinforces the approach of other arbitral tribunals in dismissing the claims over illegal investments in their entirety.

6.4 Spentex v. Uzbekistan

The arbitral award[95] in the Spentex Netherlands, B.V. ("**Spentex**") against Uzbekistan case[96] is one of the more recent ICSID cases where the arguments of corruption were outcome decisive. The arbitral tribunal's analysis in this case seems to reflect a creative and, perhaps, revolutionary approach to the issues of corruption and bribery of public officials in international investment arbitration. It, for the first time,

> reprimanded the Respondent State by urging it to make a substantial payment to an international anti-corruption institution, under threat of an adverse costs order.[97]

[95] At the time of the publication of this textbook, the decision of the arbitral tribunal has not yet been published. From the attended scientific conferences, it is my understanding that the award is not going to be made public. This section is, therefore, largely based on the information provided in open source articles at Investment Arbitration Review portal (https://www.iareporter.com/) and a detailed summary of the award in Betz (2017), pp. 128–136.

[96] Spentex Netherlands, B.V. v. Republic of Uzbekistan, ICSID Case No. ARB/13/26, Award, 27 December 2016.

[97] Alekhin and Shmatenko (2018), p. 151.

6.4.1 Factual and Procedural Background

On 27 September 2013, Spentex registered a request for arbitration against Uzbekistan with ICSID. The claimant is a company incorporated under the laws of the Netherlands. The request for arbitration was based on Article 9 of the Netherlands-Uzbekistan BIT.[98] On 27 December 2016, the arbitral proceedings were completed with the arbitral tribunal's decision on jurisdiction.

Spentex is a subsidiary of an Indian company called Spentex Industries Limited.[99] It is known that in 2006 it established investment in Uzbekistan by purchasing three textile manufacturing plants. Under the claimant's case its operations in Uzbekistan faced serious financial crisis. Moreover, according to Spentex,

> unable to operate profitably, and to remain current with its loans, the claimant professes to have been pushed into bankruptcy due to the actions of Uzbek authorities.[100]

Notably, while having its Indian "origin", the claimant, nevertheless, chose to take recourse under the Netherlands-Uzbekistan BIT by using its corporate presence in the Netherlands.

6.4.2 Findings and Analysis of the Tribunal

The respondent's primary defence and objection to the jurisdiction of the ICSID tribunal was based on the allegations of corruption. Similarly to what was put forward by Uzbekistan in the Metal-Tech case, the respondent submitted that Spentex Industries Limited (being a parent company of the claimant) made corrupt payments to public officials through two intermediate companies called Trade Development Ltd. and First Finance Solutions (collectively – consultants) prior to its investment's acquisition via a public tender in 2006.[101]

---

[98] "Each Contracting Party hereby consents to submit any legal dispute arising between that Contracting Party and a national of the other Contracting Party concerning an investment of that national in the territory of the former Contracting Party to the International Centre for Settlement of Investment Disputes for settlement by conciliation or arbitration under the Convention on the Settlement of Investment Disputes between States and Nationals of other States opened for signature at Washington on 18 March 1965. A legal person which is a national of one Contracting Party and which before such a dispute arises is controlled by nationals of the other Contracting Party shall in accordance with Article 25 (2) (b) of the Convention for the purpose of the Convention be treated as a national of the other Contracting Party.", Article 9 of the Agreement on encouragement and reciprocal protection of Investments between the Kingdom of the Netherlands and the Republic of Uzbekistan.

[99] *See,* corporate website of Spentex Industries Ltd. at http://www.clcindia.com/our_ethos.html.

[100] *See,* Djanic (2017), available at https://www.iareporter.com/articles/indian-company-invokes-dutch-bit-rather-than-indian-treaty-in-new-arbitration-over-withdrawn-subsidies-in-uzbekistan/.

[101] *Id.*

The respondent's case hinged upon certain circumstances, which were collectively named as *red flags* and, which were displayed and highlighted for the arbitral tribunal during the written and oral submissions. In particular, the respondent submitted that:

- the consultants were promised substantial consulting fees only two days prior to when Spentex submitted its tender bid to purchase two textile plants in Uzbekistan;
- the consultants lacked any relevant experience which would have been necessary for preparing a bid;
- the claimant had increased its bid by USD 6 million shortly after retaining the consultants.[102]

As a result of the alleged existence of the above-mentioned *red flags*, the respondent asked the arbitral tribunal to decide that the investor could not benefit from the protection that was offered under the Netherlands-Uzbekistan BIT. This argument was primarily based on the reasoning that the investor's allegedly corrupt conduct was against the public policy and the principle of clean hands.[103]

Spentex denied all allegations and explained that both consultants acted as legitimate advisors and provided proper services, such as on-ground support, logistical management, local market study and investment banking.[104] Finally, the claimant also disputed the legal aspects of the respondent's argument by indicating that there was no limitation within the BIT that required the investment to be made in compliance with the host State's law, while bad faith and unclean hands could not serve as standalone reasons in public international law for refusing to admit and hear claims.[105]

6.4.2.1 Effects of Corruption on Arbitration

From the available sources it appears that the initial question before the tribunal was whether corruption, if proven, can have an effect on the entire arbitration and result in dismissal of the investor's claims.[106] Relying on the existing case law as well as on the principles of international public policy and clean hands doctrine, the arbitral tribunal found that corruption would be dispositive of the entire claim.[107]

---

[102] *Id.*

[103] Spentex Netherlands, B.V. v. Republic of Uzbekistan, ICSID Case No. ARB/13/26, Award, 27 December 2016, para. 818 as referenced in Betz (2017).

[104] Djanic (2017), available at https://www.iareporter.com/articles/indian-company-invokes-dutch-bit-rather-than-indian-treaty-in-new-arbitration-over-withdrawn-subsidies-in-uzbekistan/.

[105] *Id.*

[106] *Id.*

[107] *Id.*

In its finding, the arbitral tribunal emphasized that the investment system is established in order to protect foreign investors against actions that violate the rule of law. Its purpose is therefore to promote the rule of law and it cannot be used in cases where the investor itself had engaged in conduct that goes against this principle.[108] Thus, the arbitral tribunal decided that if the foreign investment was obtained through illicit activity, such as corruption, it could not benefit from the protection that is being offered under international investment agreements.

The significance and importance of the Spentex tribunal's finding is that it was not hinged upon the existence of the legality requirement in the applicable BIT. In other words, the tribunal decided that the legality of the investment was a general standard that had to be applied irrespective of the scope of definition of investment in the applicable legal instrument.[109]

Another significance of this case is that the tribunal differed in opinions as to the procedural outcome of the finding of corruption. While the (undisclosed) majority of the tribunal believed that such a finding would be a matter of the admissibility of claims, one other (undisclosed) arbitrator dissented with the opinion that corruption would ultimately deprive the tribunal of its jurisdiction. It was concluded that no resolution of this discussion was necessary, since both approaches would lead to the dismissal of the claims in their entirety.

The conflict of opinions, as it was seen in the Spentex decision, does not seem to be met in other arbitral decisions that involved the analysis of findings of corruption. While having a debate on the question "how the claims shall be dismissed" rather than on the question "whether the claims shall be dismissed at all" indicates that the modern case law progressively moves into the "*right*" direction, there nevertheless seems to be lack of legal certainty as to the proper procedural outcome in such situations.

As for the definition of corruption, the tribunal found it appropriate to seek guidance from the Anti-Bribery Convention and the 2003 United Nations Convention against Corruption.[110]

---

[108] *Id.*

[109] The legality requirement is usually being derived from the words "in accordance with host State law" in the definition of the "investment" in international investment agreements.

[110] Ultimately, the tribunal settled on the understanding that "(a)ny promise, offering or giving to a (foreign) public official, directly or indirectly, of an undue financial or other advantage in order that the official act or refrain from acting in the exercise of his or her official duties, for the purpose of obtaining business advantages falls under the notion of corruption." *See,* Djanic (2017), available at https://www.iareporter.com/articles/indian-company-invokes-dutch-bit-rather-than-indian-treaty-in-new-arbitration-over-withdrawn-subsidies-in-uzbekistan/.

6.4.2.2 Burden and Standard of Proof

In the situation of absence of the agreement of the parties and/or of the relevant norms in the applicable legal instruments, the Spentex arbitral tribunal recalled its wide powers to determine the applicable burden and standard of proof.

Following the submissions of the respondent, the tribunal agreed that the use of the strict standard of proof (such as “clear and convincing” evidence) would make the allegations of corruption almost impossible to prove or disprove.[111] Therefore, the tribunal decided to adopt a flexible approach to the standard of proof without accepting the standards that were suggested by the parties. In light of the opaque nature of acts through which corruption is executed, the tribunal took the position that a method known as “connecting the dots” would be the most appropriate for this purpose.[112] In other words, the tribunal decided that it was necessary to review and analyse each individual piece of evidence and have a look at the greater picture in the context of other established facts. According to the tribunal, this would enable a nuanced approach capable of considering all of the relevant circumstances and facts in relation to the allegations of corruption.[113]

As to the application of the burden of proof, while the tribunal decided that it should give consideration to the way the parties had cooperated during the fact-finding exercise, it had, nevertheless, found that the starting point should be the established principle that each party needs to prove the facts on which it relies.

6.4.2.3 Red Flags

When assessing the evidence of corruption that was presented by Uzbekistan, the arbitral tribunal noted that there is an

> inherent danger to dispose of the problem [of corruption] by resorting to strict evidentiary rules that may take proving or disproving corruption practically impossible.[114]

In light of this, the arbitral tribunal decided to rely on circumstantial evidence and the accumulation of *red flags* that it identified - in particular, the following:

---

[111] Spentex Netherlands, B.V. v. Republic of Uzbekistan, ICSID Case No. ARB/13/26, Award, 27 December 2016, para. 856 as referenced in Betz (2017), p. 131.

[112] Djanic (2017), available at https://www.iareporter.com/articles/indian-company-invokes-dutch-bit-rather-than-indian-treaty-in-new-arbitration-over-withdrawn-subsidies-in-uzbekistan/.

[113] As we have seen, this approach also finds its support in legal literature. *See*, Partasides (2010); Malik and Kamat (2018), available at https://paperity.org/p/185990736/corruption-in-international-commercial-arbitration-arbitrability-admissibility, p. 17; Karadelis (2010), available at https://globalarbitrationreview.com/print_article/gar/article/1029476/corruption-and-the-standard-of-proof.

[114] Gaillard (2019), p. 8 with reference to Betz (2017), pp. 128–136.

- Unconventionally high fees for services;
- Lack of qualifications of the consultants to provide services that they were expected to provide under the consultancy agreements;[115]
- The lack of clarity about the services that were to be provided under the consultancy agreements;[116]
- No evidence that could display the specific services that were rendered and their economic added value;
- Finally, the tribunal also voiced its concern over the lack of transparency, as the controversial payments were made to accounts in Luxembourg and the British Virgin Islands, countries known for providing "discreet banking services".[117]

As a result of this analysis, and after "[c]onnecting the dots", the tribunal concluded that the making of the investment was "*clearly*" done through "corrupt activities on the part of the investor and of officials of the Respondent."[118]

6.4.2.4 "It Takes Two to Tango..."

The tribunal noted that, where corruption is involved, "it takes two to tango";[119] therefore, any allegation of corruption necessarily implies that the respondent's own officials were also implicated.[120] The missing link, however, was the absence of direct evidence that bribes were destined to the Uzbek government officials.

The tribunal had nevertheless drawn conclusions from other *red flags* and established that the bribes were indeed destined and paid to the Uzbek public officials. In particular, the tribunal reportedly based this finding on one main circumstance, namely that the USD 6 million "fee" had been paid to one of the consultants just a few days before the public tender took place.[121] Subsequently, the tribunal found that both the claimant and the respondent were involved in the corrupt activity that led to the establishment of the investment in question.[122]

---

[115] In particular, the First Finance Solutions was headed by the then 22-year-old brother of the President of the Kazakh British Chamber of Commerce.

[116] According to the tribunal's analysis the contracts only offered vague descriptions, such as "ensuring good support for the bid" and "ensuring good relations" with the Uzbek authorities.

[117] Djanic (2017), available at https://www.iareporter.com/articles/indian-company-invokes-dutch-bit-rather-than-indian-treaty-in-new-arbitration-over-withdrawn-subsidies-in-uzbekistan/.

[118] Spentex Netherlands, B.V. v. Republic of Uzbekistan, ICSID Case No. ARB/13/26, Award, 27 December 2016, para. 934 as quoted in Betz (2017), p. 134.

[119] *See*, Kulkarni (2013), available at www.transnational-dispute-management.com/article.asp?key=1957, p. 47; Alekhin and Shmatenko (2018).

[120] Djanic (2017), available at https://www.iareporter.com/articles/indian-company-invokes-dutch-bit-rather-than-indian-treaty-in-new-arbitration-over-withdrawn-subsidies-in-uzbekistan/.

[121] *Id.*

[122] The conduct of the undisclosed public official who received the bribe seems to have been attributed to the conduct of the state. This is consistent with the general public international law norms. *See*, Crawford (2002), pp. 106–109; Shaw (2008), p. 786.

As a result of the analysis and findings described above, the arbitral tribunal in its majority decided that the claims related to the investment that had been established through corrupt activity were inadmissible.

6.4.3 Tribunal's Criticism and Cost Assessment

In addition to looking at strictly legal questions of the raised corruption defense by the respondent, it is reported that the Spentex tribunal also made a couple of observations on the flow of the process and made several proposals for the future development of IIL.

6.4.3.1 Lack of Cooperation from the Respondent

The Spentex tribunal reportedly found it inappropriate that Uzbekistan did not agree to cooperate with the tribunal in finding the "missing link" in the chain of corrupt schemes, namely in finding the person from the Uzbek Government's side who may have been bribed by the claimant. In omitting to cooperate, it appears that Uzbekistan had actually filled in this "missing link" with, what some authors call, a "logical nexus between the probable nature" of the information that was withheld and "the inference derived therefrom".[123] The respondent's argument was that there was no need for the tribunal to know the name of the exact governmental official in order to dismiss the claims of the investor on the determined grounds.[124]

The tribunal also seemed to be displeased by the reluctance of the respondent to investigate and/or prosecute the officials who "tangoed" with the investor in its corruption scheme.[125] Uzbekistan alleged that the State had no resources to initiate such investigation, but the tribunal was not satisfied with this reasoning and instead concluded that the Uzbek Government was simply unwilling to investigate and prosecute the relevant individuals.[126]

In the arbitral tribunal's view, the respondent's conduct, if accepted without consequences would have an adverse effect on the entire system:

---

[123] Craig et al. (2000), p. 451.

[124] Djanic (2017), available at https://www.iareporter.com/articles/indian-company-invokes-dutch-bit-rather-than-indian-treaty-in-new-arbitration-over-withdrawn-subsidies-in-uzbekistan/.

[125] *Id.* The expert of the respondent testified that no criminal proceedings were initiated at the time of arbitration in relation to the Claimant's investment.

[126] Spentex Netherlands, B.V. v. Republic of Uzbekistan, ICSID Case No. ARB/13/26, Award, 27 December 2016, para. 941 as referenced in Betz (2017), p. 134.

> Such an approach would reinforce perverse incentives for respondent States in the context of corruption. It would ask an investment tribunal to dismiss a claimant's claim, while granting impunity to a respondent State both in respect of the alleged corruption and the claimant's investment claims.[127]

6.4.3.2 Creative Cost Assessment

The decision on costs made it impossible for any party to proclaim victory over the dispute. It has also opened another range of questions in relation to arbitral tribunal's powers in cases where the allegations of illicit misconduct have been made and, perhaps, generally in any ISDS case.

It is stated that the tribunal urged Uzbekistan to make certain reforms in its anti-corruption policy and to make a monetary contribution to an international program targeting to fight corruption. While the tribunal recognized that it did not possess the power to order Uzbekistan to make such a donation, it, nonetheless, offered a strong incentive for the State to do so by conditioning the cost order on such contribution.[128]

It is reported that the tribunal's majority consisting of *Prof. August Reinisch* and *Stanimir Alexandrov*, stressing the Respondent's own responsibility for corrupt practices in Uzbekistan, offered a choice of two options:

- Either Uzbekistan donates USD 8 million to one of the United Nations' anti-corruption funds within 90 days in addition to covering its own legal fees and 50% of the costs of the proceedings;
- Or Uzbekistan pays 75% of more than USD 17 million of the claimant's legal fees and 100% of the costs of the proceedings in addition to its own legal fees.[129]

In relation to the first option, the figure of USD 8 million was chosen by the arbitral tribunal after giving due considerations to the amount of the bribes in question, the costs that Uzbekistan was willing to undertake to defend its position in arbitration and the possibility of making a significant change with the help of the contribution.[130]

In addition to the careful consideration of the exact sum of the contribution, the tribunal also carefully selected the potential recipients of the contribution—namely, either the UNDP Global Anti-Corruption Initiative or the UNDP "Anti-corruption for Peaceful and Inclusive Societies" project. The arbitrators also evaluated other organisations such as OECD and Transparency International but decided that the UNDP programs had more suitable targets. As was noted before, it is stated that the tribunal found that such a decision was appropriate and fair in light of the fact that

[127] *Id.* with reference to para. 940.

[128] Djanic (2017), available at https://www.iareporter.com/articles/indian-company-invokes-dutch-bit-rather-than-indian-treaty-in-new-arbitration-over-withdrawn-subsidies-in-uzbekistan/.

[129] *Id.*

[130] *Id.*

the State was also responsible for the initial corruption, and it failed (at the time) to duly investigate and prosecute the parties that were involved in bribery on the side of the State.

It has been reported that Uzbekistan has since made a contribution to the United Nation's anti-corruption program and has initiated joint projects aiming at combating corruption in the country.[131]

Notwithstanding the fact that initiating anti-corruption programs in collaboration with international organisations is a positive development, the question that arises in connection with this decision and remains yet unanswered is whether the Spentex tribunal remained within the boundaries of its competences, or not. The questions on uncertainty of tribunal's powers in this respect seem to have arisen already during the arbitration itself with one of the arbitrators dissenting in opinion on whether the tribunal had a right of issuing such a decision.

In *Brigitte Stern's* view, the conditioning of the cost order on the respondent's fulfilment of the recommendation essentially equates such a recommendation to an order, which falls outside of the tribunal's competence.[132] Moreover, *Stern* expressed concerns that a situation where States are ordered to bear a part or the entirety of the costs of claimants in cases involving corruption could have negative effects on the entire system. Thus, she opined that claimants, who are engaged in corruption, would have a "free-ride" in their pursuit of damages without the risk of baring additional costs of the arbitration procedures.[133]

So far, it seems to be an unprecedented decision on the costs in ISDS and in arbitration in general.

6.4.3.3 Proposals for Subsequent Treaty Drafting

In addition to deciding on the merits of the dispute between the parties, the arbitral tribunal made several propositions as to the future development of IIL. In particular, the Spentex tribunal stated the following:

> On the one hand, the claimant cannot have its claim entertained (due to a lack of jurisdiction or admissibility). On the other hand, a tribunal should be able to entertain the claim as if no corruption had occurred and, in case it finds the State liable, calculate the damages that a claimant having made an investment without resort to corruption would have been entitled to and then order that such amount be transferred not to the claimant, but to an appropriate body of the UN, the OECD, or any other body fighting against corruption.[134]

---

[131] Article of the United Nation's Development Program's cooperation with Uzbekistan's Ministry of Justice and General Prosecutor's Office is available at http://www.uz.undp.org/content/uzbekistan/en/home/presscenter/pressreleases/2018/04/20/undp%2D%2Dministry-of-justice-and-general-prosecutor-office-launch-a.html.

[132] Djanic (2017), available at https://www.iareporter.com/articles/indian-company-invokes-dutch-bit-rather-than-indian-treaty-in-new-arbitration-over-withdrawn-subsidies-in-uzbekistan/.

[133] *Id.*

[134] Spentex Netherlands, B.V. v. Republic of Uzbekistan, ICSID Case No. ARB/13/26, Award, 27 December 2016, para. 941 as referenced in Betz (2017), p. 134.

The arbitral tribunal suggested that such mechanisms should be introduced during the subsequent drafting of international investment treaties in order to ensure its effective and binding application.

6.4.4 Analysis of the Award

The Spentex case is, so far, one of its kind. It is unique and important due to the fact that the arbitral tribunal decided on a wide range of questions, provided analysis to different matters of direct relevance to the present scientific research and elaborated on the potential future legal framework for cases involving illicit misconduct, such as corruption and bribery. It is a rare example when the arbitral tribunal took an extra-proactive position in deciding on the merits of the dispute and attempting to revisit the current legal situation in international investment law and arbitration. It is also unique in a sense that it decided to "penalize" both the investor and the State for engaging in corrupt practices.[135]

The most important take away-s from the Spentex case for the purposes of the present monograph are summarised below.

6.4.4.1 Application of the Legality Requirement

The legality requirement shall be applied irrespective whether it is enshrined in the applicable treaty or not. It was found that the legality requirement is a general standard directly applicable in international investment law and arbitration. In the context of corruption, the tribunal's analysis is consistent with the doctrinal views that contracts that are tainted by corruption are unenforceable.[136]

6.4.4.2 Standard of Proof

The arbitral tribunal may apply a more flexible standard of proof for allegations of illicit conduct especially when these allegations concern conduct, which is non-transparent *per se*, such as corruption and bribery. In this case the arbitral tribunal applied the so-called "connecting the dots" approach, which is less strict than "clear and convincing evidence" and, perhaps, as flexible as the "balance of probabilities" standard.

---

[135] Alekhin and Shmatenko (2018), p. 151.

[136] Teachout (2011), pp. 681–682.

6.4.4.3 Red Flags as Evidence

Due to the above-mentioned choice of approach, the arbitral tribunal found that it was appropriate to admit *red flags* as the basis for its findings of corruption. Furthermore, the Spentex tribunal attempted to list and define a series of different events, which are to be recognized as *red flags* under its analysis. The use of such evidence in proving corruption and fraud, as will be seen, is also welcomed by some authors.[137]

6.4.4.4 Burden of Proof

While due regard must be given to the way the parties cooperate in the disclosure of documents and fact-finding exercises, the initial burden of proof is to be carried by the party that asserts a certain argument. At the same time, it seems like that the Spentex tribunal had intentionally left room for further discussion on the possibility of shifting and/or sharing the burden of proof to/with the defending party.

On the question of Uzbekistan's role in the corrupt scheme, the tribunal seems to have drawn adverse inferences from the omission of the State to cooperate and to disclose certain information. The drawing of negative inferences is indeed not a rare "guest" in arbitration and is recognized in the academic world.[138]

6.4.4.5 State's Liability/Responsibility

It was noted that in the event of corruption and bribery, it usually "takes two to tango". In other words, both parties must be at some degree of guilt for the illicit act. The tribunal found that since bribery had to involve government officials (either directly or indirectly), neither party shall benefit from the tribunal's award.

Another take-away in this regard would be the opinion that was expressed by the dissenting arbitrator, who voiced certain concerns as to the future cases with similar narratives. *Brigitte Stern* was of the opinion that by obliging the State to take a large part in covering the costs of arbitration and the legal costs of the investor the tribunal could incentivise corrupt investors to initiate disputes without fearing to carry a heavy financial burden. In parallel to the arbitrator's dissenting views, the call for considering holding States responsible/liable for corrupt practices in international arbitration has been previously voiced in legal literature.[139]

---

[137] *See for instance*, Alekhin and Shmatenko (2018), p. 162 with reference to Amerasinghe (2005), p. 138.

[138] *See*, Born (2014), p. 2311; Mills (2003), p. 295; Lamm et al. (2010), pp. 704–705; Fathallah (2010), pp. 73–77; Clouet (2018).

[139] *See for instance*, Cremades (2005); Wilske (2010); Meshel (2013a).

The Spentex tribunal's approach is in line, although not explicitly, with some authors' views that the State, whose officials solicited and/or received bribes, cannot successfully raise the so-called "corruption defence" under the *venire contra factum proprium* principle.[140] This is in line with the expressed opinion that the imposition of consequences for States for participating in and/or tolerating corrupt practices could be the realisation of the "zero tolerance" approach in investment arbitration.[141] Moreover, it is certain that in post-Spentex era, some States will be more cautious in "tainting" investments with corruption, as it may become a "two-way street" with consequences for both parties.[142]

6.4.4.6 International Investment Law Reform

The arbitral tribunal in the Spentex case made a step further with the suggestion of revisiting the IIL in order to fight corruption effectively *inter alia* through the means of arbitration. The tribunal's analysis and its decision open up a whole new range of potential questions for further research in the field of ISDS. One of such questions could be the rights and/or obligations of arbitrators to report or take any other positive action if they become aware of corrupt practices. At the moment, the view is that "[a]ny duty of disclosure can only arise from national legislation to which tribunal members are subject."[143] It must, however, be noted that this topic is not straightforward and requires separate attention, in particular, in light of the duties of confidentiality that are owed towards parties.[144]

6.5 Sanum v. Laos

The award in this case (dated 6 August 2019) reflects a very interesting analysis of the questions of evidence and proof. It includes findings on the consequences of illicit misconduct during the operation of the investment rather than during its establishment. Some of the arbitral tribunal's conclusions were also based on the conduct of the parties during the arbitration itself.

---

140 Kulick and Wendler (2010), p. 98; *See also,* Llamzon (2008), p. 81.

141 Fernández-Armesto (2015), p. 31: "Investment arbitration has initiated and led the movement of zero tolerance towards corruption."

142 Losco (2014a), pp. 37–52, available at https://scholarship.law.duke.edu/cgi/viewcontent.cgi?referer=&httpsredir=1&article=1004&context=dlj_online, p. 48.

143 Clouet (2018) with reference to Cremades and Cairns (2003), p. 85.

144 On the questions of confidentiality duties, *see* Lew (2011).

6.5.1 *Factual and Procedural Background*

In 2007, two United States entrepreneurs became involved in the gambling business in Laos, for the purposes of which they incorporated two companies—Lao Holdings NV in the Netherlands and Sanum Investments ("**Sanum**") in Macau (collectively—claimants).[145] Through these two companies, the claimants partnered with a Laotian conglomerate in two casino projects and three slot machine clubs in Laos.[146] After several years, the claimants' partners initiated litigations against Sanum and excluded it from one of the most profitable casino projects. According to the claimants, the steps taken by their local partners were "orchestrated" and "designed" by the Government of Laos ("**Laos**").[147]

As a result, Sanum submitted its Notice of Arbitration against Laos to the Permanent Court of Arbitration under the China—Laos BIT on 14 August 2013.[148]

6.5.2 *Findings and Analysis of the Arbitral Tribunal*

The tribunal in this case was met with several arguments relating to alleged bad faith conduct of both parties. The respondent argued

> that the Tribunal should dismiss all claims because of the illegal activities in which the Claimants allegedly engaged, including bribery, embezzlement and money laundering.[149]

The claimants denied illicit misconduct and, in event, denied any causal link between the investment and alleged illegality.[150] At the same time, the claimants pointed out that the respondent failed to prosecute any of its public officials for alleged corruption, which according to it should have an effect on the tribunal's assessment of the respondent's illegality case.

Both parties confirmed that "[t]here is no doubt that bribery and corruption are contrary to the domestic laws of Laos",[151] therefore the tribunal did not have to assess the effects of illicit conduct on the investment and arbitration in general. However, the tribunal still needed to assess whether illicit conduct during the operation of the investment, rather than during its establishment, could trigger the dismissal of the investors' claims.

---

[145] Sanum Investments Limited v. the Lao People's Democratic Republic, PCA Case No 2013-13, Award, 6 August 2019, para. 1.

[146] *Id.*

[147] *Id.*, para. 2.

[148] *Id.*, para. 3.

[149] *Id.*, para. 86.

[150] *Id.*, para. 101.

[151] *Id.*, para. 95.

6.5.2.1 Jurisdiction v. Merits

The respondent's arguments of bribery, embezzlement and money laundering were connected with the request for dismissal of the investors' claims and it was presented in light of the alleged lack of tribunal's jurisdiction over illegal investments. However, the arbitral tribunal did not perceive this argument as a defence against its jurisdiction, but found it to be "an *affirmation* of the Tribunal's jurisdiction to consider the claims on their merits".[152] Notably, the tribunal decided not to elaborate on this point. This could partly be due to the reason that the tribunal had previously already confirmed its jurisdiction.[153] Such an approach, although quite abrupt, does find certain support in academic writings.[154]

6.5.2.2 Burden and Standard of Proof

There was no apparent debate between the parties as to the burden of proof and it was accepted that the burden of proof for the allegations of corruption laid with the respondent, i.e. the party alleging the illegality.[155] However, the parties disagreed on the applicable standard of proof and the tribunal had to decide whether the standard of "balance of probabilities" was sufficient for allegations of illicit conduct or whether it required "clear and convincing evidence".

At the very outset, the Sanum tribunal acknowledged the difficulty of establishing corruption, while at the same time recognizing "the importance of exposing corruption where it exists."[156] This mixture of ideas led the arbitral tribunal to admitting both standards of proof (i.e. balance of probabilities and clear and convincing evidence). It stated that "there need not be "clear and convincing evidence" on every element of each allegation of corruption, but such "clear and convincing evidence" as exists must point clearly to corruption."[157] Furthermore, the tribunal continued that

> [a]n assessment must then be made of which elements of the alleged act of corruption have been established by clear and convincing evidence, and which elements are left to reasonable

[152] *Id.*, para. 87 [emphasis added].

[153] Sanum Investments Limited v. the Lao People's Democratic Republic, PCA Case No 2013-13, Award of Jurisdiction, 13 December 2013.

[154] *See for instance,* Fathallah (2010)pp. 40–41 and 65-70, *see also*, Clouet (2018).

[155] In this regard, *see,* Hunter (1992), pp. 204–211; Alekhin and Shmatenko (2018), pp. 157–158. *See also,* Haugeneder (2009), pp. 323–339; Lamm et al. (2010), pp. 699–731; and Rosell and Prager (1999), pp. 329–348.

[156] Sanum Investments Limited v. the Lao People's Democratic Republic, PCA Case No 2013-13, Award, 6 August 2019, para. 107.

[157] *Id.,* para. 108.

> inference, and on the whole whether the alleged act of corruption is established to a standard higher than the balance of probabilities but less than the criminal standard of beyond reasonable doubt, although, of course proof beyond reasonable doubt would be conclusive.[158]

In other words, the arbitral tribunal recognized that the evidence of corruption must be clear and convincing, however it admitted the possibility of proving certain elements of corruption by reasonable inferences, i.e. "balance of probabilities".

6.5.2.3 Timing of Illicit Conduct

Remarkably, the Sanum tribunal considered that "proof of corruption *at any stage* of the investment may be relevant depending on the circumstances".[159] In relation to the "clean hands" doctrine, the tribunal decided not to opine on its general stance in public international law and investment arbitration. It, however, did emphasise that

> serious financial misconduct by the Claimants incompatible with their good faith obligations as investors in the host country (such as criminality in defrauding the host Government in respect of an investment) *is not without Treaty consequences*, both in relation to their attempt to rely on the guarantee of fair and equitable treatment, as well as their entitlement to relief of any kind from an international tribunal.[160]

Consequently, the arbitral tribunal decided not to brush away the possible proven instances of illegality after the establishment of the investment.

6.5.2.4 Application of the UN Convention Against Corruption

The arbitral tribunal considered that while

> the UNCAC applied to States rather than private parties, it [nevertheless] embodies what has become a principle of customary international law applicable ... to root out corruption

that was used to "obtain or retain business or other undue advantage in relation to the conduct of international business."[161] As a result, it appears that the arbitral tribunal found that the UNCAC is to be applied as customary international law. This is

---

[158] *Id.* According to the Sanum tribunal, "[t]his approach reflects the general proposition that the "graver the charge, the more confidence there must be in the evidence relied on."

[159] *Id.*, para. 103 [emphasis added].

[160] *Id.*, para. 104 [emphasis added].

[161] *Id.*, para. 103 with references to the UN Convention Against Corruption, Article 16(1), and Anti-Bribery Convention, Article 1(1): "Each Party shall take such measures as may be necessary to establish that it is a criminal offence under its law for any person intentionally to offer, promise or give any undue pecuniary or other advantage, whether directly or through intermediaries, to a foreign public official, for that official or for a third party, in order that the official act or refrain from acting in relation to the performance of official duties, in order to obtain or retain business or other improper advantage in the conduct of international business"; and ICC Dossier: Addressing Issues of Corruption in Commercial and Investment Arbitration, Chapter 11, at para. 34: "It is now

consistent with the general position that tribunals enjoy wide discretion on the application of law.[162]

6.5.2.5 Findings of Illegality

The respondent alleged that the claimants were engaged in a number of illicit schemes. Some of the respondent's allegations related to bribery of former governmental officials that were extended in exchange of the termination of the audit of their business. The claimants denied these allegations and stated that the payments to such persons, the existence of which was undisputed, had legitimate purposes.

The arbitral tribunal did not find the claimants' explanation to be credible, however, at the same time, it found that there was lack of clear and convincing evidence to establish corruption in these instances. While not making the findings on corruption, the tribunal was nevertheless satisfied that on the balance of probabilities, there was enough evidence proving that investors were involved in "serious financial illegalities", "fraud" *and* "chicanery".[163]

6.5.2.6 Finding of Bad Faith

Based on the available facts and evidence, the tribunal found that the claimants acted in bad faith during the operation of their investment, as well as during the arbitration proceedings.

With regards to bad faith during the operation of the investment, the arbitral tribunal made note of (i) the misrepresentations made to the Government as to the intent to make multi-million investments, and (ii) possibly making illicit payments to the government officials.[164] As to the bad faith conduct during the arbitration, the Sanum found that the claimants were "likely attempting to obstruct justice" by paying a witness so that she does not testify.[165] The tribunal also opined that it was plausible that the claimants were "attempting to mislead the Treaty Tribunals with" certain "sham" commercial offers.[166]

---

undisputed that a finding of corruption when making or performing an investment will lead to dismissal of claimant's claims and to a loss of any protection afforded by the treaty."

[162] *See for instance,* Kreindler (2002), p. 253; Hwang, M. S.C. and Lim, K., Corruption in Arbitration — Law and Reality, available at https://www.arbitration-icca.org/media/4/97929640279647/media013261720320840corruption_in_arbitration_paper_draft_248.pdf.

[163] Sanum Investments Limited v. the Lao People's Democratic Republic, PCA Case No 2013-13, Award, 6 August 2019, para. 138.

[164] *Id.*, para. 176.

[165] *Id.*, para. 176.

[166] *Id.*

It further stated that the claimants' efforts were directed "to manipulate the Government", as well as "to manipulate the arbitration process itself".[167] On the legal side, the tribunal found that "it is well established that the bad faith conduct of the investor is relevant to the grant of relief under an investment treaty".[168]

6.5.2.7 Lack of Internal Investigation by the Respondent

While denying corruption, the claimants submitted that Laos was inconsistent with its own allegations as it failed to hold anyone accountable for purported corruption.[169] The claimants specifically pointed out that corruption allegations emerged after the commencement of the arbitration.

The arbitral tribunal, without displaying its analysis, decided that "[c]onviction of its own officials *would not estop* the Government from pursuing the Claimants as bribe-givers".[170] However, at the same time, the tribunal found it "disturbing" that Laos did not take any steps to prosecute or investigate any persons who had allegedly received bribes from the claimants.[171] Considering such a "disturbing" element, the tribunal questioned the respondent's position in relation to several instances where there was no clear and convincing evidence of corruption and subsequently rejected them.[172]

6.5.3 *Analysis of the Award*

The arbitral tribunal's decision in the Sanum v. Laos case is innovative and progressive with respect to several questions that have been raised and that are of direct relevance for the purposes of this monograph.

---

[167] *Id.*, para. 177.

[168] *Id.*, para. 175.

[169] *Id.*, paras. 109, 147, 166.

[170] *Id.*, para. 110.

[171] *Id.*, para. 111.

[172] *See for instance,* Sanum Investments Limited v. the Lao People's Democratic Republic, PCA Case No 2013-13, Award, 6 August 2019, para. 122: "Moreover, no one was prosecuted in this affair. Even if Madam Sengkeo did not cooperate with the Government, why was her daughter (the owner of the bank account) not investigated? What is the daughter's explanation?"; para. 126: "There is no evidence that Madam Manivone (the presumed recipient) or anyone else was prosecuted."

6.5.3.1 Standpoint of Examination

The arbitral tribunal in this case found that illegality is not necessarily an obstacle to its jurisdiction. The tribunal acknowledged that depending on the circumstances proven illicit conduct may be relevant to either jurisdiction, or merits. This way, from the very outset, the arbitral tribunal remained open-minded in its analysis. Interestingly, the arbitrators understood the respondent's illegality arguments as an actual recognition of the tribunal's jurisdiction to examine those arguments on the merits.

6.5.3.2 Standard of Proof

Despite the fact that ICSID tribunals tend to apply stricter standards of proof for allegations of corruption,[173] the arbitral tribunal chose to be flexible in the application of the standard of proof. It recognized both the difficulty and importance of proving corruption, which is why it decided to assess and evaluate any allegations that can be proven by either "clear and convincing evidence" and "balance of probabilities" together. Thereby, the tribunal decided to be open to any possible findings that it could have made under either of the standards. As was seen from the detailed analysis above, the arbitral tribunal did, in fact, consider the findings that stemmed out from the lowered standard of proof.

6.5.3.3 Illegality & Bad Faith During the Investment Operation and Arbitration

Unlike the popular position that illegal acts during the operation of the investment shall not be determinative to the admission of the claims, the Sanum tribunal confirmed that illicit and bad faith conduct at any stage can be relevant for treaty claims. Moreover, the arbitral tribunal found that bad faith during the arbitration itself shall also be taken into account. In making these observations, the arbitral tribunal did not fully recognize them to be a product of the "clean hands" doctrine. However, at the same time, the reasoning behind its findings appears to be heavily connected to the elements of this doctrine.

6.5.3.4 Respondent's Failure to Investigate & Prosecute

Similarly, as was seen in other cases, the Sanum tribunal did not shy away in making negative comments towards a State for not taking investigatory steps against the persons who, according to the State itself, received bribes from the investors. The

[173] Losco (2014b), p. 2. *See also,* Haugender and Liebscher (2009).

failure to take such actions had led the tribunal to a number of findings that were adverse to the position of the respondent.[174]

At the same time, and opposite to some scholars' views,[175] the tribunal explicitly found that failure to take reasonable investigatory steps by a State would not cause estoppel in relation to its defence against treaty claims. This further enhances the launch of the open discussion of whether arbitral tribunals should "penalize" States for tolerating corrupt practices[176] and, nevertheless, bringing up the anti-corruption policies as defence in investment disputes. Such penalization could make certain States to "be less inclined" to run illegality arguments without substantial factual and legal basis, so as to avoid the "back-firing" of such arguments.[177]

References

Alekhin S, Shmatenko L (2018) Corruption in investor-state arbitration – it takes two to Tango. In: Asoskov AV et al (eds) New horizons of international arbitration, Issue 4, Collection of Articles, p 161

Amerasinghe F (2005) Evidence in international arbitration. Martinus Nijhoff Publishers, Leiden/Boston, p 138

Betz K (2017) Proving bribery, fraud and money laundering in international arbitration. University of Basel, Cambridge University Press

Born G (2014) International commercial arbitration, vol II, 2nd edn. Kluwer Law International, Hague, p 2311

Broches A (1972) The convention on the settlement of investment disputes between states and nationals of other states. Recueil des cours 136:331–410

Catti C (2013) The arbitrability of corruption claims. In Young arbitration review, 8th edn, pp 36–38

Clouet LM (2018) Arbitrating under the table: the effect of allegations of corruption in relation to the jurisdiction of the arbitral tribunal and the enforcement of foreign arbitral awards. https://nyu.academia.edu/LuisMar%C3%ADaClouet

Craig WL, Park WW, Paulsson J (2000) International chamber of commerce arbitration, 3rd edn, p 451

Crawford J (2002) The international law commission's articles on state responsibility: introduction, text and commentaries. Cambridge University Press, pp 106–109

Cremades BM (2005) Corruption and investment arbitration. Aksen G et al (eds) Global reflections on international law, commerce and dispute resolution: Liber Amicorum in Honour of Robert Briner, ICC Publication No. 693

Cremades BM, Cairns DJA (2003) Transnational public policy in international arbitral decision making: the cases of bribery, money laundering and fraud. In: Karsten K, Berkeley A (eds) Arbitration: money laundering, corruption, and fraud. Dossiers of the ICC Institute of World Business, p 85

[174] *See*, Sharp (2006); Mills (2003), p. 295; and Born (2014), p. 2311.

[175] *See*, Kulick and Wendler (2010), p. 98; Llamzon (2008), p. 81.

[176] Alekhin and Shmatenko (2018), p. 151.

[177] Losco (2014a), pp. 37–52, available at https://scholarship.law.duke.edu/cgi/viewcontent.cgi?referer=&httpsredir=1&article=1004&context=dlj_online, p. 48.

Crivellaro A (2003) Arbitration case law on bribery: issues of arbitrability, contract validity, merits and evidence. In: Karsten K, Berkeley A (eds) Arbitration, money laundering, corruption and fraud. Dossiers - ICC Institute of World Business Law, p 21

Djanic V (2017) In newly unearthed Uzbekistan ruling, exorbitant fees promised to consultants on eve of tender process are viewed by tribunal as evidence of corruption, leading to dismissal of all claims under Dutch BIT. Glob Arbitr Rev

Fathallah R (2010) Corruption in international commercial and investment arbitration: recent trends and prospects for Arab countries. Int J Arab Arbitr 2(3):73

Fernández-Armesto J (2015), The effects of a positive finding of corruption. In: Baizeau D, Kreindler RH (eds) Addressing issues of corruption in commercial and investment arbitration, in Dossiers of the ICC Institute of World Business Law, Vol 13. ICC Publication No. 768E, p 31

Gaillard E (2019) The emergence of transnational responses to corruption in international arbitration. J Int Arbitr 35(1):8

Haugender F, Liebscher C (2009) Chapter V: international arbitration - corruption and investment arbitration: substantive standards and proof. In: Klausegger C et al (eds) Austrian Arbitration Yearbook, pp 539–564

Haugeneder F (2009) Corruption in investor-state arbitration. J World Invest Trade 10(3):323–339

Hunter JM (1992) Modern trends in the presentation of evidence in international commercial arbitration. Am Rev Int Arbitr 3:204–211

Karadelis K (2010) Corruption and the standard of proof. Glob Arbitr Rev

Kreindler R (2002) Aspects of illegality in the formation and performance of contracts. In: 11th International Council for Commercial Arbitration Congress, p 253

Kulick A, Wendler C (2010) A corrupt way to handle corruption? Thoughts on the recent ICISD case law on corruption. Legal issues of economic integration. Kluwer Law International 37(1): 98

Kulkarni SA (2013) Enforcing anti-corruption measures through international investment arbitration. Transnatl Disp Manage 3

Lamm CB, Pham HT, Moloo R (2010) Fraud and corruption in international arbitration. In: Fernandez-Ballesteros A, Arias D (eds) Liber Amicorum Bernardo Cremades. Kluwer, pp 699–731

Lamm CB, Greenwald BK, Young KM (2014) From the world duty free to metal-tech: a review of international investment treaty arbitration cases involving allegations of corruption. ICSID Rev

Lew JDM (2011) The arbitrator and confidentiality. In: Dossier of the ICC institute of world business law: is arbitration only as good as the arbitrator? Status, power and role of the arbitrator

Llamzon A (2008) The control of corruption through international investment arbitration: potential and limitations. In: Proceedings of the American Society of International Law on 9-12 April, 2008, 102:81

Llamzon A (2014) Corruption in international investment arbitration. Oxford University Press

Losco MA (2014a) Charting a new course: metal-tech v. Uzbekistan and the treatment of corruption in investment arbitration. Duke Law J 64:37–52

Losco MA (2014b) Streamlining the corruption defense: a proposed framework for FCPA-ICSID Interaction. Duke Law J Online 64:2. Available at https://dlj.law.duke.edu/article/streamlining-the-corruption-defense-losco-vol63-iss5/

Lund-Turner K (2015) The corruption defense in Investment-Treaty Arbitration: tempering the zero-tolerance approach, p 5. https://pacific.academia.edu/KastleLund

Malik D, Kamat G (2018) Corruption in international commercial arbitration: arbitrability, admissibility & adjudication. The Arbitration Brief

Meshel T (2013a) The use and misuse of the corruption defence in international investment arbitration. J Int Arbitr 30

Meshel T (2013b) Metal-Tech Ltd. v. Republic of Uzbekistan – 'Strike Two' against investor claimants facing the corruption defense. IntLawGrrls, Available at https://ilg2.org/2013/12/18/metal-tech-ltd-v-republic-of-uzbekistan-strike-two-against-investor-claimants-facing-the-corruption-defense/

Michael Hwang SC, Lim K (2012) Corruption in arbitration—law and reality. https://www.arbitration-icca.org/media/4/97929640279647/media013261720320840corruption_in_arbitration_paper_draft_248.pdf
Mills K (2003) Corruption and other illegality in the formation and performance of contracts and in the conduct of arbitrations relating thereto. ICCA Congress Series No. 11, p 295
Nappert S (2013) Nailing corruption: thoughts for a gardener. A comment on World Duty Free Company Ltd. v. the Republic of Kenya. Transnatl Disp Manage
Odumosu I (2011) International investment arbitration and corruption claims: an analysis of world duty Free v. Kenya. Law Dev Rev 4(3):88
Partasides C (2010) Proving corruption in international arbitration: a balanced standard for the real world. ICSID Rev Foreign Invest Law J 25(1)
Perry S (2013) Uzbek claim dismissed because of corruption. Glob Arbitr Rev. Available at https://globalarbitrationreview.com/article/1032822/uzbek-claim-dismissed-because-of-corruption
Rosell J, Prager H (1999) Illicit commissions and international arbitration: the question of proof. J Int Arbitr 15(4):329–348
Scherrer M (2002) Circumstantial evidence in corruption cases before international arbitral tribunals. Int Arbitr Law Rev 5(2):34–35
Schreuer C, Malintoppi L, Reinisch A, Sinclair A (2009) The ICSID convention: a commentary. Cambridge University Press, p 669
Sharp J (2006) Drawing adverse inferences from the non-production of evidence. J Int Arbitr 22
Shaw MN (2008) International law, 6th edn. Cambridge University Press, p 786
Teachout Z (2011) The unenforceable corrupt contract: corruption and nineteenth century contract law, symposium issue: money, politics, and the constitution. N Y Univ Rev Law Soc Change 35:681–682. Available at https://ir.lawnet.fordham.edu/cgi/viewcontent.cgi?article=1431&context=faculty_scholarship
Torres-Fowler Z (2012) Undermining ICSID: how the global antibribery regime impairs investor-state arbitration. Virginia J Int Law 52
Waibel M (2014) Investment arbitration: jurisdiction and admissibility. In: Legal Studies Research Paper Series, Paper No 9/2014. University of Cambridge, p 50
Wiebecke M (2018) Evidence and proof. In: Legum B (ed) The investment treaty arbitration review, 3rd edn. p 97
Wilske S (2010) Sanctions for unethical and illegal behavior in international arbitration: a double-Edged Sword. Contemp Asia Arbitr J, 3

Chapter 7
Arbitral Tribunals Not Upholding Corruption and Fraud Arguments

In this chapter, analysis of five cases in which arbitral tribunals did not uphold allegations of fraud or corruption is provided. These cases have been selected as they reflect different and, at times, opposite approaches undertaken by arbitral tribunals in investment disputes.

7.1 Sistem v. Kyrgyzstan

Although, the arbitral tribunal in the present case did not uphold the findings of corruption or fraud, its decision is, nevertheless, relevant for the present research. Questions of the definition of bribery in the scope of international arbitration and its determination were raised and analysed by the arbitral tribunal, which had prompted some remarkable findings.

7.1.1 Factual and Procedural Background

Sistem Mühendislik Insaat Sanayi ve Ticaret A.S ("**Sistem**"), a company incorporated under the laws of the Republic of Turkey, filed a request for arbitration against the Kyrgyz Republic ("**Kyrgyzstan**") to ICSID on 11 October 2005. The ICSID arbitration clause was included in the Kyrgyzstan-Turkey BIT.[1] Sistem concluded

[1] Article VII(2) of the Agreement between the Republic of Kyrgyzstan and the Republic of Turkey concerning the reciprocal promotion and protection of investments dated 28 April 1992: "If these disputes cannot be settled in this way within six months following the date of the written notification mentioned in paragraph 1, the dispute can be submitted as the investor may choose, to: (a) the International Center for Settlement of Investment Disputes (ICSID) set up by the "Convention on

A. Tussupov, *Corruption and Fraud in Investment Arbitration*, EYIEL Monographs - Studies in European and International Economic Law 22,
https://doi.org/10.1007/978-3-030-90606-1_7

several contracts in Kyrgyzstan for construction, management and operation of a hotel in Bishkek.

The dispute arose over the alleged physical and legal take-over of control of a hotel which was previously owned and managed by the claimant. The respondent, in turn, argued that Sistem's investment should not be protected because the claimant purportedly bribed government officials in order to acquire rights over the disputed asset.

7.1.2 Findings and Analysis of the Tribunal

It was submitted that in 1995, the claimant voluntarily and at no cost refurbished the official residency of the President of Kyrgyzstan. The respondent suggested that such an act constituted an attempt to bribe the Kyrgyz President. It was further suggested that the free refurbishment led the claimant to the award of the contract that was concluded in 1999, which subsequently granted Sistem one hundred percent control over a hotel in the capital.[2]

However, the tribunal was not satisfied with the presented illegality arguments. Although the tribunal found "no explanation of the [1999] main agreement" and how it came about, it was still of the opinion that there was no proof that the refurbishment of the official residence of the President constituted a bribe.[3]

As a first step, the arbitral tribunal found that the official residence of the President of a State was not a private dwelling and constituted a public property. In connection with this, the tribunal found that refurbishing a public building could well qualify as a normal corporate *good will* practice, which was aimed at promoting the reputation of a company.[4] Developing this idea, the arbitral tribunal turned to the definition of bribery incorporated in the Anti-Bribery Convention, which was invoked by the respondent and which defines bribery as

> undue pecuniary or other advantage, whether directly or through intermediaries, to a foreign public official, for that official or for a third party, in order that the official act or refrain from acting in relation to the performance of official duties, in order to obtain or retain business or other improper advantage in the conduct of international business.[5]

As a next step, the tribunal analysed whether the refurbishment of the presidential residence procured undue or improper advantage for the claimant. This is closely

Settlement of Investment Disputes between States and Nationals of other States", (in case both Parties become signatories of this Convention.)"

[2] Sistem Mühendislik Insaat Sanayi ve Ticaret A.S. v. the Kyrgyz Republic, ICSID Case No. ARB (AF)/06/1, Award, 9 September 2009, para. 40.

[3] *Id.*, para. 43.

[4] *Id.*, para. 41.

[5] Article 1 of the OECD Convention on Combating Bribery of Foreign Public Officials in International Business Transactions.

connected to the question of existence of the causal link between the alleged bribe and the contract that underlined the dispute. The arbitrators stated that they found no such link (nor was it explained by the respondent) because no private person (in contrast to public) benefited from the refurbishment and that no advantage was granted to Sistem in exchange to its *good will.*[6]

7.1.3 Analysis of the Award

Similarly to other cases that are analysed in the present textbook, the Sistem tribunal did not have to go into the questions of applicable law and standard of proof. However, unlike the World Duty Free case where parties voluntarily provided hard evidence of corruption, in this case the tribunal found that it had absolutely no evidence to support the allegations of bribery. Nevertheless, the Sistem v. Kyrgyzstan award is significant for several of its findings, in particular the following:

i. *Good will* or Bribery?
The tribunal recognized the existence of *good will* practices that are exercised by corporate entities, that are designed and destined for the benefit of a whole State, rather than private parties. This finding can potentially blurry the line between a legitimate donation to the State (as was alleged in the World Duty Free case, for instance) and an attempt to bribe a public official.

ii. Definition of Bribery
The tribunal considered it appropriate to define "bribery" in accordance with international legal instruments. In this case, the tribunal sought guidance from the Anti-Bribery Convention. This reiterates the position of other tribunals who also referred to international legal instruments, regardless of the fact whether the concerned States are parties or signatories to such instruments. Although, as will be seen further below (infra Sect. 7.4 of Part B), there may be alternative approaches to this.

iii. Genuine Link
Even though the arbitral tribunal in this case found that considerable amount of time elapsed after the alleged bribe had been made, it was still aware of the possibilities that in "some circumstances it may happen that regular payments over a period of time effectively "buy" the long-term goodwill of the recipient, so as to make it difficult to establish a causal link between the bribe and the advantage that it procures."[7]

---

[6] Sistem Mühendislik Insaat Sanayi ve Ticaret A.S. v. the Kyrgyz Republic, ICSID Case No. ARB (AF)/06/1, Award, 9 September 2009, para. 41.

[7] *Id.*, para. 44.

7.2 EDF v. Romania

The EDF Services Limited v. Romania case is unique in a sense that allegations of illicit misconduct were used as a "sword" by the investor rather than as a "shield" by the State.[8] In this regard, the arbitral tribunal had to analyse whether the request to pay a bribe made by the State is contrary to its obligations under international investment agreements.

7.2.1 *Factual and Procedural Background*

EDF Services Limited ("**EDF**") filed a request for arbitration against Romania on the basis of the UK-Romania BIT,[9] which ICSID received on 14 June 2005. EDF is incorporated at the Bailiwick of Jersey,[10] it maintained investments in Romania through participation in two joint ventures with Romanian state-owned enterprises. The operations of the joint ventures were centred at the airport resale business.

EDF argued that after the election of the new Government in Romania, the joint ventures were subjected to harassment and were solicited to pay bribes in the amount of USD 2.5 million. According to EDF, the solicitation was made by two senior government officials, namely the Chief of Cabinet to the then Prime Minister of Romania and the then Secretary of State. The claimant submitted that by soliciting bribes, the respondent failed to accord fair and equitable treatment over its investment under the applicable BIT.[11]

The respondent denied all the allegations and referred to the completed domestic judicial proceedings that were earlier initiated by the claimant in Romania and where a final and irrevocable decision was made, dismissing EDF's bribery complaints.

[8]Various authors concluded that the illegality arguments are much more often used by states as a "shield" against claims in investment arbitration. *See*, Alekhin and Shmatenko (2018), pp. 164–168. *See also*, Menaker and Greenwald (2015), pp. 77–102; Low (2019), p. 341.

[9]Article 7(2) of the Agreement between the Government of the United Kingdom of Great Britain and Northern Ireland and the Government of Romania for the Promotion and Reciprocal Protection of Investments dated 13 July 1995: "(2) Where the dispute is referred to international arbitration, the national or company concerned may choose to refer the dispute either to: (a) the International Centre for the Settlement of Investment Disputes. . ."

[10]Bailiwick of Jersey is a Crown dependency.

[11]*Id.*, Article 2(2): "Investments of nationals or companies of each contracting party shall at all times be accorded fair and equitable treatment."

7.2.2 *Findings and Analysis of the Tribunal*

The nature of the act itself, such as "a request for a bribe", was analysed by the tribunal and it came to the conclusion that the act would be in violation of the fair and equitable treatment standard under the UK-Romania BIT, as well as in violation of international public policy. In this regard the arbitral tribunal noted that "exercising a State's discretion on the basis of corruption is a [...] fundamental breach of transparency and legitimate expectations".[12]

7.2.2.1 Standard of Proof

At the very outset, the EDF tribunal started with confirming that "corruption ... is notoriously difficult to prove since, typically, there is little or no physical evidence."[13] However, while acknowledging the notorious difficulty to prove such acts, the arbitral tribunal found that "[t]he seriousness of the accusation of corruption in the present case, considering that it involves officials at the highest level of the Romanian Government at the time, demands clear and convincing evidence."[14] Such a finding was substantiated with the reference to other arbitral tribunals, stating that "[t]here is general consensus among international tribunals and commentators regarding the need for a high standard of proof of corruption."[15]

In light of the standard of proof that was found to be applicable by the arbitral tribunal, it decided that the evidence that was presented as proof for solicitation of bribes was "far from being clear and convincing."[16] The tribunal reasoned its findings based on detailed analysis of each type of evidence that was submitted by the parties:

i. Witness Statements

The tribunal made note of the fact that some of the claimant's testimonies were merely based on hearsay evidence without support of direct evidence. While the arbitrators stressed that "hearsay testimonies" are admissible as evidence in arbitration, confirmatory evidence is, nevertheless, normally required.[17] The other witness

[12] Malik and Kamat (2018), p. 16 with reference to EDF Services Limited v. Romania, ICSID Case No ARB/05/13, Award, 8 October 2009, para. 221.

[13] EDF Services Limited v. Romania, ICSID Case No ARB/05/13, Award, 8 October 2009, para. 221. The same point is often raised in legal literature, *see for instance*, Alekhin and Shmatenko (2018), p. 164.

[14] EDF Services Limited v. Romania, ICSID Case No ARB/05/13, Award, 8 October 2009, para. 221.

[15] *Id.*

[16] *Id.*

[17] *Id.*, para. 224.

statements, in the tribunal's view, were either inconsistent with parallel testimonies or lacked credibility.[18]

ii. Manipulated Emails?

The claimant alleged that once the request for a bribe was made, the claimant's managers exchanged emails, in which such a request was mentioned and described. However, the tribunal did not find this piece of evidence to be admissible due to the fact that in earlier domestic criminal proceedings the witness could not concede whether he indeed drafted or sent that email, and also because there was counter-evidence that suggested that the email was manipulated. "Again, the evidence was not clear and convincing."[19]

iii. Secret Audio Tape

In an attempt to further substantiate its allegations of bribery solicitation, the claimant requested that new evidence be admitted. The new evidence consisted of a secret audio tape, with the transcript, that allegedly contained a recording of the conversation when a bribe was requested. The new evidence was declared inadmissible by the tribunal for various reasons, including lack of authenticity of the audio tape. Just as in the case with the allegedly manipulated email, there was evidence that the audio tape did not display the full conversation.

However, notwithstanding the other grounds on which the respondent objected the admission of the tape as evidence, the arbitral tribunal, nevertheless, stated that if the audio tape had been complete and without discontinuities, it would have been admitted to the record of the proceedings.

7.2.2.2 Burden of Proof

Consistently with the overall practice and a range of doctrinal views,[20] the tribunal decided that the burden of proof rests with the claimant as the party alleging the solicitation of bribery. It was noted that the burden of proof was not only in relation to the fact that a bribe had been requested from the claimant's manager, but also that such request had been made not in the private interest of the person soliciting the

---

[18] *Id.*, para. 223: "The testimony of Mr. Marco Katz, a witness for Claimant, is of doubtful value. He denied initially, in 2002, when questioned by the PNA (later replaced by the DNA) having any knowledge of the person who solicited the bribe. But he said in his written statement to the Tribunal in these proceedings, dated July 2, 2007 that he had been immediately informed by Mr. Weil that the bribe request had been made by Mr. Sorin Tesu. On May 18, 2006, in a Statement delivered to the DNA, Mr. Katz mentioned the name of Mr. Sorin Tesu as the person who requested the payment of USD2.5 million from Mr. Weil. The obvious question for the Tribunal is in which of these statements was Mr. Katz telling the truth. There is no way to know. The evidence is not clear and convincing."

[19] *Id.*, para. 224.

[20] In this regard, *Hunter* stated that placing the burden of proof on the alleging party is necessary to negate the baseless contentions. *See*, Hunter (1992), pp. 204–211. *See also*, Haugeneder (2009), pp. 323–339; Lamm et al. (2010), pp. 699–731; Rosell and Prager (1999), pp. 329–348.

bribe, but on behalf and for the account of the government authorities in Romania, so as to make the State liable in that respect.[21] In the absence of such evidence, the arbitral tribunal drew the conclusion that the claimant did not sustain its burden of proof.

7.2.3 Analysis of the Award

Some of the findings that were expressed by the tribunal seem to be significant for the subject of the present research. In particular, the EDF v. Romania award displays the arbitral tribunal's examination of the standard of proof, admissibility of evidence, the effects of the domestic court proceedings in relation to the same subject matter and, more importantly, whether bribery solicitation is contrary to international investment treaty obligations.

An interesting feature of this dispute is that the claim on illicit misconduct (i.e. solicitation of bribery) was made on behalf of the claimant rather than the respondent. It is the investor who alleged criminal conduct of the State, which was suggested to be contrary to fair and equitable treatment standard that was enshrined in the UK-Romania BIT.

i. Solicitation of Bribery v. State Obligations

The highlight of the award is that the tribunal generally supported the theoretical idea that if a State requests an investor to pay a bribe, that would constitute a breach of the fair and equitable treatment standard and would also be contrary to international public policy and legitimate expectations of a foreign investor.[22] However, in coming to such conclusion the arbitral tribunal did not refer to any international legal instruments, domestic law or other arbitral awards. Seemingly enough, the tribunal's analysis was rather intuitive and self-explanatory.

ii. Private Interest v. Public Interest

In determining the possible State's responsibility in this case, the tribunal noted that it had to be proven that the alleged bribe was made "for the account of the Government", rather than in private interest of a public official.[23] This element, in the arbitral tribunal's view, was decisive in establishing State responsibility.

iii. Standard of Proof and Admissibility of Evidence

Another important feature of this case is the determination of the standard of proof and admission of evidence. Despite the existence of various academic opinions to the contrary,[24] the EDF tribunal found that "clear and convincing" evidence had to

[21] EDF Services Limited v. Romania, ICSID Case No ARB/05/13, Award, 8 October 2009, para. 232.

[22] *Id.*, para. 221.

[23] *Id.*, para. 232.

[24] *See*, Alekhin and Shmatenko (2018), p. 161.

be applied to support corruption claims.[25] The tribunal stated that there was a general consensus on this point among other arbitral tribunals that examined corruption claims, which is why it has not elaborated on how it came to such a conclusion itself. Indeed, from various publications, as well as from the analysis conducted in this monograph, the application of stricter standards of proof by arbitral tribunals for allegations of corruption and/or fraud is witnessed.[26] However, this is not an universal approach and other standards of proof are applied as well.

Additionally, it is to be noted that some of the evidence was either not admitted or was accorded only limited weight by the tribunal based on international legal standards, rather than national law of the host State. In other words, the arbitral tribunal felt it appropriate to make use only of international law, as well as the IBA Rules,[27] in order to determine the weight of the submitted evidence.

iv. Burden of Proof

As to the burden of proof, the arbitral tribunal decided that the claimant bared the burden of proof for its claims. The respondent was not required to disclose documents or submit any counterevidence, perhaps, this is partly because the arbitral tribunal felt that no *prima facie* case was made on behalf of the claimant. In any event, the respondent did provide witness statements in support of its defence against the corruption allegations.

7.3 Siag and Vecchi v. Egypt

In the present case the tribunal was asked to decide on the allegations of fraud committed on the tribunal itself by the claimant. Allegations of such character are less frequent in ISDS cases than allegations of fraud at the establishment or operation of the investment. Additionally, one of the arbitrators dissented with his findings on fraud, while making some innovative proposals on engaging third (investigatory) parties for the identification of truth.

7.3.1 Factual and Procedural Background

Waguih Elie George Siag ("**Mr. Siag**") and Clorinda Vecchi (collectively—the claimants), both citizens of Italy, filed a request for arbitration to ICSID against

[25] The stricter standard of proof for allegations of illegality are more commonly met in ISDS cases. *See*, Losco (2014), pp. 37–52, available at https://scholarship.law.duke.edu/cgi/viewcontent.cgi?referer=&httpsredir=1&article=1004&context=dlj_online.

[26] *See for instance,* Crivellaro (2006), p. 109.

[27] EDF Services Limited v. Romania, ICSID Case No ARB/05/13, Award, 8 October 2009, para. 47.

the Arab Republic of Egypt ("**Egypt**") on the basis of the Italy–Egypt BIT. As Clorinda Vecchi deceased on 16 October 2007, her claims were advanced by the executors of her estate.

The claimants were the principal investors in Touristic Investments and Hotels Management Company (SIAG) S.A.E. and Siag Taba Company. It was alleged that through a series of acts and omissions directed against the claimants, Egypt destroyed the value of the claimants' investments.[28]

Egypt advanced several positions in defence against the investors' claims. Egypt alleged that Mr. Siag was at all relevant times a national of Egypt, thus precluding him from succeeding in a claim against Egypt under the BIT.[29] The failure to be a citizen of another contracting State could pull the brakes on the entire arbitration.[30] This requirement is so absolute that it is argued that it cannot be waived by parties.[31] Even though this argument was rejected in the arbitral tribunal's decision on jurisdiction, Egypt pursued the same contention during the merits stage after reformulating some of its arguments and providing some additional evidence. Egypt asserted that by denying his Egyptian citizenship Mr. Siag committed fraud on the arbitral tribunal.

7.3.2 *Findings and Analysis of the Tribunal*

Even though the question of Mr. Siag's nationality was successfully resolved at the jurisdictional stage, the tribunal, nevertheless, decided to look at it again at the merits following a reformulated allegation of the respondent. The question before the tribunal was whether Mr. Siag indeed through "fraud, deception or other dishonest behaviour" acquired the Lebanese passport.

7.3.2.1 Burden of Proof

While the arbitral tribunal acknowledged that following the usual practice the burden of proof is with the asserting party, at the merits stage it noted that Mr. Siag would have been nevertheless required to provide some evidence of his citizenship:

> ...while it is clear that the burden of proof in respect of all jurisdictional objections lies with Egypt, at the merits phase Mr Siag must first prove on the balance of probabilities that he acquired Lebanese nationality, assuming that his acquisition of Lebanese nationality is a relevant factor.[32]

[28] Waguih Elie George Siag and Clorinda Vecchi v. the Arab Republic of Egypt, ICSID Case No ARB/05/15, Award, 1 June 2009, para. 2.

[29] *Id.*, para. 5.

[30] Waibel (2014), p. 34.

[31] Schreuer et al. (2009), para. 213.

[32] Waguih Elie George Siag and Clorinda Vecchi v. the Arab Republic of Egypt, ICSID Case No ARB/05/15, Award, 1 June 2009, para. 316.

At the same time, the above finding appears to have been of merely theoretical nature as the tribunal was immediately satisfied with the evidence that was already provided to it earlier during the jurisdictional stage, in particular the Lebanese passport:

> The Tribunal finds that as at 27 February 2008, even before the merits hearing and before Mr Siag had given oral evidence and defences, Mr Siag had provided extensive prima facie evidence of his Lebanese nationality.[33]

Considering the above, the tribunal reiterated that the burden of proof was still with Egypt and had not shifted to the claimants. As was concluded by a number of other legal scholars, this is the most common position in relation to the burden of proof generally in international arbitration.[34]

7.3.2.2 Standard of Proof and Evidence

The question that was raised in the arbitration and was disputed by the parties is "what does Egypt have to prove?"[35] In this regard, the arbitral tribunal found that the respondent had to prove fraud on the part of Mr. Siag and this finding appears to be mostly based on the respondent's own submissions who *inter alia* asserted that "the issue before the Tribunal is not the procedural one as to whether there has been a waiver or not. Rather, the far more important question is whether this Tribunal has been deceived by the principal claimant before it as to his basis for presenting a claim. . . ."[36]

The answer to the question raised above led the parties and the tribunal to the identification of the applicable standard of proof. In the tribunal's view, the applicable standard of proof for allegations of such serious nature must be considerably higher than for ordinary claims. In that analysis, the arbitral tribunal followed the submission of the claimants where it was suggested that the applicable standard of proof was "the American standard of "clear and convincing evidence".[37] It was explained that this standard was somewhere in between the traditional civil standard of "preponderance of the evidence" (otherwise known as the "balance of probabilities"), and the criminal standard of "beyond reasonable doubt".[38]

Egypt did not suggest any lesser standard of proof as it believed that the burden rested with the claimants. In the absence of Egypt's arguments in that regard and

[33] *Id.*, para. 316.

[34] Alekhin and Shmatenko (2018), pp. 157–158. *See also*, Haugeneder (2009), pp. 323–339; Lamm et al. (2010), pp. 699–731; Rosell and Prager (1999), pp. 329–348.

[35] Waguih Elie George Siag and Clorinda Vecchi v. the Arab Republic of Egypt, ICSID Case No ARB/05/15, Award, 1 June 2009, para. 319.

[36] *Id.*, para. 321.

[37] Alekhin and Shmatenko (2018), p. 161.

[38] Malik and Kamat (2018), p. 18.

with reference to other arbitral tribunal's decisions,[39] it was upheld that "clear and convincing evidence" was necessary to prove the respondent's assertion of fraud on the part of Mr. Siag.

Following this analysis, the arbitral tribunal turned to the evidence submitted by the respondent. It appears from the award, that the tribunal was provided with a note from a Lebanese state organ stating that there was no record of Mr. Siag's Lebanese nationality in the civil registry. In response to this, Mr. Siag submitted reports of international organisations that discussed problems of Lebanon in the administrative sphere, which included the problem of poorly managed state registries.[40]

The arbitral tribunal was satisfied with the counterevidence and subsequently found that the evidence submitted by Egypt was neither clear, nor convincing.

7.3.3 *Analysis of the Award*

From the findings of the arbitral tribunal in this case, it is observed that the tribunal went into considerations and analysis of the burden of proof, the standard of proof, admission and effects of certain evidence, which are all areas of interest for the topic of the present textbook.

i. Burden of Proof

As to the burden of proof, it was agreed that the burden of proof was with the party asserting the claim. However, notwithstanding the general finding on the burden of proof, the arbitral tribunal, nevertheless, felt comfortable with idea of the defending party providing at least some evidence in support of its counter-arguments.

ii. Positive Evidence v. Negative Evidence

In assessing the evidence that was put before it, the arbitral tribunal made an interesting statement saying that a party against whom an allegation of illicit misconduct was made is not necessarily obliged to provide negative evidence thereof. The tribunal appreciated the fact that it is more difficult to provide evidence over acts that you have *not* committed. In this sense, the tribunal was satisfied with the provision of the so-called "positive evidence".

iii. Standard of Proof

As to the issue of the standard of proof, the tribunal applied a stricter standard. According to the tribunal, the stricter standard of proof was to be applied due to the

[39] Wena Hotels Limited v. the Arab Republic of Egypt, ICSID Case No ARB/98/4, Award, 8 December 2000.

[40] Waguih Elie George Siag and Clorinda Vecchi v. the Arab Republic of Egypt, ICSID Case No ARB/05/15, Award, 1 June 2009, para. 256. For instance, one of the reports was the Final Report of the European Union Election Observation Mission in the Parliamentary Elections of Lebanon in 2005, which stated that the Lebanon's state registry suffered from "chronic structural, procedural and material deficiencies".

nature and degree of the assertions that had been made, especially if the claims suggest that certain immoral, criminal conduct was undertaken. Due to these reasons, the Siag tribunal found that "clear and convincing evidence" was needed to substantiate Egypt's allegations of fraudulent conduct.

It generally seems that the arbitral tribunal in this case was very cautious and sceptical of the respondent's allegations of fraud. It might be that the majority arbitrators were of the opinion that Egypt was trying to adopt a tactical manoeuvre aimed at defeating investors' claims without looking at the merits. Notably, arbitral tribunals had been warned of such possibilities and the need to cautiously approach illegality claims in scholarly writings.[41]

7.3.4 Analysis of the Dissenting Opinion of Professor Francisco Orrego Vicuña

One of the arbitrators, *Prof. Francisco Orrego Vicuna*, did not accept the reasoning of the majority of the tribunal and provided his opinion on several issues. *Prof. Vicuna* dissented on the findings that were made in the decision on jurisdiction and in the final award. In relation to the points discussed above, *Prof. Vicuna* dissented on all of them:

i. Burden of Proof

Firstly, Professor stated that he still believed that the burden of proof was supposed to be shifted to the claimants, as there was (in his view) enough evidence to suggest that Mr. Siag's citizenship was tainted by fraud and corruption.

ii. Standard of Proof and Evidence

As a second step, *Prof. Vicuna* disagreed with the heavy standard of proof that was applied by the majority and opined that the tribunal was "to choose the most relevant rules in accordance with the circumstances of the case and the nature of the facts involved, as it has been increasingly recognized."[42] He further added that

> [t]he facts of this case, difficult as they are to establish with absolute certainty, could be best judged under a standard of proof allowing the Tribunal "*discretion in inferring from a collection of concordant circumstantial evidence* (faisceau d'indices) the facts at which the various indices are directed."[43]

[41] *See for instance,* Fathallah (2010), p. 73.

[42] Waguih Elie George Siag and Clorinda Vecchi v. the Arab Republic of Egypt, ICSID Case No ARB/05/15, Dissenting Opinion of Professor Francisco Orrego Vicuña to the Final Award, 11 May 2009, p. 4, with reference to Sayed (2004), pp. 89–92.

[43] Waguih Elie George Siag and Clorinda Vecchi v. the Arab Republic of Egypt, ICSID Case No ARB/05/15, Dissenting Opinion of Professor Francisco Orrego Vicuña to the Final Award, 11 May 2009, p. 4 [emphasis added].

Prof. Vicuna also suggested to weigh in the evidence based on its source. The arbitrator proposed to put the information coming from state organs of a sovereign on one scale and the evidence of the claimant in the proceedings on the other. The dissenting arbitrator had "not the slightest doubt that" that the information of the third (non-interested) State should have been accorded more weight.[44]

iii. Intervention of Interpol?

Moreover, *Prof. Vicuna* made another suggestion, which in his view should have been undertaken by the tribunal in the light of the evidence that was submitted by Egypt:

> The only other choice would have been *to request the intervention of Interpol* in support of the Tribunal's task to establish the true facts, which was not asked for nor in my view appeared necessary in view of the evidence on record.[45]

From the academic point of view and for the purposes of the present research, the suggestions of *Prof. Vicuna* (in particular, the final one) are of significant interest. Unfortunately, in his opinion, the arbitrator did not provide any substantial reasoning for his suggestions and did not provide record of prior similar experience in other arbitrations (either commercial or investment). Neither has the author found any explicit support for such ideas. However, at the same time, the author has also not identified any explicit opposition against them.

7.4 Kim and Others v. Uzbekistan

In this case Uzbekistan raised arguments against the jurisdiction of the arbitral tribunal based on the allegations of illegality and corruption. However, this case differs from the other two Uzbekistan cases that were analysed in the scope of the present research[46] because here the arbitral tribunal did not find the investors' conduct to be tainted by corruption or by any other illegality so as to make the investors' claims inadmissible or to find that the tribunal lacks jurisdiction. Remarkably, the State referred to both fraud and corruption in the present case.

7.4.1 Factual and Procedural Background

On 25 March 2013, the ICSID Centre received the request for arbitration signed by Vladislav Kim and eleven other citizens of the Republic of Kazakhstan (collectively

[44] *Id.*

[45] *Id.* [emphasis added].

[46] *I.e.*, Metal Tech v. Uzbekistan and Spentex v. Uzbekistan.

"**Investors**") against Uzbekistan.[47] As the Investors in this case are the nationals of the Republic of Kazakhstan, the request for arbitration was submitted on the basis of the Kazakhstan-Uzbekistan BIT.[48] The dispute is related to the claimants' ownership interests in two large cement plants located in the territory of Uzbekistan.[49]

Uzbekistan had several lines of argumentation that it put forward in defence of its position against the claims of the Investors and the jurisdiction of the arbitral tribunal. In particular, the respondent alleged that:

- the claimants did not provide sufficient evidence as to their citizenship of the Republic of Kazakhstan;[50]
- the claimants were not "investors" who made an "investment" under the meaning of the Kazakhstan-Uzbekistan BIT;[51]
- the claimants' investment was not made in compliance with the Uzbek legislation and that, therefore, such investment could not enjoy protection under the BIT;[52]
- the claimants' investment was procured by corruption and therefore the claims were not admissible.[53]

While the tribunal decided negatively on all the above-mentioned jurisdictional objections of the respondent, for the purposes of the current research the final two arguments and their analysis by the tribunal are of particular interest and are closely reviewed in the subsequent paragraphs.

7.4.2 *Findings and Analysis of the Tribunal*

In this section, the most relevant and important (for the purposes of the present monograph) findings of the Kim tribunal are analysed.

---

[47] Vladislav Kim and others v. the Republic of Uzbekistan, ICSID Case No. ARB/13/6, Decision on Jurisdiction, 8 March 2017, para. 28.

[48] "Each Contracting Party hereby agrees that any legal dispute arising between one of the Contracting Parties and an investor from the State of the other Contracting Party in relation to investments made by him or her in the State territory of the first Contracting Party shall be submitted for consideration to one of the following organizations [. . .] (c) International Centre for Settlement of Investment Disputes, if both Contracting Parties are parties to the Convention on the Settlement of Investment Disputes between States and Nationals of Other States, opened for signature on 18 March 1965 in Washington." Article 10 of the Agreement between the Government of the Republic of Kazakhstan and the Government of the Republic of Uzbekistan on Promotion and Reciprocal Protection of Investments dated 2 June 1997.

[49] Vladislav Kim and others v. the Republic of Uzbekistan, ICSID Case No. ARB/13/6, Decision on Jurisdiction, 8 March 2017, para. 3.

[50] *Id.*, paras. 181–236.

[51] *Id.*, paras. 237–357.

[52] *Id.*, paras. 358–540.

[53] *Id.*, paras. 543–617.

7.4.2.1 Legality Requirement

Due to the fact that the Kazakhstan-Uzbekistan BIT contains an explicit wording in Article 12 that suggests the existence of the legality requirement, the arbitral tribunal decided not to make any findings on its possible implicit application.[54]

In relation to the interpretation of the legality requirement, the arbitral tribunal was not persuaded that it was to follow the "rule-like statements" contained in decisions of other tribunals in similar cases. The Kim tribunal decided that the application of the "rule-like statements" was not proper *inter alia* because the Kazakhstan-Uzbekistan BIT was not applied in cases where such statements were made. Subsequently, the arbitral tribunal undertook its own attempt to interpret the text of Article 12 of the BIT through the rules envisaged in the Vienna Convention on the Law of Treaties.[55]

As a result of its interpretation, the tribunal came to the conclusion that

> the legality requirement in the BIT denies the protections of the BIT to claims when the investment involved was made in noncompliance with a law of Uzbekistan where together the act of noncompliance and the content of the legal obligation results in a compromise of a correspondingly significant interest of Uzbekistan.[56]

Due to the serious nature of the consequences of the finding of illegality, the tribunal made a note stating that the allegations of illegality must be undertaken on the case-by-case analysis and are to be guided by the principle of proportionality.[57]

7.4.2.2 Findings on Fraud

After establishing the meaning and the scope of the legality requirement in the context of the Kazakhstan-Uzbekistan BIT, the tribunal applied its analysis and interpretation onto the arguments and facts that were presented by the parties. The respondent submitted several grounds for the alleged breach of the legality requirement *inter alia* claiming that the investment was made through fraud. Uzbekistan pursued (i) fraud in violation of Uzbek Securities Law,[58] (ii) false disclosure and

---

[54] "This Agreement shall apply to investments within the territory of one Contracting Party's State, made in compliance with its legislation by investors from the other Contracting Party's State, regardless of whether they were made before or after the entry into force of this Agreement.", Article 12 of the Agreement between the Government of the Republic of Kazakhstan and the Government of the Republic of Uzbekistan on Promotion and Reciprocal Protection of Investments dated 2 June 1997.

[55] *See*, Vladislav Kim and others v. the Republic of Uzbekistan, ICSID Case No. ARB/13/6, Decision on Jurisdiction, 8 March 2017, paras. 386–404.

[56] *Id.*, para. 404.

[57] *Id.*

[58] *Id.*, para. 419.

concealment in registering the sales-purchase agreement,[59] and (iii) fraud causing significant harm to the State, minority shareholders and the brokers.[60]

While deciding on the fraud allegations, the arbitral tribunal found that an act of fraud generally had a great impact on the host State's interests and it was, therefore, significant enough to be considered for the breach of the legality requirement. In this regard, the tribunal stated that a proven allegation of fraud would likely be sufficient to cause the investment to fall outside the scope of the legality requirement under Article 12 of the Kazakhstan-Uzbekistan BIT.[61]

Subsequently, after analysing the arguments and evidence that were presented by the respondent, the tribunal's majority found that Uzbekistan failed to prove fraud on the side of the Investors. In its finding, the tribunal's majority decided that the claimants had no fraudulent intent, which was found to be an essential element of the act of fraud itself.[62] It is for this reason that Uzbekistan's "fraud objection" was dismissed.

It appears that similar reasoning was *mutatis mutandis* applied in relation to the alleged false disclosure and concealment in registering the commercial contracts.[63] The tribunal's majority found that Uzbekistan did not provide sufficient evidence to support its allegations.[64]

As an overall result, the majority of the arbitral tribunal found that the "Respondent either has failed to establish that Claimants acted in noncompliance with various laws or that such acts of noncompliance do not result in a compromise of an interest that justifies, as a proportionate response, the harshness of denying application of the BIT".[65]

For completeness, it is to be noted that on the other hand, the tribunal minority's view was that the respondent established the intent required to conclude that the claimants acted in noncompliance with various laws. The dissenting arbitrator was of the opinion that such acts of noncompliance—particularly the nondisclosure of the price paid for the shares—should have resulted in the compromise of a correspondingly significant interest of Uzbekistan that would render proportionate the exclusion of the investment from the protection of the BIT.[66]

[59] *Id.*, para. 421.

[60] *Id.*, para. 422.

[61] *Id.*, para. 435.

[62] *Id.*, para. 439. The minority of the tribunal found the opposite; the description of the position of the minority may be found in paragraph 440 of the Decision on Jurisdiction.

[63] *Id.*, paras. 466–476.

[64] *Id.*, paras. 515–536. The minority of the tribunal found the opposite; the description of the position of the minority may be found in paragraph 537 of the Decision on Jurisdiction.

[65] *Id.*, para. 541.

[66] *Id.*, para. 541.

7.4.2.3 *Red Flags* and Proof

In making assessment of the corruption arguments, the tribunal did not consider the burden of proof issue in detail and moved on to comment on the matters of *red flags* that were raised by the respondent first. In the arbitral tribunal's opinion, *red flags* most often provide only circumstantial, as opposed to direct evidence, and that as circumstantial evidence, *red flags* can play an important *supporting* role in the assessment of guilt.[67] Moving onto the questions whether *red flags* can directly establish an element of crime, the tribunal found that it should depend on the applicable legal system and that there was no universal answer to that effect.[68] Nevertheless, the arbitral tribunal was of the opinion that *red flags* were useful in triggering awareness that a certain business transaction did not conform with the customary characteristics that are usually found in a comparable transaction and in triggering closer examination of such circumstances surrounding the business transaction in question.[69]

While examining the *red flags* that were put forward by the respondent, the arbitral tribunal considered the context and the environment, in which the investment and the particular business transaction took place. The tribunal followed the explanation of the claimants who argued that certain *western red flags* might not be regarded as *red flags* in the CIS countries. In particular, the tribunal found it reasonable to take into account that the political and economic regimes in the CIS countries justified taking of extra measures so as not to call attention to any individual's wealth or business dealings.[70] In other words, the Kim tribunal found it appropriate to look into the allegation of illicit conduct in light of the surrounding circumstances of the host region. The end effect of this analysis is that *red flags* may differ from jurisdiction to jurisdiction and there is no universally exhaustive list of events that shall qualify as *red flags* for the purposes of IIL.

As to the standard of proof, the arbitral tribunal followed neither of the parties submissions and it noted that since the respondent alleged the breach of certain criminal laws of Uzbekistan, it could potentially seek guidance from the Uzbek legislation and the standard of proof that was applicable before the courts of Uzbekistan.[71] However, the arbitral tribunal decided not to make a finding on the applicable standard of proof since under its analysis there was no sufficient evidence of bribery.

---

[67] *Id.*, para. 548.

[68] *Id.*

[69] *Id.*, para. 549.

[70] *Id.* The analysis was made in the light of the Respondent's argument that the Claimants made payments through a complicated web of off-shore companies.

[71] *Id.*, para. 545.

7.4.2.4 Findings on Corruption

The essence of the respondent's argument was that the claimants' investment was procured by corruption through payments to *Ms. Gulnar Karimova*, a daughter of the then-President of Uzbekistan and to *Mr. Bizakov*, a well-connected entrepreneur in the Republic of Kazakhstan.

When evaluating the merits of the arguments and evidence put forward by the parties, the tribunal put it in context of Uzbek law, in particular in context of the provisions of criminal law, which *inter alia* defined the terms "corruption" and "bribery". While conducting analysis of Uzbek law requirements and definitions of "bribery", the arbitral tribunal found that the allegations of the respondent did not stand scrutiny due to a number of reasons.[72]

One of the reasons was that *Ms. Gulnar Karimova*, who purportedly received an overpayment of USD 8 million, was not a state official and did not hold a position in the Uzbek Government at the relevant times. The same finding was made in respect of *Mr. Bizakov*. In context of Uzbek law it meant that no bribery took place, because "bribery" is committed only when undue advantage is extended to a public official according to the Uzbek criminal law provisions. Looking back at what was discussed by scholars before this case, *Kulick* and *Wendler* seem to have been right in finding that corruption may not always serve as a ground for refusing jurisdiction even if the "in accordance with the law" clause applies.[73]

In relation to the respondent's argument that the payments to *Ms. Karimova* and *Mr. Bizakov* were contrary to the international public policy, the arbitral tribunal did not find the relevant nexus between the alleged payments and the necessary characteristics of the definition of "bribery" and/or "corruption" under international law.[74]

Interestingly, on the allegations of corruption during the operation of the investment the Kim tribunal opined that "matters [of] bribery or corruption that arose later are more appropriately addressed at the merits stage."[75]

7.4.3 *Analysis of the Award*

The arbitral tribunal's decision in Kim et al. v. Uzbekistan case is similar in some ways and, at the same time, different in many other ways from the decisions of other arbitral tribunals in similar cases where the allegations of corruption, bribery and fraud were put forward. Some of the relevant findings of the Kim tribunal are summarised below:

---

[72] *Id.*, para. 615.

[73] Kulick and Wendler (2010), p. 78, as referred in Kulkarni (2013), p. 17.

[74] Vladislav Kim and others v. the Republic of Uzbekistan, ICSID Case No. ARB/13/6, Decision on Jurisdiction, 8 March 2017, paras. 554–591.

[75] *Id.*, para. 593.

i. The Application of the Legality Requirement

Under the tribunal's analysis it is implied that the legality requirement is applicable notwithstanding the fact whether it is incorporated in the text of the treaty. However, in the event when the legality requirement is present in the text of the applicable treaty in a certain form and/or context, the tribunal does not need to address the implicit legality requirement. The later finding of the tribunal was reasoned with the fact that the explicit requirement in the text of the agreement is a special rule, which should override a more general (implicit) rule under the principle *lex specialis derogate lex generalis*.

ii. The Scope of the Legality Requirement

The arbitral tribunal conducted its own interpretation of the legality requirement enshrined in Article 12 of the Kazakhstan-Uzbekistan BIT using the interpretation rules of the Vienna Convention on the Law of Treaties. Other than the conclusion that the legality requirement applies only to the period of the making of the investment, the tribunal's finding was that for one to breach of the legality requirement a certain algorithm of steps has to be undertaken. The Kim tribunal's algorithm is three-folded and consists of the following stages:

1. First, the tribunal must assess the significance of the allegedly violated obligation.[76]
2. Second, the tribunal must assess the degree of negative effect of the investor's conduct.[77]
3. Third, the tribunal must evaluate whether the combination of the investor's conduct and the law involved results in a compromise of a significant interest of the host State to such an extent that the harshness of the sanction of placing the investment outside of the protections of the BIT is a proportionate consequence for the violation.[78]

Each of the above items has a non-exhaustive list of other deliverables that the tribunal found necessary to undertake. As a result of the analysis under each item (and sub-item) of the algorithm the tribunal made its own finding on the legality contention.

As seen from the approach of the Kim tribunal, the scope of the legality requirement and its fulfilment or non-compliance is heavily dependent on the internal factors of the host State, in particular on the degree at which the host State itself treats the alleged misconduct under its own legislation and procedures. The fact that the Kim tribunal decided to assess the alleged corrupt practices strictly under the

---

[76] *Id.*, para. 406.

[77] *Id.*, para. 407.

[78] *Id.*, para. 408.

[79] Kreindler (2002), p. 253. *See also*, Hwang, M. S.C. and Lim, K., Corruption in Arbitration—Law and Reality, available at https://www.arbitration-icca.org/media/4/97929640279647/media013261720320840corruption_in_arbitration_paper_draft_248.pdf.

laws of Uzbekistan, without references to international law or international public policy might be criticised by the international legal community, in particular by scholars who previously expressed the views that tribunals must also take into account public policy so as to ensure the enforceability of awards.[79]

Additionally to the above, there is also a risk that the duty of the arbitrators to the "international business community at large"[80] can be compromised by a rather formalistic approach to acts that are clearly illicit but *de jure* lawful.

iii. The Effects of Fraud

The tribunal's general opinion was that a proven act of fraud would deprive the investment of the treaty protection. The definition and the scope of fraud were mostly determined by the norms of the host State's legislation.

iv. The Effects of Corruption

The idea that a proven act of corruption at the making of the investment could deprive the investment of treaty protection was accepted by the tribunal. Moreover, the tribunal also opined that allegations of corruption after the establishment of the investment are to be reviewed at the merits stage. In defining corruption and its required elements the tribunal sought guidance from the norms of the host State's laws and (as a second step) from international conventions.

v. The Standard of Proof

As to the questions of the applicable standard of proof, while the arbitral tribunal did not find it necessary to decide on this question, its opinion appears to be consistent with the opinions of the tribunals in the Metal-Tech v. Uzbekistan and World Duty Free v. Kenya cases. In other words, the tribunal did not object and accepted that a lowered standard of proof (i.e. reasonable certainty) could potentially be applied for allegations of corruption. At the same time, the arbitral tribunal opined that it was also keen on receiving elaborations of the parties on the applicable standard of proof in such situations under the laws of the host State.

vi. Red flags

In contrast to other matters such as the standard of proof and effects of corruption/fraud in investment arbitration, the tribunal's position in this case was not entirely clear. The Kim tribunal was of the opinion that *red flags* could not be regarded as direct evidence and could only be treated as evidence of circumstantial nature. As to the question whether a number of *red flags* could serve as an exclusive basis for the finding of corruption, the arbitral tribunal did not provide a determinative answer.[81]

---

[79] Kreindler (2002), p. 253. *See also*, Hwang, M. S.C. and Lim, K., Corruption in Arbitration— Law and Reality, available at https://www.arbitration-icca.org/media/4/97929640279647/media013261720320840corruption_in_arbitration_paper_draft_248.pdf.

[80] Beale and Esposito (2009), p. 361.

[81] The arbitral tribunal stated: "There is not a universal answer", Vladislav Kim and others v. the Republic of Uzbekistan, ICSID Case No. ARB/13/6, Decision on Jurisdiction, 8 March 2017, para. 548.

vii. Appreciation of Circumstances

An interesting and a very important feature of the Kim tribunal's analysis is that it paid very close attention to the political and business environment of the relevant region. The arbitral tribunal evaluated the context in which the investment was made and accepted that in this particular region it might be reasonable for private businesses to be less transparent in their commercial transactions. It is recalled that a similar reasoning was suggested by the claimants in the World Duty Free[82] and Metal-Tech cases, where the arbitral tribunals had not accepted such lines of argumentation. Certainly, there is a very thin line, which must be observed when deciding on certain untraditional ways of conducting business in different parts of the world.

In general terms, while being one of the latest decisions involving the allegations of fraud and corruption, the Kim et al. v. Uzbekistan case once again displays that there is no consensus and uniformed approach in ISDS when it comes to the way the allegations of illicit conduct are being treated. It reinforces the view expressed by *Tweeddale* and *Tweeddale,* stating that there is no internationally agreed opinion on the arbitrable and non-arbitrable matters, as "each country has its own perspectives on legality and illegality".[83]

7.5 Karkey v. Pakistan

Similarly to the case that was discussed previously, in this case the tribunal did not find the claimant's investment to be tainted by corruption. Nevertheless, this arbitral tribunal made a series of important findings on the way the allegations of corruption were to be treated and assessed. Being one of the recent arbitration disputes, the Karkey v. Pakistan tribunal had a chance to analyse the findings of other tribunals and incorporate some of them in its award.

7.5.1 Factual and Procedural Background

The claimant is Karkey Karadeniz Elektrik Uretim A.S. ("**Karkey**"), a power generation company established under the laws of Turkey.[84] The respondent is the Islamic Republic of Pakistan ("**Pakistan**"). The dispute relates to power generation

[82] In the World Duty Free case, the Claimant argued that the alleged bribery was in fact part of the local custom.

[83] Malik and Kamat (2018), p. 5 with reference to Tweeddale and Tweeddale (2007), para. 4.23.

[84] *Id.*, para. 2.

equipment.[85] ICSID received the claimant's request for arbitration on 16 January 2013.

One of the lines of the respondent's defence was an argument that Karkey's investment into power generation business in Pakistan was tainted by fraud. According to the respondent, Karkey's investment in Pakistan existed only as a result of its participation in a public tender. In other words, under Pakistan's case, Karkey could only become an investor if its bid in the public tender was responsive to the tender documentation. It stated that any fraud committed during this tender process, which induced the authorities to issue Karkey with its letter of award, would therefore preclude the tribunal's jurisdiction because Karkey's investment would not be established "in conformity with" Pakistani law.[86] The respondent's fraud case was centred upon alleged intentional misrepresentation of facts made during the tender process. Pakistan argued that such an act would constitute fraud under both national and international law.[87] As has been previously discussed, such a position could indeed lead to the denial of jurisdiction over the claims relating to such an "investment".[88]

Moreover, Pakistan also argued that Karkey's investment was procured through corruption. Pakistan's corruption allegations were based on the fact that prior to winning the public tender, Karkey engaged a consultant, who did not possess any expertise, and made several unreasonable payments to him. Under the respondent's case, the consultant was related to the wife of Pakistan's Head of Government, although not closely, and that his engagement and payment of more than USD 100,000 could not have been justified. It was also alleged that a series of other payments for the total sum exceeding USD 300,000 were made to an undisclosed source just days before the investment was made.

The respondent also noted that in the framework of a separate lawsuit, the Supreme Court of Pakistan issued a judgment, in which the Court found that the national procurement laws were violated. The respondent requested the arbitral tribunal to take the Supreme Court's decision into account.

Remarkably, the claimant did not produce any documents or offer any witnesses to substantiate the legitimacy of the consultants' engagement. In relation to the above-mentioned Supreme Court's judgement, the claimant submitted that there was a settlement agreement concluded after the Supreme Court's judgement, which effectively revoked the findings of illegality of the public procurement process.

As to the procedural matters, Pakistan did not deny that the burden of proof in relation to its claims was with the party asserting it. However, given the secret nature

[85] Karkey Karadeniz Elektrik Uretim A.S. v. Islamic Republic of Pakistan, ICSID Case No. ARB/13/1, Award, 22 August 2017, para. 1.

[86] *Id.*, para. 297.

[87] *Id.*, para. 306.

[88] *See for instance,* Fernández-Armesto (2015); Lamm et al. (2014); Alekhin and Shmatenko (2018).

of corruption and fraud, Pakistan argued that it was practically impossible for it to obtain all the relevant evidence, which could be decisive for the examination of corruption allegations.[89] In support of its line of argumentation, Pakistan referred to tribunals and commentators who had previously supported the idea that a duty to rebut specific allegations of corruption should be borne by a party possessing relevant information. For instance, as was analysed by a commentator in an academic piece, "plausible evidence of corruption, offered by the party alleging illegality, should require an adequate evidentiary showing by the party denying the allegation."[90]

Following the above, it was argued that considering the difficulty of proving corruption, the arbitral tribunal could have accepted circumstantial or indirect evidence as proof for a finding of corruption.[91]

7.5.2 *Findings and Analysis of the Tribunal*

As was noted above, the Karkey v. Pakistan arbitration is one of the latest investor-state disputes, which involved the allegations of fraud and corruption. Notwithstanding the fact that other tribunals analysed certain questions in similar disputes, the Karkey tribunal had its own approach and determination of procedural and material issues that were put before it. Below is a collection of findings of the Karkey tribunal that are relevant for the topic of this book.

7.5.2.1 Burden of Proof

In respect of the burden of proof, the arbitral tribunal's primary conclusion was that a party that asserts a certain fact must prove it in accordance with the principle *onus probandi incumbit actori.* As has been observed by *Alekhin* and *Shmatenko*, this is the most common approach taken by arbitral tribunals, including in cases with allegations of corruption.[92] Consequently, the tribunal found that Pakistan was to bear the burden of proof with respect to its allegations of corruption and fraud.[93] However, the tribunal also took into account the arguments that were made by the respondent and found that "the burden of proof with respect to corruption and fraud

[89] Karkey Karadeniz Elektrik Uretim A.S. v. Islamic Republic of Pakistan, ICSID Case No. ARB/13/1, Award, 22 August 2017, para. 309.

[90] Partasides (2010), para. 66.

[91] Karkey Karadeniz Elektrik Uretim A.S. v. Islamic Republic of Pakistan, ICSID Case No. ARB/13/1, Award, 22 August 2017, para. 309.

[92] Alekhin and Shmatenko (2018), pp. 157–158.

[93] Karkey Karadeniz Elektrik Uretim A.S. v. Islamic Republic of Pakistan, ICSID Case No. ARB/13/1, Award, 22 August 2017, para. 497.

[could shift] to Karkey should the Tribunal be satisfied that there is unequivocal (or unambiguous) prima facie evidence in this regard."[94]

7.5.2.2 Standard of Proof

The Karkey tribunal opined that many international tribunals required "clear and convincing evidence" for allegations of corruption.[95] The increasing application of a stricter standard of proof for allegations of illegality has also been observed by some authors.[96] On this basis, the arbitral tribunal found that the applicable standard of proof in this case required "clear and convincing evidence", in particular due to the fact that the allegation of corruption "involves officials at the highest level of the Pakistani Government at the time".[97]

Although the Karkey tribunal disregarded the arguments that were put forward by the respondent for a lowered standard of proof (i.e. "balance of probabilities"), the arbitral tribunal nevertheless stated that its conclusion would have remained the same regardless of the applicable standard of proof.[98]

7.5.2.3 Findings on Fraud

In relation to Pakistan's claim that Karkey's alleged misrepresentations in the public tender constituted fraud at the making of the investment, the arbitral tribunal found that Pakistan had failed to evidence the occurrence of fraud or misrepresentations.[99]

---

[94] *Id.* The possibility of shifting the burden of proof has been discussed in scholarly writings with some level of support, *see for instance,* Schreuer et al. (2009), p. 669; *See also,* Fathallah (2010), p. 73; Schlaepfer (2015), pp. 127–133.

[95] The tribunal referenced the following: EDF Services Limited v. Romania, ICSID Case No ARB/05/13, Award, 8 October 2009, para. 221 (noting that the "seriousness of the accusation of corruption … demands clear and convincing evidence" and that "[t]here is general consensus among international tribunals and commentators regarding the need for a high standard of proof of corruption"); Oostergetel v. Slovak Republic, UNCITRAL, Final Award, 23 April 2012, ¶ 303 ("Mere insinuations cannot meet the burden of proof [for allegations of corruption]"); Liman Caspian Oil BV and NCL Dutch Investment BV v. Republic of Kazakhstan, ICSID Case No ARB/07/14, Award, 22 June 2010, paras. 422, 424 ("The Tribunal emphasizes that corruption is a serious allegation, especially in the context of the judiciary. The Tribunal notes that both Parties agree that the standard of proof in this respect is a high one. . .It is not sufficient to present evidence which could possibly indicate that there might have been or even probably was corruption. Rather, Claimants have to prove corruption.")

[96] *See for instance,* Losco (2014), pp. 37–52, available at https://scholarship.law.duke.edu/cgi/viewcontent.cgi?referer=&httpsredir=1&article=1004&context=dlj_online; Summerfield (2009).

[97] Karkey Karadeniz Elektrik Uretim A.S. v. Islamic Republic of Pakistan, ICSID Case No. ARB/13/1, Award, 22 August 2017, para. 492.

[98] *Id.*, para. 493.

[99] *Id.*, para. 620.

The facts, which had been presented by Pakistan as fraud and misrepresentations, were understood by the tribunal as matters of contractual commitments, which could potentially cause "contractual penalties".[100]

7.5.2.4 Findings on Corruption

In relation to the allegations of corruption in the context of the consultancy agreement and questionable payments, the tribunal did not find enough evidence to make the finding of corruption. The arbitral tribunal was not satisfied with the *red flags* that Pakistan raised, stating that *red flags* constituted mere questions and such questions were not sufficient to shift the burden of proof to the claimant.

In particular, the Karkey tribunal stated that it was not convincing that the government official (i.e. a minister) could have been corrupted by an amount of AED 350,000 (less than USD 100,000) in relation to a project of a value of several hundreds of millions of US dollars.[101] The previous finding was made notwithstanding Pakistan's submission that the average standard of living in Pakistan did not exceed USD 1000.

As was noted before, the arbitral tribunal had to examine the judgment of the Supreme Court of Pakistan, which allegedly made the findings that the national laws were violated during the procurement process, by means of which Karkey made its investment in Pakistan. The tribunal decided that its assessment of the Supreme Court's judgment should be undertaken in light of international law and that it was not bound by this (or any other national court) judgment. Notably, such an approach by international tribunals has been explicitly confirmed by the International Court of Justice in the *Diallo case*.[102]

After assessing the Supreme Court's judgment, as well as the Supreme Court's conduct,[103] the arbitral tribunal held that corruption was neither proven by standalone evidence, nor by the Supreme Court's judgment. It was for these reasons that the tribunal did not consider itself to be bound, as an international tribunal, by the findings of Pakistan's Supreme Court.[104] However, the arbitral tribunal stated that it was not going to dismiss the judgment in general and would, nevertheless, consider

---

[100] *Id.*, para. 616.

[101] *Id.*, para. 521.

[102] *Id.*, para. 552. The arbitral tribunal referenced the following quote of the ICJ in the Diallo case: "Exceptionally, where a State puts forward a manifestly incorrect interpretation of its domestic law, particularly for the purpose of gaining an advantage in a pending case, it is for the Court to adopt what it finds to be the proper interpretation"—Case concerning Ahmadou Sadio Diallo (Republic of Guinea v. Democratic Republic of the Congo), Judgment, 30 November 2010, ICJ Reports 2010, p. 639, para. 70.

[103] *Id.*, para. 560: "Last but not least, the Tribunal notes that the Supreme Court played an active part in several of the acts attributable to Pakistan and that are presented by Karkey as a general pattern of breaches of the BIT."

[104] *Id.*

the judgment as a fact. In this regard, the conduct of the Karkey tribunal gives at least some comfort to scholars who opined that arbitral tribunals are to carefully assess the outcome of internal investigations and court decision on the questions of corruption.[105]

Additionally to the above, one of the arguments raised by the claimant, i.e. *estoppel,* deserves separate attention. Karkey asserted that the State was to be estopped from its illegality claims due to the fact that it had known or should have been aware of the alleged circumstances before the arbitration proceedings and, nevertheless, did not react to them. In other words, Karkey put forward the position that is advocated by some scholars in legal literature stating that States whose officials solicited and/or received bribes cannot use corruption as defence against its own wrongdoings.[106]

Interestingly, the respondent raised a rather theoretical point to rebut the *estoppel* argument by questioning whether a person who committed fraud or corruption should be allowed to raise *estoppel* at all. Pakistan submitted as follows:

> This argument fails for a number of reasons, inter alia, because Pakistan cannot be estopped from raising objections to the Tribunal's jurisdiction on the basis of fraud and corruption because, as a matter of logic, Karkey cannot have relied on a statement or course of conduct by Pakistan in good faith (as required by Pope & Talbot) if it is guilty of fraud or corruption.[107]

Although not directly referring to the doctrine of "clean hands", Pakistan's general position to the above was that a party who committed an illegal act cannot claim *estoppel* because it cannot have reasonably relied on the other party's responsive conduct in good faith.

Unfortunately, the arbitral tribunal decided not to make any substantial finding on the claimant's *estoppel* argument, which might be due to the fact that the illegality claims were not made out in the first place.

7.5.3 Analysis of the Award

The Karkey v. Pakistan case provides several important insights into the arbitral tribunal's analysis and conclusions on certain matters of both procedural and substantive nature that are enlisted below.

i. Burden of Proof

The Karkey tribunal found that in a situation of a plausible *prima facie* case presented by the asserting party, the burden of proof could shift to the other party.

---

[105] Losco (2014), pp. 37–52, available at https://scholarship.law.duke.edu/cgi/viewcontent.cgi?referer=&httpsredir=1&article=1004&context=dlj_online, p. 50.

[106] *See*, Kulick and Wendler (2010), p. 98; Llamzon (2008).

[107] Karkey Karadeniz Elektrik Uretim A.S. v. Islamic Republic of Pakistan, ICSID Case No. ARB/13/1, Award, 22 August 2017, para. 337.

It is especially relevant and important because such an idea had been argued by many other parties who attempted to prove illicit misconduct on the part of their opponents.

As record indicates, the shifting of the burden of proof has not been widely accepted in practice so far. The concept could generally be a practical solution for situations where the opposing party is reluctant to provide negative evidence and when no direct evidence of illegality is available. This concept could serve as a balancing tool between lowered and heightened standards of proof (e.g. "balance of probabilities" v. "clear and convincing evidence") by some arbitral tribunals.

ii. Standard of Proof

Unlike the decisions that were made lately by arbitral tribunals in other investor-state disputes, the Karkey tribunal concluded that due to the fact that corruption (and fraud) is a serious allegation, which bears serious consequences, a heightened standard of proof (i.e. "clear and convincing evidence") was applicable. As discussed before, this position is not without support in the academic world.[108] At the same time, as was noted above, the heightened standard of proof was balanced with the finding that the burden of proof could, in principle, be shifted to the responding party if the asserting party presents a plausible *prima facie* case.

iii. Relevance of Domestic Court Decisions

In this case, the tribunal found that, although domestic court decisions may be used by international tribunals, they are not bound by them under international law. In particular, the Karkey tribunal concluded that a number of events may preclude an international tribunal from taking a judgment of a national court into account, including the denial of justice and "where a State puts forward a manifestly incorrect interpretation of its domestic law."[109]

iv. Fraud and Misrepresentations in Contractual Relationships

The allegations of misrepresentations during a public tender process had been reviewed under a certain angle that was different from what the respondent tried to pursue. The tribunal's decision in this regard implicitly suggests that not every misrepresentation, even if made knowingly, could lead to findings of fraud for the purposes of international arbitration. Additionally, as was explicitly noted before, even if intentional misrepresentations did take place in this case, they could have been remedied by contractual means, for instance, by way of a contractual penalty.

The conclusion that is to be made in this regard is that non-compliance with procurement rules or laws does not automatically lead to fraud or corruption.

v. The Relevance of the Sum of the Payment

One of the findings of the Karkey tribunal, which was made very briefly in a couple of sentences and that is different from one other case that is analysed in detail in this

---

[108] Kulkarni (2013), p. 26 with reference to Summerfield (2009), p. 123.

[109] Karkey Karadeniz Elektrik Uretim A.S. v. Islamic Republic of Pakistan, ICSID Case No. ARB/13/1, Award, 22 August 2017, para. 551.

monograph,[110] is the assessment and the conclusion on the size of the alleged bribe. The Karkey tribunal found that the sum of USD 100,000 was not a significant amount considering the value of the whole investment project and the Minister's high ranking position with the government. In other words, it appears as if the tribunal assumed that this amount would have likely been insufficient to bribe a high ranking governmental official. It is possible that the tribunal treated the payment as if it was of minor gravity.[111]

While reserving from making statements whether corruption indeed took place, it appears that the Karkey tribunal did not attempt to assess the facts in light of the circumstances that were typical for the socio-economic environment of the relevant region.

References

Alekhin S, Shmatenko L (2018) Corruption in investor-state arbitration – it takes two to tango. In: Asoskov et al (eds) New horizons of international arbitration, Issue 4, Collection of Articles

Beale KD, Esposito P (2009) Emergent international attitudes towards bribery, corruption and money laundering. Arbitration 360 75:361

Crivellaro A (2006) Arbitration case law on bribery: issues of arbitrability, contract validity, merits and evidence. Dossiers of the ICC Institute of World Business Law, p 109

Fathallah R (2010) Corruption in international commercial and investment arbitration: recent trends and prospects for Arab countries. Int J Arab Arbitr 2(3):73

Fernández-Armesto J (2015) The effects of a positive finding of corruption. In: Baizeau D, Kreindler RH (eds) Addressing issues of corruption in commercial and investment arbitration. Dossiers of the ICC Institute of World Business Law, vol 13, ICC Publication No. 768E

Haugeneder F (2009) Corruption in investor-state arbitration. J World Invest Trade 10(3):323–339

Hunter JM (1992) Modern trends in the presentation of evidence in international commercial arbitration. Am Rev Int Arbitr 3:204–211

Kreindler R (2002) Aspects of illegality in the formation and performance of contracts. In: 11th International Council for Commercial Arbitration Congress, p 253

Kulick A, Wendler C (2010) A corrupt way to handle corruption? Thoughts on the recent ICISD case law on corruption. In: Legal Issues of Economic Integration. Kluwer Law International, vol 37(1)

Kulkarni SA (2013) Enforcing anti-corruption measures through international investment arbitration. Transnatl Dispute Manag 3, available at www.transnational-dispute-management.com/article.asp?key=1957

Lamm CB, Pham HT, Moloo R (2010) Fraud and corruption in international arbitration. In: Fernandez-Ballesteros, Arias (eds) Liber Amicorum Bernardo Cremades. Kluwer, pp 699–731

Lamm CB, Greenwald BK, Young KM (2014) From the world duty free to metal-tech: a review of international investment treaty arbitration cases involving allegations of corruption. ICSID Rev

Llamzon A (2008) The control of corruption through international investment arbitration: potential and limitations. In: Proceedings of the American Society of International Law on 9–12 April, 2008, vol 102

[110] *See*, the Metal-Tech v. Uzbekistan case.

[111] On the requirement of severity of illegal conduct, *see*, Summerfield (2009); Kulick and Wendler (2010), p. 98; Kulkarni (2013), p. 25.

Losco MA (2014) Charting a new course: Metal-Tech v. Uzbekistan and the treatment of corruption in investment arbitration. Duke Law J Online 64:37–52

Low L (2019) Dealing with allegations of corruption in international arbitration. Am J Int Law Unbound 113:341

Malik D, Kamat G (2018) Corruption in international commercial arbitration: arbitrability, admissibility & adjudication. In: The Arbitration Brief, available at https://paperity.org/p/185990736/corruption-in-international-commercial-arbitration-arbitrability-admissibility, p 16

Menaker AJ, Greenwald BK (2015) Proving corruption in international arbitration. In: Baizeau D, Kreindler RH (eds) Addressing issues of corruption in commercial and investment arbitration. Dossiers of the ICC Institute of World Business Law, vol 13, ICC Publication No. 768E, pp 77–102

Partasides C (2010) Proving corruption in international arbitration: a balanced standard for the real world. ICSID Rev 25(1)

Rosell J, Prager H (1999) Illicit commissions and international arbitration: the question of proof. J Int Arbitr 15(4):329–348

Sayed A (2004) Corruption in international trade and commercial arbitration. Kluwer Law International, pp 89–92

Schlaepfer AV (2015) The burden of proof in international arbitration. In: van den Berg AJ (ed) Legitimacy: myths, realities, challenges, in ICCA Congress Series No. 18, pp 127–133

Schreuer C, Malintoppi L, Reinisch A, Sinclair A (2009) The ICSID Convention: a commentary. Cambridge University Press

Summerfield JN (2009) The corruption defense in investment disputes: a discussion of the imbalance between international discourse and arbitral decisions. Transnatl Dispute Manag 6(1)

Tweeddale A, Tweeddale K (2007) Arbitration of commercial disputes: international and English law and practice. Oxford University Press

Waibel M (2014) Investment arbitration: jurisdiction and admissibility. In: Legal Studies Research Paper Series, Paper No 9/2014. University of Cambridge, p 34

Chapter 8
Learned Lessons

The beauty of case law is that it develops even in a situation of a legal vacuum, when no written or customary norms have been established and dispute settlement bodies have to create certain unwritten rules in delivering justice over matters that have no textbook solutions. This is in particular important for investment treaty arbitration, as its "baby boom" of cases took place within the last couple of decades.[1]

The analysis of cases relating to the present topic as conducted in Part II and to some extent in Part I, as well as other cases that have been studied, can indicate the vector of development of international investment law in addressing fraud and corruption. The case law analysis identifies established practices accepted by arbitral tribunals and displays possible issues in certain areas.

This chapter provides an overview of the current trends that have been developed through a growing number of ISDS cases.

8.1 Ability of Investment Tribunals to Address the Issues of Corruption and Fraud

Despite its party autonomy setting that was shaped to accommodate matters of rather civil nature, it is evident that international investment arbitration is generally capable of dealing with the allegations of illicit misconduct. In line with the analysed cases, many scholars seem to agree on this point.[2]

---

[1] Alexandrov (2005), pp. 19–59.

[2] *See for instance,* Gaillard (2019), p. 3; *see also*, Llamzon (2014), paras. 9.04–9.07; Raouf (2009), pp. 116–136; Cremades and Cairns (2003), pp. 78–79; Kreindler (2002), pp. 252–253; Eriksson (1993); Wetter (1994).

A. Tussupov, *Corruption and Fraud in Investment Arbitration*, EYIEL Monographs - Studies in European and International Economic Law 22,
https://doi.org/10.1007/978-3-030-90606-1_8

The general practice indicates that in cases where arbitral tribunals are convinced that materially illicit acts did take place, they do not shy away from penalizing the offender. As a general rule, in such cases, investments were deemed to be illegal and therefore found to be outside of the scope of international investment treaty protection. Whereas, the result may usually seem to be the same in such scenarios, arbitral tribunals have often differed in their approach from the procedural perspective. The general examination of the "illegality" allegations usually goes through the same routine.

An arbitral tribunal is often invited to assess certain allegations of illegality by one of the parties. Although, as has been seen in previous chapters,[3] there are examples where tribunals inquired on issues of illegality at their own initiative, thereby inviting parties to make submissions and produce evidence relating to those issues. However, the latter does not seem to be a mainstream approach—at least for the time being.

The next usual step for an arbitral tribunal to make is a preliminary (or, in other words, *prima facie*) determination of possible legal implications of the indicators or allegations of illegality for the purposes of investment arbitration. To put this in simple terms—the arbitral tribunal usually decides whether the illicit conduct, if proven, could matter for the case at hand. For this, the arbitral tribunal does not need to make a final determination on the merits, but rather undertake a summary assessment, so as to investigate whether to entertain such arguments or not.

Clearly, if allegations are manifestly not relevant for the purposes of an investment dispute, the tribunal does not have to entertain and/or to take into account such issues when considering the administration of the arbitration process. It is to be noted that arbitral tribunals might want to exercise a heightened level of care when brushing away certain arguments, so as not to infringe the parties' right to be heard. This is indeed a very delicate topic, in particular in investment arbitration, where one of the parties is a sovereign.

If the allegations do appear to be relevant for an arbitral tribunal, it could then proceed to the examination of such matters on their merits. It is always up to a tribunal how to organize its decision-making process over the submitted claims—however, the case law indicates that it is not foreign for tribunals to order a separate round of submissions and/or oral hearings dedicated to corruption and fraud grounds only.[4] The reason for this is that positive findings on the basis of corruption and fraud might be outcome determinative for the whole arbitration, which is why tribunals find it reasonable to first consider them before moving to the merits of investment claims (unless corruption and fraud are used as a "sword" by a claimant[5]).

As has been seen before, the central issue for the examination of allegations of illegality is the question of evidence, on which an arbitral tribunal is expected to make a decision, even though in some cases it has been observed that tribunals did

---

[3] *See for instance,* Metal-Tech v. Uzbekistan in Sect. 6.2 of Part II.

[4] *Id.*

[5] *See for instance,* EDF v. Romania in Sect. 7.2 of Part II.

not live up to that expectation and did not provide any answer in that regard. The evidentiary questions would not only include the admissibility and credibility of evidence issues, but also the applicable standards and burden of proof.

Finally, the arbitral tribunal would be expected to assess the legal implications of a possibly positive finding of corruption or fraud. Although, this step is being displayed as one of the last items of the algorithm, it is indeed quite possible (and practical) that a tribunal makes the determination of legal consequences in the very beginning. This would include matters relating to the scope and application of the legality requirement under a relevant investment treaty. If, at the very outset of arbitration, a tribunal decides that the legality requirement does not apply for any reason, then it may be less motivated to dive into the investigation of the illegality matters.

The general algorithm, as has been seen from the analysis of case law in the chapters above, does not always include the question of determination of applicable law. At the same time, it might not be best for parties and tribunals to completely disregard this matter, as in some cases the applicable law considerations played a major role when examining the legal relevance of allegations or when analysing the evidence that was submitted by parties in support of their respective cases.[6]

For the avoidance of doubt, it is noted that the discussed algorithm is not universal for all arbitral tribunals in ISDS cases. This is simply because no universal approach appears to exist at this stage.

8.2 Use of Fraud and Corruption Arguments as a "Shield"

The arguments of illegality are much more often invoked by host States as a "shield" from all possible liability related arguments that are put forward by foreign investors.[7] Despite the semi-philosophical considerations of the necessity to protect the rule of law and the system of international protection of foreign investments from possible abuse, the popularity of the use of illegality arguments as a "shield" by States can also be quite pragmatic—such a "shield" can defeat all "swords". In other words, if proven, corruption and fraud can make all investment claims go away, even if they indeed have merit.

As seen from scholar opinions, as well as from the chronology of the analysed cases in the chapters above, it remains true that the number of cases where States allege corruption and fraud has become more frequent than before.[8]

---

[6] *See for instance*, Kim et al. v. Uzbekistan in Sect. 7.4 of Part II.

[7] Alekhin and Shmatenko (2018), pp. 164–168. *See also*, Menaker and Greenwald (2015), pp. 77–102; Low (2019), p. 341.

[8] *See*, Gaillard (2019), p. 2.

Finally, the illegality arguments can also be used by different actors for a different purpose. Although quite rare, but still evident, foreign investors can also allege solicitation of bribes as part of their treaty violation case.[9] Thus, solicitation of bribery can be regarded as harassment or even discrimination, if such solicitation is exercised specifically because of the foreign origin of the investor.

To put this all into the perspective of international investment law, such acts could be regarded as a breach of fair and equitable treatment. Because of the possible broad application of this standard, some commentators have created categories that can be used when assessing State conduct under this standard. These are the following:

a. Legality;
b. Administrative Due Process and Denial of Justice;
c. Protection of Legitimate Expectations;
d. Stability, Predictability, Consistency;
e. Non-Discrimination;
f. Transparency;
g. Proportionality and Reasonableness.[10]

Depending on the circumstances, solicitation of bribery by States may well fall under almost any of the above categories.

Furthermore, skilled advocates might argue that by obligating a foreign investor to pay a bribe, a host State violates the full protection and security obligation (if, of course, present under the relevant investment treaty). Although some may say that the traditional interpretation of the full protection and security standard is limited to protecting the investment against physical damage caused by organs of the State or third parties,[11] there are views that the standard could be interpreted much wider and could also include a duty to provide legal protection too.[12] Therefore, if a State does not or cannot provide effective legal protection against corruption, an argument that it does not respect the full protection and security standard under the relevant investment treaty may be expected.

Finally, and to reflect on all the above, according to one other scholar research, the average (and selective) ratio between the instances where a State is alleging

[9] An example of a situation where a foreign investor (unsuccessfully) alleged corruption on the part of the State is Rumeli Telekom A.S. and Telsim Mobil Telekomunikasyon Hizmetleri A.S. v. Republic of Kazakhstan, ICSID Case No. ARB/05/16, Award, 29 July 2008. *See also,* EDF Services Limited v. Romania discussed previously.

[10] Jacob and Schill (2015), pp. 719–743.

[11] *See for instance,* Suez, Sociedad General de Aguas de Barcelona, S.A.and Vivendi Universal, S.A. v. Argentine Republic, ICSID Case No. ARB/03/19, Decision on Liability, 30 July 2010, para. 173: "In this respect, this Tribunal is of the view that the stability of the business environment and legal security are more characteristic of the standard of fair and equitable treatment, while the full protection and security standard primarily seeks to protect investment from physical harm."

[12] *See for instance,* Azurix Corp. v. The Argentine Republic, ICSID Case No. ARB/01/12, Award, 14 July 2006, para. 406 et seq; Biwater Gauff (Tanzania) Ltd. v. United Republic of Tanzania, ICSID Case No. ARB/05/22, Award, 24 July 2008, para. 724 et seq.

corruption and a foreign investor alleging solicitation of bribes is 3 to 1.[13] This ratio evidences the existence of a growing trend for the use of illegality arguments by States as a "complete defence"[14] against practically everything, i.e., jurisdiction, admissibility, liability and quantum, rather than as an investment protection claim.

8.3 Evidence & *Red Flags*

As can be observed from the analysis of case law provided in this Part above, the questions of evidence and its relevance are of importance in disputes where the allegations of corruption and fraud are being made. In such situations two possible scenarios have been witnessed:

- when the evidence of illicit misconduct is being presented by a party that was involved in illicit conduct itself (i.e. by way of a witness statement, direct or cross examination during a hearing or production of documents);[15]
- when an arbitral tribunal has been provided with circumstantial evidence and/or an aggregate of *red flags* only.[16]

The analysis of case law indicates that when arbitral tribunals are presented with direct evidence of illicit misconduct by a party, there is usually no further discussion on its admissibility and credibility. In that sense, obtaining direct evidence of corruption or fraud can be crucial for parties and the tribunal's decision making. Although, production of direct or even self-inflicting evidence has proven to be extremely rare and difficult in practice for objective reasons.[17]

The situation is, however, the opposite when an arbitral tribunal has only been provided with circumstantial evidence or a number of *red flags* to rely on. Parties are usually not in agreement on the admissibility, credibility and relevance of these kinds of evidence. However, what matters even more—an arbitral tribunal would have to carefully decide what to do with such evidence and how to assess it—and there appears to be no universal answer to these questions among various investment tribunals.

As has been witnessed—when presented with indirect evidence and *red flags*, some arbitral tribunals required that this evidence was supported by *direct* evidence.[18] Looking back at Sect. 7.2 of Part II, it is to be recalled that the arbitral

[13] Llamzon (2014), para. 7.10.

[14] *Id.*, paras. 7.10–7.13.

[15] *See for example*, World Duty Free v. Kenya and Metal-Tech v. Uzbekistan discussed in Part II.

[16] *See for instance*, Spentex Netherlands B.V. v. Uzbekistan in Sect. 6.4 of Part II.

[17] *See for instance*, Mills (2003), p. 295; Alekhin and Shmatenko (2018), p. 164.

[18] "The Arbitral Tribunal cannot find it established, on the basis of available materials, that the Concession was illegally obtained and that, for this reason, it is not protected under the BIT. On the other hand, investigations and proceedings in Argentina are still going on.", TSA Spectrum de

tribunal in the EDF v. Romania case was presented with three pieces of evidence, which under the claimant's case, were to prove illegality of the respondent's conduct. In particular, the claimant submitted a witness statement, an email of an agent of the respondent and a secret audio tape. As was displayed, none of the named pieces of evidence, although being clear *red flags*, were admitted by the arbitral tribunal due the fact that they were not supported by direct evidence.

The notion of *red flags* deserves special attention. Although being a relatively common notion in other areas of law, such as anti-trust legislation,[19] its place in international investment law and arbitration is still quite novel. This explains absence of an uniformed approach and application of *red flags* by investment tribunals, irrespective of the fact that it has been subjected to discussion by parties and arbitral tribunals in the analysed ISDS cases.[20]

At the same time, and despite different approaches vis-à-vis evidentiary value of *red flags,* it shall be recognized that *red flags* as means of proving certain facts (especially fraud and corruption) do have a place in international arbitration.[21] Remarkably, in two analysed ISDS cases where *red flags* were used as basis for factual examination, the arbitral tribunals did eventually make findings of corruption, as well as took up certain "disciplinary" measures against States for tolerating corruption.[22] This could (although arguably) serve as evidence of the effectiveness of *red flags* as means of proving illicit misconduct.

However, the "effectiveness" has not been appreciated by all tribunals in ISDS cases so far, in particular as seen in the Kim et al. v. Uzbekistan case. There, it was opined that *red flags* can provide only circumstantial evidence, which is of solely *supportive* nature, and that such *red flags* are useful for merely triggering attention to certain aspects of the case.[23] Even though the arbitral tribunal did not go strong on what appeared to be convincing indicators of corruption (i.e. payments to the daughter of the then-President of Uzbekistan) and without necessarily agreeing with the outcome in that case, the opinion expressed by the Kim tribunal with regards to the nature of *red flags* does sound reasonable. When walking in the shoes of a party who has to defend itself against the allegations of corruption and/or fraud, it would indeed feel unjust if that party was to be found guilty on mere indicators, as this is what *red flags* essentially are.

Argentina S.A. v. Argentine Republic, ICSID Case No. ARB/05/5, Award, 19 December 2008, para. 174–175. *See also,* EDF Services Limited v. Romania discussed in Part II.

[19] *See e.g.,* U.S. Department of Justice, Antitrust Division, Federal Trade Commission (2016), Antitrust Guidance for Human Resource Professionals, Antitrust Red Flags for Employment Practices, available at https://www.justice.gov/atr/file/903511/download.

[20] *See for instance,* Metal-Tech v. Uzbekistan and Spentex v. Uzbekistan discussed in Part II.

[21] Low (2019), p. 343.

[22] In Metal-Tech v. Uzbekistan, the State was penalized with the decision on the allocation of costs, whereas in Spentex v. Uzbekistan, the State was "incentivized" to donate USD 8 million to international anti-corruption programs.

[23] Vladislav Kim and others v. the Republic of Uzbekistan, ICSID Case No. ARB/13/6, Decision on Jurisdiction, 8 March 2017, paras. 548–549.

Furthermore, the analysis of case law displays that the notion of *red flags* has to be "formless", as they may differ from jurisdiction to jurisdiction, from industry to industry, or more particularly, from dispute to dispute. The bigger question here is whether *ref flags* are to be treated differently, and perhaps with more diligence, in investor-state disputes rather than in international commercial arbitration, due to the public nature of the ISDS mechanism. Given that (i) a sovereign is involved in the process, (ii) the tribunal is usually constituted under a public international law instrument (e.g. BITs or MITs), and (iii) the decision of the investment tribunal may affect the well-being of the whole nation—would it not be reasonable to accord (a more) special attention to *red flags* of corruption and fraud? This is the question that is reserved for Sect. 9.3 of Part III below, however what can be concluded already now is that consistency in approach in relation to the application of *red flags* would make exposing of corruption and fraud a lesser challenge in investment arbitration.

Finally, another important lesson learned when speaking of evidence and lack of consistency is that not every direct evidence can be treated as credible and this should be evaluated by the circumstances in which such evidence exists or existed.[24]

8.4 Burden & Standards of Proof: Different Approaches

Similarly to the evidentiary issues discussed above, the determination of the applicable burden and standard of proof has also proven to be of central importance and relevance in cases where an arbitral tribunal is to examine the allegations of corruption and fraud.

As seen from the analysed cases in this Part, the question of the burden of proof is often being disputed by parties. At the same time, the matters and arguments that parties raise in relation to the burden of proof catch only limited attention of arbitral tribunals and legal scholars, or so it seems.

The analysed case law indicates that there is a widely accepted practice as recognized by tribunals[25] and legal scholars[26] that the burden of proof lays with the party that is asserting a certain fact. At the same time it has been witnessed that some arbitral tribunals[27] and authors[28] accept the possibility of shifting the burden of

[24] *See for instance*, Siag v. Egypt case where the arbitral tribunal found that a document from a third party state's registry was not to be fully trusted due to reports that indicated its poor information management (discussed in Part II).

[25] *See for example*, EDF v. Romania, and Churchill & Planet v. Indonesia discussed previously.

[26] *See*, Hunter (1992), pp. 204–211; Haugeneder (2009), pp. 323–339; Lamm et al. (2010), pp. 699–731; Rosell and Prager (1999), pp. 329–348.

[27] *See for example*, Siag v. Egypt and Karkey v. Pakistan, discussed at Sects. 7.3 and 7.5 of Part II respectively.

[28] *See for instance*, Schreuer et al. (2009), p. 669; *See also*, Fathallah (2010), p. 73; Schlaepfer (2015), pp. 127–133.

proof to the responding party. The approach taken in the Karkey v. Pakistan case is similar to the approach that is exercised in common law jurisdictions, where a responding party is expected to provide negative evidence in a situation where an asserting party has presented a prima facie case.[29] Such an approach appears to be justifiable, especially in light of the fact that acts of corruption and fraud are usually well hidden and cannot be easily proven.

In contrast to the burden of proof question, the applicable standard of proof remains to be a debated and sometimes a heated topic in arbitration regardless of whether a case involves allegations of corruption or fraud. Unsurprisingly, the determination of the applicable standard of proof for allegations of fraud and corruption is an ever more sensitive topic for parties. This may be partly because the actors of illicit schemes do not tend to act openly and leave a paper-trail behind. "[L]ike most crimes and intentional misconduct, and perhaps more so, acts of corruption and collusion are specifically designed not to be able to be identified or detected."[30] As a result, achieving a certain level of proof of committed acts can be a difficult undertaking in international arbitration.

The chronological analysis of case law and legal doctrine in the present textbook indicates that there are two (generalised) ways arbitral tribunals approach the determination of the applicable standard of proof in disputes where the allegations of fraud and corruption have been made.

The first identified approach indicates that some arbitral tribunals tend to apply what has been defined as "**heightened standards of proof**", which would include "clear and convincing evidence" and "beyond reasonable doubt" standards. The term "heightened" is being used because the mentioned examples of such standards usually exist in litigation matters of other than civil nature. In other words, these standards are often used in criminal proceedings, whereas in civil proceedings, including in arbitration, parties are usually expected to prove their cases on standards that require a lesser level of proof.

The rationale for invoking a heightened standard of proof has been stated to be the serious legal consequences that the findings of corruption and fraud may trigger in international investment arbitration matters. For this reason, some tribunals were reluctant to make determinative conclusions on the allegations of fraud and corruption on the basis of evidence that was not "clear and convincing" or "beyond reasonable doubt".

The second analysed approach displays that other arbitral tribunals choose to refer to what has been termed as "**lowered standards of proof**", which would include "balance of probabilities" or "intime conviction" standards. Although the term "lowered" is being used to identify this group of evidentiary standards, in

[29] "[T]he burden of proof with respect to corruption and fraud [could shift] to Karkey should the Tribunal be satisfied that there is unequivocal (or unambiguous) prima facie evidence in this regard"—Karkey Karadeniz Elektrik Uretim A.S. v. Islamic Republic of Pakistan, ICSID Case No. ARB/13/1, Award, 22 August 2017, para. 497.

[30] Mills (2003) and Partasides (2010).

reality such standards are commonly used in international arbitration and domestic civil litigation. By that token, various tribunals and national courts have often found it sufficient to base its findings on civil matters on the basis of *lowered* standards of proof.

One of the reasons of the "clash" of the two approaches is the focal question that is being raised by arbitral tribunals and legal scholars—whether to apply traditional civil law standards of proof for allegations of criminal nature (i.e. corruption and fraud), or rather seek guidance from the criminal legal practice and seek "clear and convincing evidence" or proof that is "beyond reasonable doubt".

In the previous chapters it has been witnessed that in three out of ten cases arbitral tribunals decided that the applicable standard of proof for allegations of corruption and fraud must be "clear and convincing" evidence, i.e. a heightened standard of proof.[31] While three cases out of the total ten that have been analysed in the frames of this Part does not seem to be a big number, it is to be noted that only in eight discussed cases[32] arbitral tribunals actually assessed the question of an applicable standard of proof for allegations of corruption and fraud. In one of the eight cases, the arbitral tribunal did not even have to assess this question simply because the investor admitted the existence of illicit commissions on the voluntarily basis.[33] In the Sanum case, the arbitral tribunal practically chose and applied both standards. This effectively leaves us with a ratio of 3:3, or 50% × 50%. The ratio is certainly not representative for all cases in investment arbitration, as the general tendency of applying a heightened standard of proof is much more common than the application of a lowered one.[34] However, what may be representative is the fact that in all three cases where the standard of proof was heightened, arbitral tribunals did not uphold the allegations of corruption and fraud. They were deemed to be unproven.

As was observed above, in four out of eight analysed cases where arbitral tribunals had to decide on the applicable standard of proof for allegations of corruption and fraud, the choice was made for the lowered standards of proof (e.g. balance of probabilities, reasonable certainty and "connecting the dots"). Remarkably, in three out of these four cases, arbitral tribunals upheld the allegations of corruption. They were deemed to be proven. In the remaining one the arbitral tribunal did confirm the allegations on the factual basis but decided that they had no relevance from the legal point of view.[35]

---

[31] *See*, EDF v. Romania, Siag v. Egypt and Karkey v. Pakistan discussed in Part II.

[32] The other five cases are Metal-Tech v. Uzbekistan, Churchill and Planet Mining v. Indonesia, Spentex v. Uzbekistan, Kim et al. v. Uzbekistan and Sanum v. Laos, discussed throughout Part II.

[33] *See*, Metal-Tech v. Uzbekistan in Sect. 6.2 of Part II.

[34] *See*, Menaker and Greenwald (2015); Hwang, M. S.C. and Lim, K., Corruption in Arbitration — Law and Reality, available at https://www.arbitration-icca.org/media/4/97929640279647/media013261720320840corruption_in_arbitration_paper_draft_248.pdf, p. 15 with references to Crivellaro (2003), pp. 115–117; Volkov (2015), p. 4.

[35] Kim et al. v. Uzbekistan discussed in Sect. 7.4 of Part II. By way of reminder, the arbitral tribunal found that the alleged (and confirmed) facts were not to be regarded as "bribery" under Uzbek law,

Finally, the Sanum tribunal decided to enjoy the best of the two worlds and remain open-minded—it applied both standards: the *lowered* together with the *heightened*. However, it must be noted that the Sanum arbitral tribunal was only able to make findings on the balance of probabilities standard, while the "clear and convincing evidence" standard has not been satisfied by the alleging party.

As a result of this "learned lesson", one can observe that where arbitrators treat the illegality allegations with more flexibility, the arguments of corruption and fraud do, in fact, become outcome determinative.

8.5 Addressing States' Responsibility for Illicit Acts

In several landmark cases analysed in this Part, arbitral tribunals looked both ways when examining the allegations of illicit misconduct, especially in cases that involved allegations of corruption. As was stated before, "it takes two to tango" in corruption scenarios,[36] therefore in some cases it could be reasonable to argue that both parties should meet the legal consequences of such acts. Although the issue of States' responsibility for corrupt practices in international investment arbitration did not attract wide attention, there were nevertheless concerns and voices raised in this regard in the legal literature before.[37]

In the World Duty Free case discussed in Sect. 6.1 of this Part, the arbitral tribunal had ultimately found the investor being at fault by pointing out that it had a choice of making or not making the illicit payment to the then President of Kenya.[38] The claimant in that case chose the path of bribery. At the same time, the arbitral tribunal made a remark that it found the whole situation "highly disturbing", in particular, because the former President of Kenya was not prosecuted for corruption by the Kenyan State.[39] Perhaps, this can be especially "disturbing" or even cynical if a State is raising allegations of corruption before an international tribunal, while it itself fails to take appropriate actions against responsible public officials at the domestic level.

which is why the legality requirement was not breached (i.e. the investment was made *in accordance with the law of the host state*).

[36] Dine (2017), pp. 81–92.

[37] *See for instance,* Cremades (2005); Wilske (2010); Meshel (2013); Alekhin and Shmatenko (2018).

[38] "[The bribe] was not procured by coercion or oppression or force by the Kenyan President not by "undue influence"; and as regards any investment, there was at the material time no "hostage factor" because there was then no investment or other commitment in Kenya by Mr Ali or his principal."—World Duty Free Company Limited v. The Republic of Kenya, ICSID Case No. ARB/00/7, Award, 4 October 2006, para. 178.

[39] *Id.*, para. 180.

Furthermore, as can be seen from the analysis of the Metal-Tech v. Uzbekistan case, the arbitral tribunal had similar (unsatisfactory) feeling of the decision it had to make to the detriment of the claimant:

> While reaching the conclusion that the claims are barred as a result of corruption, the Tribunal is sensitive to the ongoing debate that findings on corruption often come down heavily on claimants, *while possibly exonerating defendants that may have themselves been involved in the corrupt acts.*[40]

As has been discussed above, the arbitral tribunal in the Metal-Tech case found it appropriate to express its displease in the State's participation in corruption in the decision for allocation of costs.[41]

In another case against Uzbekistan, namely in the Spentex dispute, the arbitral tribunal went several steps further with punitive measures against the State for tolerating corruption. While the Spentex tribunal decided that the investor's claims were inadmissible because of corruption,[42] it reportedly made note of the fact that the respondent State was far from being cooperative in the proceedings, *inter alia* by refusing to provide information on the individuals responsible for receiving bribes and whether these individuals were subjected to criminal investigations. It was noted that Uzbekistan was rather unwilling than unable to investigate and prosecute corrupt activities in connection with this case.[43]

Importantly, it is said that the Spentex tribunal argued that such an uncooperative approach by the State could have had adverse effect on the entire system of arbitration,[44] while at the same time recognising that, for the time being, arbitral tribunals are helpless in sanctioning corrupt activities of States.[45] Nevertheless, the majority of the tribunal upheld that it would be fair and just to urge Uzbekistan to make a donation of USD 8 million to the Global Anti-Corruption Initiative of the United Nations Development Programme under the risk of being obliged to bear all costs and fees of the proceedings and 75 percent of the investor's legal fees.[46]

In the latest Sanum v. Laos arbitral award, the tribunal also took note of the respondent's reluctance to enforce its anti-corruption policies. In doing so, the

---

[40] Metal-Tech Ltd. v. Republic of Uzbekistan, ICSID Case No. ARB/10/3, Award, 4 October 2013, para. 389 [emphasis added]. In the same paragraph, the tribunal stated that "[i]t is true that the outcome in cases of corruption often appears unsatisfactory because, at first sight at least, it seems to give an unfair advantage to the defendant party…"

[41] *Id.*, para. 422.

[42] Betz (2017), p. 134 with reference to Spentex Netherlands, B.V. v. Republic of Uzbekistan, ICSID Case No. ARB/13/26, Award, 27 December 2016, para. 944.

[43] *Id.*, para. 942.

[44] *Id.*, para. 940: "Such an approach would reinforce perverse incentives for respondent States in the context of corruption. It would ask an investment tribunal to dismiss a claimant's claim, while granting impunity to a respondent State both in respect of the alleged corruption and the claimant's investment claims."

[45] Betz (2017), p. 135.

[46] *Id.*, with reference to Spentex Netherlands, B.V. v. Republic of Uzbekistan, ICSID Case No. ARB/13/26, Award, 27 December 2016, para. 981.

arbitral tribunal practically dismissed a number of illegality arguments made by the respondent because the State itself was not consistent with its position taken during the arbitration and did not produce any evidence of the initiated criminal proceedings against persons who allegedly received bribes from investors.

Finally, as was discussed in Sect. 7.2 of Part II above, a somewhat alternative view on State's responsibility for corruption was expressed in the EDF v. Romania case, where the corruption allegation was used as a "sword" by the investor, which is quite rare in ISDS cases.[47] The tribunal in the EDF case stated that an asserting party must present "clear and convincing evidence ... showing not only that a bribe had been requested" by a state official but that it was made "on behalf and for the account of the Government authorities...so as to make the State liable in that respect" and that it was not merely done in "the personal interest of the person soliciting the bribe".[48] In other words, the EDF tribunal found that as long as there was no "clear and convincing evidence" showing that the corrupt official received a bribe as an "official" of the State, it would not be most relevant for the outcome of the case.

Summarily, in five out of ten cases arbitral tribunals addressed the question of State's acts in connection with corruption allegations. One out of these five cases was the dispute where the investor alleged corruption as a claim against the State, which is why the tribunal practically had to address it. Thus, in two other researched cases arbitral tribunals decided to take certain measures against a State. Evidently, the cases where tribunals did take steps against a State are more recent than the others.

References

Alekhin S, Shmatenko L (2018) Corruption in investor-state arbitration – it takes two to tango. In: Asoskov et al (eds) New horizons of international arbitration, Issue 4, Collection of Articles

Alexandrov SA (2005) The "Baby Boom" of treaty-based arbitrations and the jurisdiction of ICSID tribunals: shareholders as "investors" and jurisdiction ratione temporis. Law Pract Int Courts Tribunals 4(1):19–59

Betz K (2017) Proving bribery, fraud and money laundering in international arbitration. University of Basel, Cambridge University Press

Cremades BM (2005) Corruption and investment arbitration. In: Aksen G et al (eds) Global reflections on international law, commerce and dispute resolution: Liber Amicorum in honour of Robert Briner. ICC Publication No. 693

Cremades BM, Cairns DJA (2003) Transnational public policy in international arbitral decision-making: the case of bribery, money laundering and fraud. In: Karsten K, Berkeley A (eds)

---

[47] Many authors have expressed views that it is much more common to see states putting forward the illegality allegations as defense against IIL claims (i.e. as a "shield") rather than investors alleging illegality to prove their case (i.e. as a "sword"). *See*, Alekhin and Shmatenko (2018), pp. 164–168. *See also*, Menaker and Greenwald (2015), pp. 77–102; Low (2019), p. 341.

[48] EDF Services Limited v. Romania, ICSID Case No ARB/05/13, Award, 8 October 2009, para. 232.

Arbitration, money laundering, corruption and fraud. Dossiers – ICC Institute of World Business Law, pp 78–79

Crivellaro A (2003) Arbitration case law on bribery: issues of arbitrability, contract validity, merits and evidence. In: Karsten K, Berkeley A (eds) Arbitration, money laundering, corruption and fraud. Dossiers - ICC Institute of World Business Law, vol 109, pp 115–117

Dine J (2017) It takes two people to tango (or more!). In: Rowley C, dela Rama M (eds) The changing face of corruption in the Asia Pacific, pp 81–92

Eriksson M (1993) Arbitration and contracts involving corrupt practices: the arbitrator's dilemma. Am Rev Int Arbitr 4

Fathallah R (2010) Corruption in international commercial and investment arbitration: recent trends and prospects for Arab countries. Int J Arab Arbitr 2(3):73

Gaillard E (2019) The emergence of transnational responses to corruption in international arbitration. J Int Arbitr 35(1)

Haugeneder F (2009) Corruption in investor-state arbitration. J World Invest Trade 10(3):323–339

Hunter JM (1992) Modern trends in the presentation of evidence in international commercial arbitration. Am Rev Int Arbitr 3:204–211

Jacob M, Schill SW (2015) Fair and equitable treatment: content, practice, method. In: Bungenberg et al (eds) A handbook on international investment law, pp 719–743

Kreindler R (2002) Aspects of illegality in the formation and performance of contracts. In: 11th International Council for Commercial Arbitration Congress, pp 252–253

Lamm CB, Pham HT, Moloo R (2010) Fraud and corruption in international arbitration. In: Fernandez-Ballesteros, Arias (eds) Liber Amicorum Bernardo Cremades. Kluwer, pp 699–731

Llamzon AP (2014) Corruption in international investment arbitration. Oxford University Press

Low L (2019) Dealing with allegations of corruption in international arbitration. Am J Int Law Unbound 113

Menaker AJ, Greenwald BK (2015) Proving corruption in international arbitration. In: Baizeau D, Kreindler RH (eds) Addressing issues of corruption in commercial and investment arbitration. Dossiers of the ICC Institute of World Business Law, vol 13, ICC Publication No. 768E

Meshel T (2013) The use and misuse of the corruption defence in international investment arbitration. J Int Arbitr 30

Mills K (2003) Corruption and other illegality in the formation and performance of contracts and in the conduct of arbitrations relating thereto. In: International Commercial Arbitration: Important Contemporary Questions, ICCA Congress Series No. 11

Partasides C (2010) Proving corruption in international arbitration: a balanced standard for the real world. ICSID Rev: Foreign Invest Law J 25(1)

Raouf M (2009) How should international arbitrators tackle corruption issues? ICSID Rev: Foreign Invest Law J 24(1):116–136

Rosell J, Prager H (1999) Illicit commissions and international arbitration: the question of proof. J Int Arbitr 15(4):329–348

Schlaepfer AV (2015) The burden of proof in international arbitration. In: van den Berg AJ (ed) Legitimacy: myths, realities, challenges, ICCA Congress Series No. 18, pp 127–133

Schreuer C, Malintoppi L, Reinisch A, Sinclair A (2009) The ICSID Convention: a commentary. Cambridge University Press, p 669

Volkov O (2015) Standard of proof in international arbitration – search for precision in considering corruption claims, available at https://uba.ua/documents/presentation/VolkovO_2015.pdf, p 4

Wetter JG (1994) Issue of corruption before international arbitral tribunals: the authentic text and true meaning of Judge Gunnar Lagergren's 1963 Award in ICC Case No. 1110. J Int Arbitr 10(3)

Wilske S (2010) Sanctions for unethical and illegal behavior in international arbitration: a double-edged sword. Contemp Asia Arbitr J 3

Part III
Challenges & Solutions

The analysis in Parts I and II of this monograph provides a clear background to the present reality in the ISDS mechanism's ability in fighting fraud and corruption. This analysis also outlines the outstanding challenges and open questions that deserve closer attention. Among such challenges some authors have indicated the question of existence of arbitral tribunals' duty to investigate/examine corruption and fraud.[1] As this point has been sufficiently debated in publications and during academic events, it does not seem to be necessary to discuss this any further in this textbook. Some of such publications date back to almost 40[2] and 20[3] years ago. For instance, *Cremades* and *Cairns* stated the following in this regard:

> The position today [2003] is that the international arbitrator *has a clear duty to address issues of bribery, money laundering or serious fraud* whenever they arise in the arbitration and whatever the wishes of the parties and to record its legal and factual conclusions in its award. This is the only course available to protect the enforceability of the award and the integrity of the institution of international commercial arbitration.[4]

---

[1] *See for instance*, opinion expressed in Gaillard (2019), p. 3: "…there is no question today that arbitrators are empowered, and indeed have the duty, to investigate and adjudicate corruption issues and thereby contribute to the global fight against corruption."; *see also*, Llamzon (2014), paras. 9.04–9.07. For further discussion of arbitrators' duties in such cases and their "two possible scenarios" *see* Raouf (2009), pp. 116–136. Views on this have also been expressed in Cremades and Cairns (2003), pp. 78–79; and in Kreindler (2002), pp. 252–253.

[2] *See for instance*, Mourre (2006) with reference to *Sieghart, P.*: "Suppose I have before me a case where an agent is claiming a commission from a supplier, expressed to be payable in the event that the supplier obtains a certain contract in a certain developing country. Suppose I begin to notice that both parties are carefully skating round the area of what the agent was actually supposed to do to earn his commission. Should I press them on it? […] In a case like that, is the arbitrator the servant of the parties, or of the truth?…"

[3] Rosell and Prager (1999), p. 331 with reference to Heuze (1993), p. 179: "Regarding the question of whether an arbitrator may or must address the issue of illicit commissions at his or her own initiative when neither party has raised the issue, there seems to be a consensus that the arbitrator should address the issue."

[4] Cremades and Cairns (2003), pp. 85–86 [emphasis added].

Bermann supported the above opinion by stating in his expert report in the Yukos Universal Limited (Isle of Man) v. the Russian Federation case that "the consensus to this effect is so strong that, as a corollary to the preceding discussion, arbitral tribunals are *required* to treat seriously allegations and evidence of fraud or illegality in connection with the cases before them and, on their own initiative, to investigate them" and that "[a]rbitral tribunals *are not free* to disregard allegations and evidence of fraud and illegality."[5]

Indeed, the duty of arbitrators (in ISDS) to examine allegations of corruption and fraud in good faith should be treated as a given; it is natural (and obligatory) for the ones who are charged with functions of delivering justice to pay close attention that the system and the laws are not abused by and with illicit elements. If this duty is not assumed or recognised, then there is something obviously wrong with the system or with the justice mechanism.

Derains answered to those who had sceptical views towards arbitrators' *capabilities* of adjudicating general matters by concluding that "arbitration is a normal forum, if not the juge naturel, as far as cross-border transactions are concerned."[6] This 'response' shall also be extended to what concerns the issues of illegality, including corruption and fraud. In fact, the ISDS tribunals' abilities in addressing corruption and fraud allegations have been witnessed in Part II above.

The tribunal's willingness or possible un-willingness to investigate/examine corruption and fraud allegations will also not be discussed within the frames of this monograph, as there should be no room for debate on this topic.[7] There may be a large number of things that one is not willing to do, but there is this overriding duty to serve justice and law as an adjudicator, in light of which one should disregard any possible subjective wishes and preferences. In this context, *Pieth* goes further by saying that passive and unwilling arbitrators may even become "accessories" to illicit dealings,[8] while *Thomson* believes that arbitrators may be even be held liable for failure to act.[9] Other authors speak of the "duties" that arbitrators owe towards "the international business community at large" to maintain the institute of arbitration as a safe and legitimate dispute settlement mean.[10]

Therefore, this textbook addresses only objective challenges of the system of international investment arbitration. As can be seen from the analysis of case law in

---

[5] Bermann (2015): paras. 136, 140. Available at https://www.italaw.com/sites/default/files/case-documents/italaw4443_1.pdf [emphasis added].

[6] Derains (1978), p. 976 referred in Malik and Kamat (2018), p. 12.

[7] *See for instance*, opinion expressed in Devendra (2019), p. 249.

[8] Pieth (2003), p. 41. The same opinion has been expressed in Neocleous (2014), p. 14.

[9] Thomson (2014) with reference to the speech of Polkinghorne, M at the GAR Live London event on 7 May 2014.

[10] Beale and Esposito (2009), p. 361. *See also*, Clouet, L.M. (2018), Arbitrating under the table: the effect of allegations of corruption in relation to the jurisdiction of the arbitral tribunal and the enforcement of foreign arbitral awards, available at https://nyu.academia.edu/LuisMar%C3%ADaClouet.

Part II, the difficulty of proving corruption and fraud before investment tribunals is one of such challenges.

It has also been observed that arbitral tribunals approach the allegations of illicit misconduct quite differently. The variety of approaches also lead to substantially different and sometimes unexpected results.[11] This has created a way for several differentiated rules-like practices for the identical scope of questions, which is why the issue of consistency is to be regarded as an outstanding challenge as well.

Another objective outstanding issue is the question of negative consequences for States in cases where corruption (i.e. bribery of public officials) is being pleaded. Most cases that have been analysed include allegations of bribery made by States as a complete defence against investors' claims. Some tribunals have tried to penalise States for tolerating corruption.[12] The silent question that should have its voice is whether such practices should be adopted more regularly by arbitral tribunals or not.

Finally, this Part will touch upon the live discussion over a hot topic of potential creation of a multilateral investment court and how such a court could help the ISDS system in its international combat against corruption and fraud.

References

Beale KD, Esposito P (2009) Emergent international attitudes towards bribery, corruption and money laundering. Arbitration 360, 75:361

Bermann GA (2015) Expert Opinion (Part B) dated 20 October 2015, Yukos Universal Limited (Isle of Man) v. The Russian Federation, UNCITRAL, PCA Case No. AA 227

Cremades BM, Cairns DJA (2003) Transnational public policy in international arbitral decision-making: the case of bribery, money laundering and fraud. In: Karsten K, Berkeley A (eds) Arbitration, money laundering, corruption and fraud. Dossiers – ICC Institute of World Business Law, pp 78–79

Cremades BM, Cairns DJA (2003) Transnational public policy in international arbitral decision making: the cases of bribery, money laundering and fraud. In: Berkeley A, Karsten K (eds) Arbitration: money laundering, corruption, and fraud. Dossiers of the ICC Institute of World Business, pp 85–86

Derains Y (1978) Chroniques de Sentences Arbitrales. Journal du Droit International 105:976

Devendra IC (2019) State responsibility for corruption in international investment arbitration. J Int Dispute Settlement 10(2):249

Gaillard E (2019) The emergence of transnational responses to corruption in international arbitration. J Int Arbitr 35(1):3

[11] *See for instance,* Odumosu (2011), p. 93: "It demonstrates that while arbitral tribunals appear to be united in their cause against corruption (it is difficult to envision them taking another view, given the near consensus of the international community on the evils of corruption), their approaches to reaching that conclusion differ."

[12] *See for instance,* Metal-Tech v. Uzbekistan and Spentex v. Uzbekistan Part II.

Heuze V (1993) La morale, l'arbitre et le juge. In: Rev. de l'Arb, p 179

Kreindler R (2002) Aspects of illegality in the formation and performance of contracts. In: 11th International Council for Commercial Arbitration Congress, pp 252–253

Llamzon A (2014) Corruption in international investment arbitration. Oxford University Press

Malik D, Kamat G (2018) Corruption in international commercial arbitration: arbitrability, admissibility & adjudication. In: The Arbitration Brief, available at https://paperity.org/p/185990736/corruption-in-international-commercial-arbitration-arbitrability-admissibility, p 12

Mourre A (2006) Arbitration and criminal law: reflections on the duties of the arbitrator. J Int Arbitr 22(1)

Neocleous N (2014) Arbitrators' investigative rights and duties, available at https://uba.ua/documents/doc/nick_neocleous.pdf, p 14

Odumosu I (2011) International investment arbitration and corruption claims: an analysis of World Duty Free v. Kenya. Law Dev Rev 4(3):93

Pieth M (2003) Transnational commercial bribery: challenge to arbitration. In: Dossier of the ICC Institute of World Business Law: arbitration – money laundering, corruption and fraud. ICC Publishing, p 41

Raouf M (2009) How should international arbitrators tackle corruption issues? ICSID Rev: Foreign Invest Law J 24(1):116–136

Rosell J, Prager H (1999) Illicit commissions and international arbitration: the question of proof. J Int Arbitr 15(4):331

Thomson D (2014) Arbitrators and corruption: watchdogs or bloodhounds? In: Global Arbitration Review, available at https://globalarbitrationreview.com/article/1033374/arbitrators-and-corruption-watchdogs-or-bloodhounds

Chapter 9
Difficulty of Proving Corruption and Fraud

Evidence and proof have a critical role in international dispute resolution of any form, including ISDS. The result in many international arbitration cases is determined by the factual background of the case and the way such facts are evaluated and examined by arbitral tribunals.[1] As yearly as in 1999, *Rosell* and *Prager* noted that

> ...it must be conceded that arbitrators and commentators in general have not developed a clear analysis with respect to said burdens and standards in cases involving allegations or suspicions of illicit commissions. It would seem, therefore, that this is a topic that requires further attention.[2]

In the following chapters you will find that the situation has not changed dramatically, especially when discussing the burden of proof.

The lessons learned as a result of case law analysis undertaken in the previous Part indicate the difficulty of proving fraud and corruption in the setting of international investment arbitration. One of the identified reasons is that at times arbitral tribunals set higher evidentiary standards for such allegations.

Looking back at Part II, it is useful to recall the way the EDF tribunal concluded that a heightened evidentiary standard was to be applicable for allegations of bribery:

> The seriousness of the accusations of corruption in the present case, considering that it involves officials at the highest level of the Romanian Government at the time, demands clear and convincing evidence.[3]

As seen above, in the EDF tribunal's opinion, the "seriousness" of the accusations of corruption and the involvement of "officials at the highest level" of a State

[1] Carreteiro (2016), p. 82 with reference to Blackaby et al. (2009), p. 384 (suggesting that perhaps 60% to 70% of cases turn on facts rather than on the application of principles of law, and that a good proportion of the remainder turn on a combination of facts and law).

[2] Rosell and Prager (1999), pp. 334–335.

[3] EDF Services Limited v. Romania, ICSID Case No ARB/05/13, Award, 8 October 2009, para. 221.

A. Tussupov, *Corruption and Fraud in Investment Arbitration*, EYIEL Monographs - Studies in European and International Economic Law 22,
https://doi.org/10.1007/978-3-030-90606-1_9

government should necessarily trigger the application of heightened evidentiary standards. Similar reasoning is provided in other cases where tribunals decided to be stricter with evidence of illicit misconduct.[4]

While such explanations are not without basis and are supported by scholar opinions,[5] there is still something that should be kept in sight. Although allegations of corruption and fraud may be of criminal nature, the setting of ISDS is of non-criminal background, i.e. *investment* arbitration. Therefore, the balance between the interests of an "accused" person and the interests of justice shall certainly be different in international investment arbitration procedures than in criminal court cases. The objective of arbitral tribunals in ISDS is not to criminally sanction a person who was found to be responsible for an illicit act, neither does an investment tribunal have such competence. Therefore, the findings of an (investment) arbitral tribunal on corruption or fraud cannot directly trigger *formal* criminal liability for those who are responsible for such illicit acts. This opinion has been confirmed by an arbitral tribunal in the Churchill Mining and Planet Mining v. Indonesia case:

> While intent and motive may be required for a criminal act of forgery or fraud, *the present proceedings are not aimed at establishing criminal liability*. Here the Tribunal must determine whether the impugned documents are authentic for purposes of an action seeking to engage the international responsibility of a State.[6]

In addition to the above, the analysis of case law and doctrine in Part II has indicated that in instances where arbitral tribunals applied heightened evidentiary standards, no corruption or fraud could have been proven in the end of the day. A very important and relevant question for the purposes of the present work was posed by *Mills*:

> It is clear that, like most crimes and intentional misconduct, and perhaps more so, acts of corruption and collusion are specifically designed not to be able to be identified or detected . . . How can we, as arbitrators sitting on tribunals established to adjudicate disputes that have arisen under such projects, ensure that *we do not allow ourselves to overlook such corruption and, by so doing, perpetuate the damage* that has been inflicted thereby?[7]

Similar opinions and concerns over the extreme difficulty of proving fraud and corruption in international arbitration have been expressed in several other

[4] *See for instance,* Wena Hotels Limited v. the Arab Republic of Egypt, ICSID Case No ARB/98/4, Award, 8 December 2000; Waguih Elie George Siag and Clorinda Vecchi v. the Arab Republic of Egypt, ICSID Case No ARB/05/15, Award, 1 June 2009; Rumeli Telekom A.S. and Telsim Mobil Telekomunikasyon Hizmetleri A.S. v. Republic of Kazakhstan, ICSID Case No. ARB/05/16, Award, 29 July 2008.

[5] *See for instance,* Born (2014).

[6] Churchill Mining PLC and Planet Mining Pty Ltd v. Republic of Indonesia, ICSID Case No. ARB/12/14 and 12/40, Award, 6 December 2016, para. 243 [emphasis added].

[7] Mills, K. (2003), Corruption and Other Illegality in the Formation and performance of Contracts and in the Conduct of Arbitrations Relating Thereto, in International Commercial Arbitration: Important Contemporary Questions, ICCA Congress Series No. 11, p. 295 [emphasis added].

publications.[8] Based on the points made above, following proposals that could potentially address the difficulty of proving corruption and fraud in international investment arbitration are put forward:

1. to consider recognizing ***red flags*** as evidence for proving corruption and fraud in ISDS cases;
2. to increase the application of **flexible** standards of proof;
3. to increase the application of **shifting or sharing** of the burden of proof (under certain circumstances);

All the listed items are elaborated in detail in the chapters below.

9.1 *Red Flags* as Means of Proof

By way of reminder, the term "red flags" was defined as "warning signs of possible illicit activity"[9] in the Introduction and Chap. 5 of Part I above. In other words, they are various forms of indicia of possible corruption, fraud, money laundering or any other illicit conduct.[10] While finding their roots in anti-trust legislation,[11] *red flags* are now codified and enlisted by various national and international bodies.[12]

As was established before, there is record of using and referring to *red flags* in international investment arbitration, in particular the two cases that have been analysed within this monograph.[13] For instance, in the Metal-Tech v. Uzbekistan case, the arbitral tribunal initiated ex officio investigation of corruption based on a number of *red flags* raised during witness examination in relation to some questionable payments under certain consulting agreements, including the following:

- high amount of payments;
- payments were made irrespective of the fact whether services were provided;

[8] Karadelis, K. (2010), Corruption and the standard of proof, Global Arbitration Review, available at https://globalarbitrationreview.com/print_article/gar/article/1029476/corruption-and-the-standard-of-proof; Mourre (2006), p. 102.

[9] Low (2019).

[10] Llamzon (2014), para. 9.11.

[11] *See e.g.*, U.S. Department of Justice, Antitrust Division, Federal Trade Commission (2016), Antitrust Guidance for Human Resource Professionals, Antitrust Red Flags for Employment Practices, available at https://www.justice.gov/atr/file/903511/download.

[12] *See e.g.*, UK Government (2017), 'Flag It Up', available at https://flagitup.campaign.gov.uk/; Woolf Committee Report on Business Ethics, Global Companies and the Defence Industry: Ethical Business Conduct in Bae Systems Plc 25-26 (2008), prepared at the request of the Board of Directors of Bae Systems Plc; Competence Center on Arbitration and Crime, Basel Institute on Governance (2019), Corruption and Money Laundering in International Arbitration: A Toolkit for Arbitrators, available at https://www.baselgovernance.org/sites/default/files/2019-05/a_toolkit_for_arbitrators_29_05_2019_single_pages.pdf.

[13] *See,* Metal-Tech v. Uzbekistan and Spentex v. Uzbekistan discussed in Part II.

- consultants had insufficient professional qualifications;
- lack of transparency of the payee;
- consultants had direct connections with public officials in charge of claimant's investments.[14]

The reason the arbitral tribunal in the Metal-Tech case, as well as in the Spentex case, had to turn to the examination and assessment on the basis of *red flags* is because they had no sufficiently direct proof that the payments under the consulting contracts were illicit and were destined to be used as bribes. As was noted before, illicit acts are often difficult to prove, primarily because the actors tend to mask the true purpose behind contractual provisions. For this reason, arbitrators at times have no real choice: either to rely on the aggregate of *red flags* or declare that the standard of proof was not satisfied, and the burden of proof was not discharged.[15]

It is argued that in international arbitration, "there will hardly ever be direct evidence for corruption and tribunals have no coercive powers."[16] Some scholars believe that it is already well established that corruption can be proven by circumstantial evidence ("faisceau d'indices"), including by *red flags*.[17] At the same time, it is observed that in international investment arbitration, the practice surrounding the application and reference to *red flags* (or as some authors and tribunals call them—"indicators") is, to the say the least, inconsistent.

The proposal that is being made in this context is the following—the international investment arbitration community needs to increase awareness of the fact that reference to and identification of *red flags* in the frames of ISDS cases is possible and welcomed. Arbitral tribunals usually have procedural means to make such call as they enjoy a wide discretion when it comes to matters of evidence in international investment arbitration.[18] Moreover, guidance and inspirations can be based on the following:

1. there is established practice of applying *red flags* by national and international specialised institutions;
2. there is established practice of applying *red flags* by tribunals in international commercial arbitration on this scope of questions;
3. there is increasing support from scholars on application of *red flags* in international arbitration.

[14] Metal-Tech Ltd. v. Republic of Uzbekistan, ICSID Case No. ARB/10/3, Award, 4 October 2013, paras. 194–227.

[15] Rosell and Prager (1999), p. 332.

[16] Competence Center on Arbitration and Crime, Basel Institute on Governance (2019), Corruption and Money Laundering in International Arbitration: A Toolkit for Arbitrators, available at https://www.baselgovernance.org/sites/default/files/2019-05/a_toolkit_for_arbitrators_29_05_2019_single_pages.pdf.

[17] *Id.*

[18] By way of reminder, *see*, Article 25(1) of the ICC Rules of Arbitration, Article 27 of the UNCITRAL Arbitration Rules and Article 34(1) of the ICSID Arbitration Rules.

Each of the these items are detailed below.

First, there are sources in different legal procedures (other than arbitration) where *red flags* are used and/or recommended to be watched for.[19] Some indicative examples of such are the following:

- 2008 Woolf Committee Report on Business Ethics, Global Companies and the Defence Industry: Ethical Business Conduct in BAE Systems Plc;[20]
- Commercial due diligence standards in public procurement process as recommended by the 2016 OECD Guidelines on Preventing Corruption in Public Procurement;
- Indicators of Commercial Fraud Prepared by the UNCITRAL Secretariat;[21]
- Guidelines of the United States Department of Justice for corruption risks under the Foreign Corrupt Practices Act.[22]

Separate attention is to be given to the ICC Guidelines on Agents, Intermediaries, and Third Parties, which identifies a number of *red flags* of corruption. By way of example, below is a selection from the total of fifteen identified *red flags*:

- Operation takes place in a country known for corrupt payments (e.g., a country that received a low score on Transparency International's Corruption Perceptions Index);
- A third party (i.e. agent or intermediary) has close personal or family relationship, or business relationship, with a public official or relative of an official;
- Due diligence reveals that a third party is a shell company or has some other non-transparent corporate structure;
- The only qualification a third party brings to the venture is influence over public officials, or a third party claims that [s/]he can help secure a contract because [s/] he knows the right people;
- The need for a third party arises just before or after a contract is to be awarded;
- A third party's commission or fee seems disproportionate in relation to the services to be rendered.[23]

---

[19] Gaillard (2019), p. 4.

[20] This report has been prepared by the committee chaired by the Rt Hon Lord Woolf of Barnes (Former Chief Justice of England and Wales) for the Board of Directors of BAE Systems Plc in May 2008, available at https://www.icaew.com/-/media/corporate/files/technical/ethics/woolf-report-2008.ashx.

[21] Indicators of Commercial Fraud Prepared by the UNCITRAL Secretariat, United Nations, 2013, available at https://www.uncitral.org/pdf/english/texts/fraud/Recognizing-and-preventing-commer cial-fraud-e.pdf.

[22] Criminal Division of the U.S. Department of Justice and the Enforcement Division of the U.S. Securities and Exchange Commission (2012), A Resource Guide to the U.S. Foreign Corrupt Practices Act, available at https://www.justice.gov/sites/default/files/criminal-fraud/legacy/201 5/01/16/guide.pdf.

[23] ICC Commission on Corporate Responsibility and Anti-corruption, ICC Guidelines on Agents, Intermediaries, and Third Parties dated 19 November 2010, pp. 4–5 quoted in Baizeau, D., and Hayes, T. (2017), The Arbitral Tribunal's Duty and Power to Address Corruption Sue Sponte, in

The above demonstrates that there is awareness of the problem of proper identification of illicit schemes in business and commerce at the national and international level and it is for this reason that various listed institutions decided to draft guidelines with lists of indicators/*red flags* for corruption and money-laundering. The existence of such lists, especially the ones adopted by international organisations, should provide more comfort for arbitrators to use them within their analysis in the ISDS setting.

Second, as *Gaillard* analysed, *red flags* are no strangers in international *commercial* arbitration.[24] This opinion is supported by several ICC arbitration cases that *inter alia* include the following:[25]

- ICC Case No 3916, the sole arbitrator noticed the short timeframe in which the "consultant" was to obtain a government contract for another party. No party could provide reasonable explanation as to what exactly the consultants' role and services constituted. The sole arbitrator then finally concluded that "the action undertaken by the [consultant] could be nothing else but the exercise of influence over those deciding who the Iranian State was going to contract;"[26]
- ICC Case No 6497, the tribunal took note that under the agreement at issue, the claimant was to receive a commission worth one third of the contract that he helped to obtain in a Middle Eastern country. The agreement at issue did not include any specific description of the necessary services that were to be provided and the claimant provided "confusing and contradictory" explanations. Upon this, the tribunal concluded that there was a "high degree of probability [that] the real object [. . .] was to channel bribes to officials in country X" and that "[s]uch probability is high enough;"[27]
- ICC Case No 8891, the arbitral tribunal based its finding that the true object under the contract in question was, in fact, a bribe. This finding was based on several *red flags* that the tribunal had identified, i.e.:
  - Short duration of a contract;
  - No evidence that actual services had been provided;
  - Manner in which the consultant was remunerated;
  - An unconventionally high success fee (18.5%).[28]
- Similarly, in the ICC Case No 13515, the arbitral tribunal based its decision on "serious and convergence indicators", such as:

Kluwer Arbitration Blog, available at https://www.lalive.law/data/publications/Duty_and_Power_to_Address_Corruption.pdf.

[24] Gaillard (2019), pp. 5–7.

[25] *Id.*

[26] French purchaser v. Dutch Seller, ICC Case No 3916, Final Award (1982), paras, 926, 929–930.

[27] Consultant v. Contractor, ICC Case No 6497, Final Award (194), para. 30.

[28] ICC Case No 8891, Award, 1998; *See also*, Rosell and Prager (1999), pp. 329–348.

  - Short duration of a contract;
  - Corruption history in the country of business;
  - An unconventionally high success fee (40%).[29]

- In the ICC Case No 13914, the arbitral tribunal used the indicators (i.e. *red flags*) that are listed in the previously mentioned guidelines to the US FCPA.[30]
- In the ICC Case No 12990, the arbitral tribunal weakened the standard of proof for allegations of corruption and based its findings on "presumption created by indicators" to decide that corruption was present.[31]

The practice of tribunals in the frames of international commercial arbitration indicates that the notion of *red flags* is far from being alien to the system of arbitration in general. Notwithstanding the essential differences in nature of parties in ISDS and commercial arbitration, both have the same general basis and both often operate under the same arbitration rules. And, finally, both often have to decide on the same scope of questions, in particular in determining whether a particular act/transaction is corrupt or fraudulent. It is for this reason that the experience within international commercial arbitration should have a spill over effect on ISDS.

In fact, it seems convincing or at least reasonable to expect that the notion of *red flags* should be accorded even larger attention and weight in international investment arbitration than in commercial, due to the presence of public elements of this dispute resolution mechanism. The public elements of ISDS are the following:

- At least one party in investment arbitration is always a State;[32]
- Claims are almost always based on States' conduct of regulatory and/or administrative character;
- Arbitration is initiated on the basis of investment treaties, that are international agreements in the meaning of public international law;
- The outcome of ISDS cases may have an impact on the well-being of the whole nation.

The final characteristic above does not only address possible economic effects of a monetary award rendered against a State, but also possible reputational consequences that may influence the flow of foreign capital into the country in the future. In other words, investment awards may have a far reaching public impact, in particular in case of developing and least developed economies.

Additionally, the fact that arbitration is initiated on the basis of public international law also speaks for *public* approach to the questions of corruption and fraud,

---

[29] ICC Case No 13515, Final Award, 2006.

[30] ICC Case No 13914, Final Award, 2008. For completeness, it is noted that the US FCPA methodology was reviewed but was declined for formal reasons (i.e. the jurisdiction of the FCPA extends only on US citizens/residents) in the ICC Case No 9333 (1998), quoted in Raouf (2009), p. 122.

[31] ICC Case No 12990, Final Award, 2005.

[32] For details on particulars of state-to-state investment arbitration, *see* Hazarika, A. (2020), State-to-State Arbitration based on International Investment Agreements – Scope, Utility and Potential.

which means that all actors, including parties and, in particular, tribunals shall have a fiduciary duty of protecting the ISDS system from abuse. International investments that are tainted by corruption or fraud may well be such abusive elements that the system needs protection from. This is especially true when looking at the above analysed case law and international legal instruments, such as the OECD Anti-Bribery Convention.

On the basis of all the above, it is therefore suggested that the place and meaning of *red flags* in international investment arbitration should be considered and viewed in light of these public elements of the dispute resolution system, thereby triggering an even stronger duty of care by investment tribunals where *red flags* of corruption and fraud exist.

Finally, there is increasing support from the academic circles on the question of application of *red flags* in international arbitration. For instance, some scholars opine that *red flags* are to be considered as part of circumstantial evidence and that "[t] ribunals may make a firm finding of corruption based on the circumstantial evidence available to them".[33]

It is, however, also recognized that *red flags* should not, always on their own, suffice to base a finding of fraud or corruption without first seeking explanations and evidence from parties.[34] What is certain is that *red flags* (or any possible indicators) can trigger an evidentiary enquiry by an arbitral tribunal. There can be no strict requirement on the number of *red flags* to be able to trigger such enquiry, but certainly the more there is, the greater the scrutiny that is merited.[35] In other words, *red flags* should alert arbitrators that further scrutiny must be applied to the facts of a dispute.[36] It is in particular true in the frames of international investment arbitration.

Moreover, if scrutiny of the facts and existing evidence by an arbitral tribunal is not possible due to an unreasonable lack of cooperation from the defending party, then, as will be discussed further below (*infra,* Sect. 9.2 of Part III), an arbitral

[33]Competence Center on Arbitration and Crime, Basel Institute on Governance (2019), Corruption and Money Laundering in International Arbitration: A Toolkit for Arbitrators, available at https://www.baselgovernance.org/sites/default/files/2019-05/a_toolkit_for_arbitrators_29_05_2019_single_pages.pdf.

[34]Baizeau, D., and Hayes, T. (2017), The Arbitral Tribunal's Duty and Power to Address Corruption Sue Sponte, in Kluwer Arbitration Blog, available at https://www.lalive.law/data/publications/Duty_and_Power_to_Address_Corruption.pdf with reference to Tschanz, P.Y. and Vulliemin, J-M. (2001), Chronique de jurisprudence étrangère: Suisse, in Rev. Arb., Volume 4, available at https://www.lalive.law/data/publications/Duty_and_Power_to_Address_Corruption.pdf.

[35]Criminal Division of the U.S. Department of Justice and the Enforcement Division of the U.S. Securities and Exchange Commission (2012), A Resource Guide to the U.S. Foreign Corrupt Practices Act, available at https://www.justice.gov/sites/default/files/criminal-fraud/legacy/2015/01/16/guide.pdf, p. 60.

[36]Competence Center on Arbitration and Crime, Basel Institute on Governance (2019), Corruption and Money Laundering in International Arbitration: A Toolkit for Arbitrators, available at https://www.baselgovernance.org/sites/default/files/2019-05/a_toolkit_for_arbitrators_29_05_2019_single_pages.pdf.

tribunal may draw adverse inferences, which would only add to circumstantial evidence and thereby raise further *red flags*.

9.2 Shifting the Burden of Proof

The topic of burden of proof too has an important place in dispute resolution in cases that involve allegations of corruption and fraud. In fact, the study that was undertaken during the 2014 biennial conference of International Council for Commercial Arbitration demonstrated that the issues connected with or resulting from the burden of proof are frequently determinative for the outcome of *any* dispute.[37]

As was observed by *Born* in 2014, there is "little authority on the allocation of burden of proof in arbitral contexts".[38] Interestingly, the same observation was made by *Reiner* already in 1994.[39] Obviously, the topic of the burden of proof in the context of international investment arbitration is not the most exciting topic among the international academic circles. The limited authority that one can find vastly supports the current approach of an alleging party carrying the entire burden of proof or *onus probandi actori incumbit*.[40] Some authors have called such approach as a "universal principle"[41] or a "general practice of virtually all international arbitral tribunals."[42]

The above is confirmed by a wide range of arbitral tribunals' decisions. For instance, in the ICSID dispute between Asian Agricultural Products Ltd. and the Republic of Sri Lanka, the tribunal went as far as stating that there existed "a general principle of law placing the burden of proof upon the [claiming party]."[43] Similar findings have been made by arbitral tribunals in a number of other cases, including Plama Consortium Limited v. Bulgaria,[44] Salini Costruttori S.p.A. and Italstrade S.p.A. v. Jordan,[45] Tokios Tokeles v. Ukraine,[46] Azurix Corporation v. the

---

[37] Franck, S.D. et al. (2014), Precision and legitimacy in international arbitration: empirical insights from ICCA, in Kluwer Arbitration Blog, quoted in Carreteiro (2016), p. 83.

[38] Born (2014), p. 2312.

[39] Reiner (1994), pp. 333, 340, *see also*, Rosell and Prager (1999), pp. 334–335: "...it must be conceded that arbitrators and commentators in general have not developed a clear analysis with respect to said burdens and standards in cases involving allegations or suspicions of illicit commissions. It would seem, therefore, that this is a topic that requires further attention."

[40] *See*, Cheng (1953), p. 327; Brown (2007), pp. 94–95; Carreteiro (2016), p. 92.

[41] Rosell and Prager (1999), p. 335 with references to various undisclosed ICC awards.

[42] Carreteiro (2016), p. 92 with reference to Blackaby et al. (2009), p. 387.

[43] Asian Agricultural Products Ltd. v. Republic of Sri Lanka, ICSID Case No. ARB/87/3, Final Award, 27 June 1990, para. 56.

[44] Plama Consortium Limited v. Republic of Bulgaria, ICSID Case No. ARB/03/24, Award, 27 August 2008, para. 249.

[45] Salini Costruttori S.p.A. and Italstrade S.p.A. v. The Hashemite Kingdom of Jordan, ICSID Case No. ARB/02/13, Award, 31 January 2006, para. 70.

[46] Tokios Tokeles v. Ukraine, ICSID Case No. ARB/02/18, Award, 26 July 2007, para. 121.

Argentine Republic,[47] Churchill and Planet v. Indonesia,[48] EDF v. Romania,[49] etc. In other words, under the most popular scholar opinions, the application of a "strict" burden of proof with "a risk of not having a certain fact to be proven"[50] always lays with the asserting party.

Unlike the situation with standards of proof, the debate over the question whether the shifting of the burden of proof should take place for allegations of corruption and fraud is minimal.[51] This may be due to the fact that the burden of proof in its classic understanding, has been within the legal minds for centuries. Precisely, it was known to ancient lawyers since the Roman law time and it is enshrined in Latin maxims such as *ei qui affirmat non ei qui negat incumbit probatio* (the burden of proof is carried by the person who affirms, not by the one who denies) and *affirmant incumbit probatio* (the person who affirms bears the burden of proof).[52] Partly, this must also be due to the fact that this principle is simply fair, just and uncontroversial. *Affirmant incumbit probatio* protects the system of justice (and therefore—arbitration) from abuse, it precludes a person from bringing unsubstantiated claims against another for whatever possible reason. The question that is being raised in this part of the textbook is whether there is a possibility to have the burden of proof shared and/or shifted after the asserting party clears a certain evidentiary minimum and, therefore, satisfies its share of the burden of proof?

It seems to be practically possible due to the following reasons:

1. Investment arbitration has the necessary legal framework.
2. There is existing case law supporting the shifting of the burden of proof.
3. Investment tribunals possess the necessary tools that could assist in limiting possible unjust consequences of shifting the burden of proof.
4. Inspirations may be drawn from tribunals in international commercial arbitration that practiced the shifting of the burden of proof.
5. Inspirations may be drawn from national courts in some legal systems.
6. Some modern scholar opinions are in support for the flexibility of the burden of proof.

First, some of the dispute resolution rules, such as the UNCITRAL Arbitration Rules and the Statute of the Iran-United States Claims Tribunal provide the following identical rule in their respective provisions:

---

[47] Azurix Corp. v. The Argentine Republic, ICSID Case No. ARB/01/12, Decision on the Application for Annulment of the Argentine Republic, 1 September 2009, para. 215.

[48] Churchill Mining PLC and Planet Mining Pty Ltd v. Republic of Indonesia, ICSID Case No. ARB/12/14 and 12/40, Award, 6 December 2016, para. 238.

[49] EDF Services Limited v. Romania, ICSID Case No ARB/05/13, Award, 8 October 2009, para. 232.

[50] Redfern (1994), p. 320. *See also*, Carreteiro (2016), p. 84.

[51] *See,* Tsatsos (2009), pp. 91–104.

[52] Waincymer (2012), p. 762 cited in Carreteiro (2016), p. 85.

> Each party shall have the burden of proving the facts relied on to support his claim or *defence*.[53]

The emphasized term above may, in fact, leave a possibility to argue that the defending party shall also carry the burden of proving its defence and, perhaps, also making it possible to impose such a burden if it denies certain allegations made by another party. For instance, if a State claims that a foreign investment was obtained by way of fraud and substantiates its claim with certain evidence, would it not be the case that denial of fraud by an investor would constitute its "defence" against such a claim? If so, according to the UNCITRAL Arbitration Rules, would it not be the case that an investor is under the burden to prove this defence? And if this defence is not proven, where does this leave the arbitral tribunal?

The mere fact that such questions can be posed indicate that these provisions are open to interpretation in a way that could allow arbitral tribunals to demand that a party substantiates its own defence with evidence and proof.

The above shall be looked at in light of the fact that arbitral tribunals usually enjoy wide discretion on the questions of proof and evidence.[54] For instance, the ICC Arbitration Rules provide the following:

> The arbitral tribunal shall proceed within as short a time as possible to establish the facts of the case by *all* appropriate means.
>
> [...]
>
> At any time during the proceedings, the arbitral tribunal may summon any party to provide additional evidence.[55]

The discussed UNCITRAL Arbitration Rules provide tribunals with a wide discretion on this scope of questions too:

> 2. The arbitral tribunal may, *if it considers it appropriate*, require a party to deliver to the tribunal and to the other party, within such a period of time as the arbitral tribunal shall decide, a summary of the documents and other evidence which that party intends to present in support of the facts in issue set out in his statement of claim or *statement of defence*.
>
> 3. At any time during the arbitral proceedings the arbitral tribunal may require the parties to produce documents, exhibits or other evidence *within such a period of time as the tribunal shall determine*.[56]

Second, as was established in Part II of the textbook, there is already a track-record of investment tribunals acknowledging the possibility of shifting the burden

---

[53] UNCITRAL Arbitration Rules adopted by the General Assembly Resolution No 31/98, Article 24(1) and the Statute of the Iran-United States Claims Tribunal, Article 24(1) [emphasis added]. An almost identical provision is also included in the International Arbitration Rules of the American Arbitration Association: "[e]ach party shall have the burden of proving the facts relied on to support its claim or defense".

[54] Unless, of course, the parties did not agree differently.

[55] Article 25 of the ICC Arbitration Rules [emphasis added].

[56] UNCITRAL Arbitration Rules adopted by the General Assembly Resolution No 31/98, Article 24(2) and (3) [emphasis added].

of proof for allegations of illicit misconduct to a defending party. For example, in the case of Karkey Karadeniz Elektrik Uretim A.S. v. the Islamic Republic of Pakistan, the tribunal found the following:

> [T]he burden of proof with respect to corruption and fraud [could shift] to Karkey should the Tribunal be satisfied that there is unequivocal (or unambiguous) prima facie evidence in this regard.[57]

Third, arbitration, being a voluntarily and private dispute settlement mechanism, is governed by the principle of cooperation. Without cooperation among parties, it would be difficult for an arbitral tribunal to deliver justice because it does not have the same powers as a state court does. This principle is *inter alia* enshrined in the ICSID Arbitration Rules that state the following:

> The parties shall cooperate with the Tribunal in the production of the evidence and in the other measures provided for in paragraph (2).[58]

Provided that arbitrators are often not able to force parties to produce evidence, arbitral tribunals may infer from established facts other facts, especially when such parties are reluctant to cooperate.[59] In other words, a tribunal could exercise its right to draw adverse inferences from the conduct of the parties if it witnesses unreasonable and unjustifiable withholding of relevant information.[60] The notion of inferences in investment arbitration is *inter alia* supported by the ICSID Arbitration Rules that state that "[t]he Tribunal shall take formal note of the failure of a party to comply with its obligations [...]".[61] For completeness, it is to be noted that the drawing of negative inferences from the lack of cooperation from one of the parties has been practiced by arbitral tribunals in a number of ISDS cases.[62]

Once and if such inferences are drawn, a tribunal could then see whether such adverse inferences in combination with the minimum evidentiary basis that has been presented by the asserting party prior to the "sharing" or "shifting" of the burden of proof, could in fact establish the basis for its findings on the facts.

It is certainly recognized that the questions of inferences are quite delicate and complex. They have been found to be "one of the most complex topics in the law of evidence" and "a sea of technicality which defies logical analysis".[63] On the other hand, inferences are easy to get rid of by a party that is in possession or control of

---

[57] Karkey Karadeniz Elektrik Uretim A.S. v. Islamic Republic of Pakistan, ICSID Case No. ARB/13/1, Award, 22 August 2017, para. 497.

[58] ICSID Arbitration Rules, 34(3).

[59] Tsatsos (2009), p. 94 with reference to Sharp (2006), p. 549.

[60] Mehren (1992), p. 110.

[61] ICSID Arbitration Rules, 34(3).

[62] *For example,* Europe Cement Investment & Trade S.A. v. the Republic of Turkey, ICSID Case No. ARB(AF)/07/2, Award, 13 August 2009; Methanex Corporation v. United States of America, NAFTA, Final Award, 3 August 2005; Rumeli Telekom A.S. and Telsim Mobil Telekomunikasyon Hizmetleri A.S. v. Kazakhstan, ICSID Case No. ARB/05/16, Award, 29 July 2008; Feldman v. Mexico, NAFTA, Award, 16 December 2002.

[63] Shreve (1998), p. 272 quoted in Rosell and Prager (1999), p. 338.

relevant evidence.[64] In order to address negative inferences, one does not have to go as far as to prove its own point to be correct, one simply has to satisfy a tribunal that the presumed inference is not true.[65] For actors of any possible illicit scheme, the question is, of course, whether they are prepared to be truthful about their illegal acts or not.

On the other hand, such an approach would bring the matter of allocation of the burden of proof for allegations of corruption and fraud in equipoise. If the matters of evidence are in equipoise, the tribunal would have a chance to properly and justifiably rule against a party that failed to carry its burden of proof (be it either the party alleging illicit misconduct or the party defending from it).[66]

Fourth, there are examples of shifting/sharing the burden of proof in international commercial arbitration. For instance, in the ICC Case No 6497, the arbitral tribunal reversed the burden of proof to the defending party once the alleging party brought in a sufficient (but yet inconclusive) evidentiary basis. The same tribunal stated that if the defending party fails to provide counter evidence, the alleged facts can be deemed to be true.[67]

Fifth, the inspiration may be drawn from the practice of national courts in some jurisdictions. For instance, in England in labour discrimination cases, once a party makes a sufficient prima facie case, the defending party shall not be unresponsive to the allegations made against it and shall contribute to the debate and evidentiary exchange on the raised issues.[68]

Also, *Hanotiau* provides an example from the Civil Codes in Belgium and in France saying that in regular contract and transaction disputes the codes require an alleging party to prove its claim while at the same time require a defending party to prove its defence and/or that the claim does not exist or it is invalid.[69]

Lastly, as a result of two annual conferences in the University of Basel on the topic of corruption and money laundering in international arbitration, a number of legal scholars and practitioners have produced the so-called "Toolkit for Arbitrators"

---

[64] *See,* Younger et al. (1991), p. 857 with reference to the Supreme Court of Oregon (source omitted): "When evidence is introduced to rebut the presumption – however weak the evidence may be – the presumption is overcome and destroyed. [...] This 'phantom of the law' has been likened to 'bats flitting about in the twilight and then disappearing in the sunshine of actual facts' and to a house of cards that topples over when rebutted by evidence."

[65] *Id.*, p. 860.

[66] *See,* Rosell and Prager (1999), p. 337. *See also,* Born (2014), p. 2311; Mills, K. (2003), Corruption and Other Illegality in the Formation and Performance of Contracts and in the Conduct of Arbitrations Relating Thereto, in ICCA Congress Series No. 11, p. 295; Lamm et al. (2010), pp. 704–705; Fathallah (2010), pp. 73–77; Clouet, L.M. (2018), Arbitrating under the table: the effect of allegations of corruption in relation to the jurisdiction of the arbitral tribunal and the enforcement of foreign arbitral awards, available at https://nyu.academia.edu/LuisMar%C3%ADaClouet.

[67] ICC Case No 6497, Award, 1994, quoted in Raouf (2009), p. 122.

[68] *See,* Ayodele v. Citylink Ltd & Anor [2017] EWCA Civ 1913.

[69] Hanotiau (1994), pp. 341–343 with reference to Article 1315 of the Civil Code in Belgium and in France.

(“**Toolkit**”) that is designed to provide guidance for arbitrators in cases where a party alleges corruption or money laundering, or in a situation where arbitrators have their own suspicions of these illicit acts.[70] The Toolkit[71] provides the following:

> If there are indicators of corruption, arbitrators may ask the party that denies the corruption allegations to produce supporting evidence to prove the facts. Such evidence could, for instance, include evidence that an allegedly corrupt transaction was legitimate and part of a normal business transaction. Arbitrators may ask both parties for further evidence to substantiate their factual assertions.[72]

Consequently, to summarise all the above, it appears to be generally possible to demand that a defending party provides positive evidence of its non-illicit conduct in investment arbitration under certain circumstances. Some authors have expressed concerns that such shifting could violate the due process.[73] However, as can been seen from the legal framework, arbitral tribunals already have all the necessary tools to share, shift and/or reverse the burden of proof under various arbitration rules (i.e. wide discretion on the questions of evidence and proof, the burden of proof of a party for its defence and the possibility of drawing adverse inferences). By agreeing to the ISDS mechanism, the parties also deem to be in agreement with the applicable arbitration rules and principles that govern the arbitral process, such as good faith and the principle of cooperation.[74]

The shifting or sharing of the burden of proof could in turn make the work of arbitral tribunals less complex and more efficient in examination of allegations of fraud and corruption. As was stated before, illicit acts “are specifically designed not to be able to be identified or detected.”[75] And in a situation where one of the parties to arbitration, that is in control or possession of relevant evidence, refuses to cooperate, the path to the truth is even less realistic.

[70] Competence Center on Arbitration and Crime, Basel Institute on Governance (2019), Corruption and Money Laundering in International Arbitration: A Toolkit for Arbitrators, available at https://www.baselgovernance.org/sites/default/files/2019-05/a_toolkit_for_arbitrators_29_05_2019_single_pages.pdf.

[71] The authors of the Toolkit are Professor Mark Pieth and Dr. Kathrin Betz acknowledged Stanimir A. Alexandrov, Stéphane Bonifassi, Nicola Bonucci, Nadia Darwazeh, Vladimir Khvalei, Gervase MacGregor, Gianfranco Mautone, Krista Nadakavukaren Schefer, Craig Orr, Anne Peters and Claus von Wobeser.

[72] *Id.*

[73] *See,* Tsatsos (2009).

[74] Unless the parties agreed otherwise.

[75] Mills, K. (2003), Corruption and Other Illegality in the Formation and performance of Contracts and in the Conduct of Arbitrations Relating Thereto, in International Commercial Arbitration: Important Contemporary Questions, ICCA Congress Series No. 11, p. 295.

9.3 Flexible Standard of Proof

There is no debate that the standard of proof and its application by a tribunal is crucial for the outcome of a case.[76] This is why it is important to identify and understand any possible issues in the process of determination of the correct standard of proof, especially within such a delicate topic as "illicit conduct".

Among the so-called landmark ISDS cases with allegations of corruption and fraud that have been analysed in Part II, it has been determined that there is an (effective) ratio of 50 × 50 for arbitral tribunals requiring what has been defined as *heightened* or *lowered* standards of proof (*supra,* Sect. 6.4 of Part II). For completeness, it is to be noted that this ratio is not the overall ratio of all ISDS cases that involved claims of illegality. However, it is clear that there is a growing (although not consistent)[77] trend for *not* setting a *heightened* evidentiary standard for allegations of corruption and fraud. For instance, in a survey of arbitral case law on corruption that was undertaken in an open source publication of years ago, it was found that "in just one out of twenty-five cases, a "low" standard of proof was applied, whereas in fourteen cases, a "high" standard of proof [was] applied, which [was] variously described as "certainty", "clear proof", "clear and convincing evidence", "conclusive evidence".[78] In other words, the difference in numbers between today and from several years ago demonstrates the change of approach among arbitral tribunals.

This is also evident from the views that have been gradually expressed by arbitrators within the last several years. For instance, the analysis of this question expressed by the EDF tribunal in **2009**:

> There is *general consensus* among international tribunals and commentators regarding *the need for a high standard of proof of corruption.*[79]

For comparison, below is the extract from the arbitral award dated **2014** in the Fraport AG Frankfurt Airport Services Worldwide v. Republic of the Philippines

> The Tribunal holds that considering the difficulty to prove corruption by direct evidence, *the same may be circumstantial. However*, in view of the consequences of corruption on the investor's ability to claim the BIT protection, *evidence must be clear and convincing* so as to

[76] Reiner (1994), pp. 333, 340, *See also*, Reymond (1994), pp. 232 and 327 as referenced in Rosell and Prager (1999), p. 334.

[77] *See for instance,* the tribunal's analysis in a relatively recent award in Karkey v. Pakistan discussed in Sect. 7.5 of Part II.

[78] Hwang, M. S.C. and Lim, K., Corruption in Arbitration — Law and Reality, available at https://www.arbitration-icca.org/media/4/97929640279647/media013261720320840corruption_in_arbitration_paper_draft_248.pdf, p. 15 with references to Crivellaro (2003), pp. 115–117. *See also*, Volkov, O. (2015), Standard of Proof in International Arbitration – Search for Precision in Considering Corruption Claims, available at https://uba.ua/documents/presentation/VolkovO_2015.pdf, p. 4.

[79] EDF Services Limited v. Romania, ICSID Case No ARB/05/13, Award, 8 October 2009, para. 221 [emphasis added].

> reasonably make-believe that the facts, as alleged, have occurred. Having reviewed the Parties' positions and the available evidence related to the period prior to Fraport's Initial Investment, the Tribunal has come to the conclusion that Respondent has failed to provide clear and convincing evidence regarding corruption and fraud by Fraport.[80]

Finally, the tribunal in the ICSID case of Churchill Mining and Planet Mining v. Indonesia issued an award dated **2016** stating the following:

> *Some tribunals have applied the higher standard* of clear and convincing evidence due to the gravity of a finding of forgery or fraud. *Others, however, have considered that the common law standard of the balance of probabilities* or its civil law counterpart of "intime conviction" is sufficiently flexible to assess an act of forgery or fraud in a commercial setting, it being understood that the evidence must be commensurate with the seriousness of the alleged conduct and the overall context [...] the Tribunal considers that ... proof [shall] be measured on a standard of balance of probabilities or intime conviction taking into account that more persuasive evidence is required for implausible facts.[81]

As seen from the three quotes that have been made within the last ten years, the observations of arbitral tribunals have been gradually evolving from the categorical choice of "clear and convincing evidence" standard to the recognition of "circumstantial evidence" and finally to the application of the "balance of probabilities" for the allegations of fraud and corruption.[82] In other words, and as was stated above, there are clear footprints of a changing trend on the approach to the determination of the applicable standard of proof for such allegations.[83]

Apart from the practice of international investment tribunals, it is also evident from the international academic community that there is a growing awareness of the existence of this problem. There is, in fact, growing criticism over the approach of some tribunals in applying a heightened standard of proof, in particular, in the discussed EDF v. Romania case where the arbitral tribunal opined as follows:

---

[80] Fraport AG Frankfurt Airport Services Worldwide v. Republic of the Philippines, ICSID Case No. ARB/11/12, Award, 10 December 2014, para. 479 [emphasis added].

[81] Churchill Mining PLC and Planet Mining Pty Ltd v. Republic of Indonesia, ICSID Case No. ARB/12/14 and 12/40, Award, 6 December 2016, para. 240 [emphasis added].

[82] It is noted once again that although there is a changing trend, it is not yet consistent. See analysis of the arbitral tribunal in a relatively recent award in Karkey v. Pakistan discussed in Sect. 7.5 of Part II.

[83] *See also,* the findings of the arbitral tribunals in Metal-Tech Ltd. v. Republic of Uzbekistan, ICSID Case No. ARB/10/3, Award, 4 October 2013, para. 243: "... the Tribunal will determine on the basis of the evidence before it whether corruption has been established with reasonable certainty. In this context, it notes that corruption is by essence difficult to establish and that it is thus generally admitted that it can be shown through circumstantial evidence."; and in Jan Oostergetel and Theodora Laurentius v. Slovak Republic, UNCITRAL, Final Award, 23 April 2012, para. 303: "While such general reports are to be taken very seriously as a matter of policy, they cannot substitute for evidence of a treaty breach in a specific instance. For obvious reasons, it is generally difficult to bring positive proof of corruption. Yet, corruption can also be proven by circumstantial evidence."; Spentex Netherlands, B.V. v. Republic of Uzbekistan, ICSID Case No. ARB/13/26, Award, para. 856 as quoted in Betz (2017), p. 131: "...there is an inherent danger to dispose of the problem by restoring to strict evidentiary rules that may make proving or disproving corruption practically impossible...".

> In any case, however, corruption must be proven and is notoriously difficult to prove since, typically, there is little or no physical evidence. The seriousness of the accusations of corruption in the present case, considering that it involves officials at the highest level of the Romanian Government at the time, demands clear and convincing evidence.[84]

As can be observed, the EDF tribunal made two statements in the quote above: (1) it is "notoriously difficult" to prove fraud, and (2) it nevertheless "demands clear and convincing evidence". *Partasides* is of the opinion that these two statements are contradictory:

> The Tribunal is telling us that allegations of this type of illegality are by definition "notoriously" difficult to prove. Yet it nevertheless proceeds to impose an enhanced standard of proof on the allegation. Its message is difficult one to accept: "Dear investor, you will inevitably find the allegation almost impossible to prove, but we are nonetheless going to raise the evidential hurdle to make it even harder."[85]

There is a healthy debate on the way arbitral tribunals should be assessing an applicable standard of proof for allegations of illicit misconduct and there are views expressed both in favour of the heightened standard of proof,[86] as well as in support for a lowered (or ordinary) standard of proof for allegations of fraud and corruption by either of the parties.[87]

Just as in the gradual change of approach in the practice of investment tribunals, one may observe a changing perception of this question among scholars. For instance, if in 2003 *Hwang* and *Lim* concluded that the then existing case law "reflect[ed] *the prevailing arbitral practice* of subjecting complainants of corruption to a high standard of proof," in 2010 one can see open and provoking questions such as "[h]ow do you fairly evaluate proof of a conversation in a car park and a living room?"[88] as well as concrete propositions, such as that "exercising the flexibility inherent in their mandates to take account of the intrinsically difficult nature of demonstrating a bribe, arbitral tribunal need not relax – but should not enhance – the civil law standard of "the balance of probabilities" or "more likely than not."[89]

---

[84] EDF Services Limited v. Romania, ICSID Case No ARB/05/13, Award, 8 October 2009, para. 221.

[85] Partasides (2010), p. 56.

[86] *See,* Born (2014).

[87] *See,* Gaillard (2019); Partasides (2010), pp. 47–62; Devendra (2019); Llamzon (2014), para. 9.26; Mills, K. (2003), Corruption and Other Illegality in the Formation and performance of Contracts and in the Conduct of Arbitrations Relating Thereto, in International Commercial Arbitration: Important Contemporary Questions, ICCA Congress Series No. 11, p. 295.

[88] Karadelis, K. (2010), Corruption and the standard of proof, Global Arbitration Review, available at https://globalarbitrationreview.com/print_article/gar/article/1029476/corruption-and-the-standard-of-proof.

[89] Partasides (2010), p. 58.

On addressing the natural difficulty of proving certain questions, the ISDS system can get inspiration from the current practice in international commercial arbitration and other international dispute settlement mechanisms.

As to commercial arbitration, there is record of using an "average" (i.e. not heightened) standard of proof for illegality allegations at least as of 1984.[90] However, for completeness, it should be noted that just like in the ISDS cases, the approach in international commercial arbitration is still not entirely consistent.[91]

Concerning other international dispute settlement institutions, attention is drawn to international tribunals that at times have to decide certain questions over which they do not have direct powers of investigation (as would national courts do) and over which it would be difficult to find clear-cut objective evidence. There are currently two possible examples that have been identified:

- The International Criminal Court does not explicitly apply the criminal standard of "beyond reasonable doubt" for awarding reparations to victims because of the difficulty of proving loss in many cases;[92]
- The UN Compensation Commission required only a "reasonable minimum" of evidence for some categories of claims brought before it.[93]

Conclusively, it is observed that there is already a slow, inconsistent but still changing approach to the question of determination of the applicable standard of proof for allegations of fraud and corruption in international investment arbitration. The change seems to be inspired by a growing number of relevant case law and scholar opinions. As was demonstrated above, this "relaxed" approach has its reflection in international commercial arbitration and other international dispute settlement mechanisms.

When the observations made above are reviewed in light of the fact that the ISDS mechanism does not have an objective to convict persons responsible for criminal wrongdoings and/or somehow deprive such persons from their freedoms and rights,[94] one may presume that there is no grave risk in applying a lowered or

---

[90] ICC Award No. 4145, Second Interim Award, Yearbook of Commercial Arbitration 1987, p. 97, para. 27.

[91] *See,* Westinghouse International Projects Company, Westinghouse Elec. S.A. and Barns & Roe Enterprise, Inc. v. National Power Corporation and the Republic of the Philippines, ICC Case No 6401, Preliminary Award, paras. 33–35, where the tribunal found that "clear" and convincing evidence of corruption amounting to "more than a mere preponderance" was necessary; *see also,* ICC Case No. 8133 (1996), Himpurna California Energy Ltd. v. Patuha Power Ltd., UNCITRAL, Award, 1999, para. 116.

[92] International Criminal Court, Finalized Draft Rules of Procedure and Evidence, available at https://undocs.org/pdf?symbol=en/PCNICC/2000/1.

[93] Decision taken by the Governing Council of the UN Compensation Commission, 27th meeting, 6th session, UN Doc. S/AC.26/1992/10, 1992, p. 19, para. 35(2)(c) quoted in Partasides (2010), p. 58.

[94] Churchill Mining PLC and Planet Mining Pty Ltd v. Republic of Indonesia, ICSID Case No. ARB/12/14 and 12/40, Award, 6 December 2016, para. 243: "While intent and motive may be required for a criminal act of forgery or fraud, the present proceedings are not aimed at

not-heightened standard of proof for allegations of fraud and corruption in investor-state disputes.

Finally and based on all the above, it is proposed that international investment tribunals are to be advised on the complications and **risks** of applying heightened standards of proof for allegations of illicit misconduct and are to be made aware of the current changing approach in applying lowered evidentiary standards for questions of illegality.

References

Betz K (2017) Proving bribery, fraud and money laundering in international arbitration. University of Basel, Cambridge University Press, p 131

Blackaby N, Partasides C, Redfern A, Hunter M (2009) Redfern and Hunter on international arbitration, 5th edn. Oxford University Press

Born G (2014) International commercial arbitration, vol II, 2nd edn. Kluwer Law International, Hague

Brown C (2007) A common law of international adjudication. Oxford University Press, pp 94–95

Carreteiro (2016) Burden and standard of proof in international arbitration: proposed guidelines for promoting predictability. Revista Brasileira de Arbitragem 13(49)

Cheng B (1953) General principles of law as applied by international courts and tribunals. Cambridge University Press, p 327

Crivellaro A (2003) Arbitration case law on bribery: issues of arbitrability, contract validity, merits and evidence. In: Karsten K, Berkeley A (eds) Arbitration, money laundering, corruption and fraud. Dossiers - ICC Institute of World Business Law, pp 115–117

Devendra IC (2019) State responsibility for corruption in international investment arbitration. J Int Dispute Settlement 10(2)

Fathallah R (2010) Corruption in international commercial and investment arbitration: recent trends and prospects for Arab countries. Int J Arab Arbitr 2(3):73–77

Gaillard E (2019) The emergence of transnational responses to corruption in international arbitration. J Int Arbitr 35(1)

Hanotiau B (1994) Satisfying the burden of proof: the viewpoint of a "civil law" lawyer. J Int Arbitr 10(3):341–343

Lamm CB, Pham HT, Moloo R (2010) Fraud and corruption in international arbitration. In: Fernandez-Ballesteros, Arias (eds) Liber Amicorum Bernardo Cremades. Kluwer, pp 704–705

Llamzon A (2014) Corruption in international investment arbitration. Oxford University Press

Low L (2019) Dealing with allegations of corruption in international arbitration. Am J Int Law Unbound 113

Mehren R (1992) Rules of arbitral bodies considered from a practical point of view. J Int Arbitr 9(3):110

establishing criminal liability. Here the Tribunal must determine whether the impugned documents are authentic for purposes of an action seeking to engage the international responsibility of a State." *See also*, the approach taken by Lord Justice Denning's analysis in a commercial dispute in the case before an English court Bater v. Bater as cited in Rosell and Prager (1999), p. 347: "The court, when considering a charge of fraud, will naturally require a higher degree of probability than that which it would require when asking if negligence is established. It does not adopt so high degree as a criminal court, even when it is considering a charge of a criminal nature; but still it does require a degree of probability which is commensurate with the occasion."

Mourre A (2006) Arbitration and criminal law: reflections on the duties of the arbitrator. J Int Arbitr 22(1):102

Partasides C (2010) Proving corruption in international arbitration: a balanced standard for the real world. ICSID Rev: Foreign Invest Law J 25(1)

Raouf M (2009) How should international arbitrators tackle corruption issues? ICSID Rev: Foreign Invest Law J 24(1):122

Redfern A (1994) The practical distinction between the burden of proof and the talking of evidence: an English perspective. J Int Arbitr 10(3):320

Reiner A (1994) Arbitral practice concerning burden and standard(s) of proof. J Int Arbitr 10(3): 333, 340

Reymond C (1994) The practical distinction between the burden of proof and taking of evidence – a further perspective. J Int Arbitr 10(3):232 and 327

Rosell J, Prager H (1999) Illicit commissions and international arbitration: the question of proof. J Int Arbitr 15(4)

Sharp J (2006) Drawing adverse inferences from the non-production of evidence. J Int Arbitr 22: 549

Shreve GR (1998) Procedure et moyens de prevue dans l'arbitrage commercial international. Rev. de l'Arb 2:272

Tsatsos A (2009) Burden of proof in investment treaty arbitration: shifting? Humboldt Forum Recht:91–104

Waincymer J (2012) Procedure and evidence in international arbitration. Kluwer Law International, p 762

Younger I et al (1991) Principles of evidence, 2nd edn. National Practice Institute, Minneapolis, p 857

Chapter 10
Consequences of Corruption for States

If one is to accept the idea that there is consensus that international tribunals are not to entertain disputes over the results of corrupt and fraudulent acts, one of the remaining and challenging questions is what this should mean for the prevailing party. In case of fraud, the answer appears to be quite straightforward. If, for instance, a State or a third party was defrauded, then there is no obvious reason to somehow penalize that party in arbitration. However, the situation could be quite different when discussing corruption.

As was found by *Judge Lagergen* in the ICC Case No 1110 in 1963, parties that ally themselves in an illicit enterprise should realize that "they have forfeited any right to ask for the assistance of the machinery of justice (national courts or arbitral tribunals) in settling their disputes."[1] However, one of the problems that arises here is that when speaking of corruption and bribery of public officials, misconduct is usually not unilateral.[2] As was previously discussed, in corruption "it takes two to tango,"[3] therefore in some cases it could be reasonable to argue that both are at fault. Although, there is an established understanding that *Potior est condition defendentis*—in equal fault, better is the position of the defendant, the question arises whether the "better position" necessarily means an absolute victory.

There is a growing concern that host States may find it attractive to further tolerate solicitation of bribes by foreign investors so that in the future they may avoid any claims under international investment agreements with the help of the so-called "corruption defence", which would ultimately lead to either the denial of jurisdiction

[1] Judge Lagergren's decision in the ICC Case No. 1110, Award, 1963, in Journal of International Arbitration (1994), Volume 3.

[2] Newcombe, A. (2010), Investor misconduct and investment treaty arbitration: mapping the terrain, in Kluwer Arbitration Blog, available at: http://arbitrationblog.kluwerarbitration.com/2010/01/25/investor-misconduct-and-investment-treaty-arbitration-mapping-the-terrain/.

[3] Dine (2017), pp. 81–92.

A. Tussupov, *Corruption and Fraud in Investment Arbitration*, EYIEL Monographs - Studies in European and International Economic Law 22,
https://doi.org/10.1007/978-3-030-90606-1_10

or dismissal of claims.[4] When we think of the current case law, this is indeed true that the current practice could potentially lead to a one-sided approach in determining the "guilt" for corruption, which would usually lay on investors (with several exceptions as discussed further below). Such an approach, if established, could have a very cynical effect of host States willing to ensure (or even "obligate") that foreign investors pay bribes to its public officials, thereby securing a "corruption defence" for a potential ISDS dispute.[5]

A possible way to address such a challenging one-sided approach could be in recognizing the possibility of taking punitive measures against a "partner in crime" for acts of corruption in investment arbitration in certain situations.

First, the question that an international lawyer would ask her/himself is whether the conduct of a public official receiving a bribe shall be equated to the conduct of a whole State. A step by step analysis of the question is warranted.

It is generally clear that a conduct of a state official is attributable to a State under the International Law Commission Articles on Responsibility of States for Internationally Wrongful Acts (the "**Articles**"). Article 4 of the Articles provides the following:

1. The conduct of any State organ shall be considered an act of that State under international law, whether the organ exercises legislative, executive, judicial or any other functions, whatever position it holds in the organization of the State, and whatever its character as an organ of the central Government or of a territorial unit of the State.
2. An organ includes any person or entity which has that status in accordance with the internal law of the State.[6]

From the above, it is evident that the conduct of any public official within the state system, holding whatever position, would be equated to the conduct of a State. This is a long established norm in international law that was confirmed in the German Settlers case by the Permanent Court of International Justice in 1923.[7] The position that a State shall be responsible for the acts of its officials/agents is without hesitations supported by public international law scholars too.[8]

The next step would be to see whether such a conduct is still attributable to a State if a public servant receives a bribe, which would naturally be outside of its authority and jurisdiction of a state official. In other words, it is hard to imagine a State where a public official has a provision in his/her job description that says, "soliciting and obtaining bribes and/or illicit commissions". The Articles seem to provide an answer to this question as well, in particular in Article 7 that says the following:

---

[4]Wilske (2010); Meshel (2013); Diel-Gligor and Nennecke (2015); Litwin (2013); Lotz and Busch (2015).

[5]Idumosu (2011).

[6]Article 4 of the Articles on Responsibility of States for Internationally Wrongful Acts, Yearbook of the International Law Commission, 2001, Volume II, Part Two.

[7]German Settlers in Poland, Advisory Opinion, 1923, P.C.I.J., Ser. B, No. 6, p. 22.

[8]*See,* Crawford (2002), pp. 106–109; Shaw (2008), p. 786.

> The conduct of an organ of a State or of a person or entity empowered to exercise elements of the governmental authority shall be considered an act of the State under international law if the organ, person or entity acts in that capacity, *even if it exceeds its authority or contravenes instructions*.[9]

The remaining question when reading Article 7 of the Articles is whether a state official "acts in that capacity" of "a person. . .empowered to exercise elements of the governmental authority" when he/she receives a bribe. The commentaries to the Articles distinguish two types of conduct of a state official, i.e. (i) "official" conduct and (ii) "private" conduct.[10] The commentaries of the International Law Commission provide the following view:

> This indicates that the conduct referred to comprises only the actions and omissions of organs purportedly or apparently carrying out their official functions, and not the private actions or omissions of individuals who happen to be organs or agents of the State. *In short, the question is whether they were acting with apparent authority*.[11]

It seems clear that a state official, when soliciting a bribe, does not act as a private person "who happens to be" an agent of a State. Such a person, in fact, acts "with apparent authority" and is in a position of power that has been inferred upon him/her by a State. Moreover, the commentaries to the draft articles go even beyond this (already very convincing) reasoning and set a very relevant example:

> One form of ultra vires conduct covered by article 7 would be for *a State official to accept a bribe* to perform some act or conclude some transaction.[12]

It is recognized that a matter of distinguishing and drawing a line between private conduct and conduct in official capacity of a public servant is quite delicate. However, there is sufficient study that has been done supporting the attribution of such conduct (i.e. illicit/corrupt) to the conduct of a State that was made in different cases before international tribunals[13] and in scholarly writings.[14]

Furthermore, a question whether a State should be held internationally responsible for the conduct of a corrupt official is a separate topic, which is partly outside of

---

[9] Article 7 of the Articles on Responsibility of States for Internationally Wrongful Acts, Yearbook of the International Law Commission, 2001, Volume II, Part Two [emphasis added].

[10] Draft articles on Responsibility of States for Internationally Wrongful Acts, with commentaries, adopted by the International Law Commission at its fifty-third session, and submitted to the General Assembly as a part of the Commission's report covering the work of that session (A/56/10), 2001, p. 46, para. 8.

[11] *Id.* [emphasis added].

[12] *Id.*, footnote 150 [emphasis added].

[13] *See,* Gustave Caire (France) v. United Mexican States, French-Mexican Claims Commission, 1929; Kenneth P. Yeager v. The Islamic Republic of Iran, Iran – United States of America Claims Tribunal, Case No. 10199, 1987; Francisco Mallén (United Mexican States) v. U.S.A., Mexico-US General Claims Commission, 1927; United States Diplomatic and Consular Staff in Tehran (United States of America v. Iran), ICJ Judgement, ICJ Reports, 1980.

[14] Devendra (2019); Llamzon (2013); Kulick and Wendler (2010), p. 78.

the scope of the present monograph.[15] It is, nevertheless, noted that the legal basis for arbitral tribunal's valuation of host State's conduct connecting to corruption can be derived from various international legal instruments dealing with corruption and bribery, such as the Anti-Bribery Convention, the 2003 United Nations Convention Against Corruption, the 1996 Inter-American Convention against Corruption, the 1997 Convention on the Fight against Corruption involving Officials of the European Communities or Officials of Member States of the European Union and the 1999 Criminal Law Convention on Corruption.

Second, from the current case law, it is evident that there is an increasing practice of investment tribunals opining on States being complicit for corruption. There are also examples where arbitrators take actual (more or less) punitive measures against States that allege and subsequently prevail with corruption arguments. Although this practice is not uniformed in its application and in its scope, there is nevertheless growing awareness that under certain circumstances States could also be held responsible for investments that were obtained through corruption and, in some rare cases—through fraud.

In addition to the case law that was analysed in Part II where arbitral tribunals took certain steps or expressed opinions on this topic, i.e. the World Duty Free, the Metal-Tech, the Spentex and the EDF cases, this (or a similar) trend can be observed in several other investor-state disputes.

For instance, in the Ioannis Kardassopoulos v. Georgia case, the arbitral tribunal found that "a host State cannot avoid jurisdiction under the BIT by invoking its own failure to comply with its domestic law."[16] It is to be noted that while the Ioannis tribunal does conclude that a State cannot use its own breach of domestic law as defence against the jurisdiction of the tribunal, it does not opine on the question whether a State may still use it as defence at the merits stage or whether the investor's claims could be later declared inadmissible, if the allegations were proven to be true. Particular attitude of the arbitral tribunal towards the State alleging illegality in this case is, nevertheless, evident.

In another ICSID case between Niko Resources Ltd and Bangladesh, the tribunal did not uphold the allegations of corruption and assumed its jurisdiction. However, in doing so, the arbitral tribunal partly referred to the State's reluctance to take

---

[15]This would include an analysis under Article 2 of the Articles, in particular whether a State (through the conduct of its corrupt public official) violated its obligation under international law.

[16]Ioannis Kardassopoulos v. Georgia, ICSID Case No. ARB/05/18, Decision on Jurisdiction, 6 July 2007, para. 182. *See also,* the Dissenting Opinion of Mr. Bernardo M. Cremades in the Fraport AG Frankfurt Airport Services Worldwide v. The Republic of the Philippines, ICSID Case No. ARB/03/25, para. 37, which also indicates a particular attitude towards states alleging corruption in ISDS cases: "In the Biblical phrase, the Tribunal must first examine the speck in the eye of the investor and defer, and maybe never address, a beam in the eye of the Host State. Such an approach does not respect fundamental principles of procedure."

appropriate steps towards alleged fraud years before the investment arbitration started:[17]

> The events were widely publicised in Bangladesh and, shortly after they had become public the Minister concerned resigned. Petrobangla and BAPEX, with the approval of the Bangladesh Government, nevertheless entered into the GPSA. If and to the extent the Claimant or its parent company had unclean hands, the Respondents disregarded this situation. They may not now rely on these events to deny jurisdiction under an arbitration agreement which they then accepted.[18]

This analysis of the Niko Resources tribunal can be paralleled with the theory that a State can be estopped from running an "unclean hands" argument against an investor, if the facts of illegality had been known to it before and it failed to take appropriate legal measures to address such illegality.

In another ISDS case between a U.K. investor, Wena Hotels Ltd. and the Arab Republic of Egypt, the arbitral tribunal recognized the ultimate consequence of corruption being the dismissal of claims.[19] However, after doing so, it did not end up deciding on the corruption arguments presented by Egypt. The arbitral tribunal chose not to look further into corruption allegations mainly because of Egypt's reluctance in disclosing the results of its internal criminal investigations against its own public official who, according to Egypt's defense, received the bribe:

> ... it is undisputed that Mr Kandil was never prosecuted in Egypt in connection with this agreement. Regrettably, because Egypt has failed to present the Tribunal with any information about the investigation requested by Minister Sultan, the Tribunal does not know whether an investigation was conducted and, if so, whether the investigation was closed because the prosecutor determined that Mr Kandil was innocent, because of lack evidence, or because of complicity by other government officials. Nevertheless, given the fact that the Egyptian government was made aware of this agreement by Minister Sultan but decided (for whatever reasons) not to prosecute Mr Kandil, the Tribunal is reluctant to immunize Egypt

---

[17] One of the main reasons in declining the State's corruption arguments was the tribunal's finding that the doctrine of clean hands had a questionable position in international law (if at all), *see* Niko Resources (Bangladesh) Ltd. v. Bangladesh Petroleum Exploration & Production Company Limited and Bangladesh Oil Gas and Mineral Corporation, ICSID Case No. ARB/10/18, Decision on Jurisdiction, para. 477 with references to Guyana v. Suriname, PCA, Award of 17 September 2007 (under UNCLOS Ch VII): "No generally accepted definition of the clean hands doctrine has been elaborated in international law. Indeed, the Commentaries of the ILC Draft Articles on State Responsibility acknowledge that the doctrine has been applied rarely and, when it has been invoked, its expression has come in many forms. The ICJ has on numerous occasions declined to consider the application of the doctrine, and has never relied on it to bar admissibility of a claim or recovery." The Niko tribunal then applied the test of the UNCLOS Arbitral Tribunal in the Guyana v. Suriname case (2007) on the (possible) application of the doctrine of clean hands, *see* para. 483 of the Decision on Jurisdiction in the Niko v. Bangladesh case and paras. 420–421 of the Award in the Guyana v. Suriname case (2007) under UNCLOS.

[18] Niko Resources (Bangladesh) Ltd. v. Bangladesh Petroleum Exploration & Production Company Limited and Bangladesh Oil Gas and Mineral Corporation, ICSID Case No. ARB/10/18, Decision on Jurisdiction, 19 August 2013, para. 484.

[19] Wena Hotels Ltd. v. Arab Republic of Egypt, ICSID Case No. ARB/98/4, Award, 8 December 2000, para. 111: "If true, these allegations are disturbing and ground for dismissal of this claim."

> from liability in this arbitration because it now alleges that the agreement with Mr Kandil was illegal under Egyptian law.[20]

Summarily, as evident from the analysis of case law in Part II and further investment tribunals' decisions in this chapter, under certain conditions tribunals are capable of taking punitive steps against States for either soliciting bribery or tolerating corruption or any other illicit act that was known to the State before arbitration.

Finally, there are increasing voices raised in legal literature, addressing the issue of States' participation in corrupt practices,[21] with some dating back to 1953.[22] *Diel-Gligor* and *Nennecke* opined that

> ...if the host State, in bad faith, has tolerated the unlawful behaviour of the investor, and the investor has subsequently relied on the validity of his investment, the host State is barred from invoking the breach of its national law.[23]

An interesting and an illustrative example on tribunal's jurisdiction despite the payment of a bribe by an investor was given by *Lotz* and *Busch*, providing that

> ...if a bribe was paid to an official who thereupon issued a necessary license, but the conditions for a lawful license were fulfilled and the administration was bound to grant the license anyway, a good argument can be put forward in favour of such an investment still being in accordance with the (substantive) laws of the host State.[24]

Similarly to what had likely triggered the negative reaction of the Spentex tribunal towards the State, *Raouf* concluded that "[i]f a host State takes no action to investigate or prosecute the corrupt acts of its own officials, it should forfeit its right to rely on corruptions as a defense."[25] In other words, this idea is not as much connected to state agent's participation in the illegal act, but a State's reluctance to take investigatory and prosecutory measures *post factum*.

As evident from various scholar opinions, as well as international investment tribunals' decisions, there are different views on this question, ranging from quite

[20] *Id.*, para. 116.

[21] *See,* Fitzmaurice (1957), p. 119.

[22] Cheng (1953); Case concerning the factory at Chorzow (Germany v. Poland), Claim for Indemnity (Jurisdiction), 1927, PCIJ, Series A, No 9, pp. 26–31.

[23] Diel-Gligor and Nennecke (2015), p. 574 with reference to Southern Pacific Properties (Middle East) Limited v. Egypt, ICSID Case No. ARB/84/3, Award, 20 May 1992, para. 81; Swembalt AB, Sweden v. Latvia, UNCITRAL, Award, 23 October 2000, para. 35; Technical Medioambientales Tecmed, S.A. v. Mexico, ICSID Case No. ARB(AF)/00/2, Award, 29 May 2003, para. 149; Tokios Tokeles v. Ukraine, ICSID Case No. ARB/02/18, Award, 26 July 2007, para. 86; International Thunderbird Gaming Corporation v. Mexico, UNCITRAL (NAFTA), Award, 26 January 2006, para. 165; World Duty Free v. Kenya, paras. 184–185; Ioannis Kardassopoulos v. Georgia, ICSID Case No. ARB/05/18, Decision on Jurisdiction, 6 July 2007, paras. 191–194; Fraport AG Frankfurt Airport Worldwide v. Philippines, ICSID Case No. ARB/03/25, Award, 16 August 2007, para. 346–347; Desert Line Projects LLC v. Yemen, ICSID Case No. ARB/05/17, Award, 6 February 2008, paras. 117–118, 120.

[24] Lotz and Busch (2015), p. 584.

[25] Raouf (2009), pp. 116 and 135.

radical to mild.[26] Such views and propositions could be substantiated with the so-called "zero tolerance approach" that is said to be developed in international investment arbitration.[27]

To summarise all the above, it could be proposed that arbitral tribunals should be made aware of their ability to take punitive measures against a State for their own wrong-doing or reluctance to investigate the wrong-doing of their public officials under certain circumstances. Such measures, in exceptional cases, may be reflected in as much as simply obliging a State to cover the costs of the proceedings or even the legal fees of another party.

In other words, arbitral tribunals are free to choose appropriate steps within their powers and jurisdiction, if such steps are just and are for the benefit of combating corruption. As was discussed before, any step taken against corruption is a step taken for the benefit of all parties, including a State itself. In this connection, the arbitral tribunal in the Metal-Tech case made a notable remark, stating that "[t]he idea . . . is not to punish one party at the cost of the other, but rather to ensure the promotion of the rule of law, which entails that a court or tribunal cannot grant assistance to a party that has engaged in a corrupt act."[28] This is exactly the point of the current chapter—it was not a default function of investment tribunals to punish parties for illicit acts, however, it happens so that such punitive measures (whether directed against an investor or a State, *or both*) is in the interest of justice and the rule of law. Accordingly, when such measures are not taken, it means that an arbitral tribunal failed to take necessary steps for the benefit of the system at large.

---

[26] The author is not in complete agreement with all ideas. However, it is, nevertheless, important to reflect on the current debate over this scope of questions. For further opinions expressed in the legal literature, *see also,* Cremades (2005); Wilske (2010); Meshel (2013); Alekhin and Shmatenko (2018); Cosar (2015).

[27] *See*, Fernández-Armesto (2015).

[28] Metal-Tech Ltd. v. Republic of Uzbekistan, ICSID Case No. ARB/10/3, Award, 4 October 2013, para. 389. *See also,* Holman v. Johnson (1775) 1 Cowp. 341, 343, cited in World Duty Free v. Kenya, para. 181: "...the objection, that a contract is immoral or illegal as between plaintiff and defendant, sounds at all times very ill in the mouth of the defendant. It is not for his sake, however, that the objection is ever allowed; but it is founded in general principles of policy, which the defendant has the advantage of, contrary to the real justice, as between him and the plaintiff, but accidentally, if I may say so. The principle of public policy is this: ex dolo malo non oritur action. No court will lend its aid to a man who founds his cause of action upon an immoral or illegal act. If, from the plaintiff's own stating of otherwise, the cause of action appears to arise ex turpi causa, or the transgression of a positive law of this country, there the court says he has no right to be assisted. It is upon that ground the court goes; not for the sake of the defendant, but because they will not lend their aid to such a plaintiff. So if the plaintiff and defendant were to change sides, and the defendant was to bring his action against the plaintiff, the latter would then have the advantage of it; for where both are equally at fault, potior est condition defendentis."

References

Alekhin S, Shmatenko L (2018) Corruption in investor-state arbitration – it takes two to tango. In: Asoskov et al (eds) New horizons of international arbitration, Issue 4, Collection of Articles

Cheng B (1953) General principles of law as applied by international courts and tribunals. Cambridge University Press

Cosar U (2015) Claims of corruption in investment treaty arbitration: proof, legal consequences and sanctions. In: van den Berg AJ (ed) Legitimacy: myths, realities, challenges, ICCA Congress Series. No. 18. Kluwer Law International

Crawford J (2002) The International Law Commission's articles on state responsibility: introduction, text and commentaries. Cambridge University Press, pp 106–109

Cremades BM (2005) Corruption and investment arbitration. In: Aksen G et al (eds) Global reflections on international law, commerce and dispute resolution: Liber Amicorum in honour of Robert Briner. ICC Publication No. 693

Devendra IC (2019) State responsibility for corruption in international investment arbitration. J Int Dispute Settlement 10(2)

Diel-Gligor K, Nennecke R (2015) Investment in accordance with the law. In: Bungenberg M et al (eds) A handbook: international investment law

Dine J (2017) It takes two people to tango (or more!). In: Rowley C, dela Rama M (eds) The changing face of corruption in the Asia Pacific, pp 81–92

Fernández-Armesto J (2015) The effects of a positive finding of corruption. In: Baizeau D, Kreindler RH (eds) Addressing issues of corruption in commercial and investment arbitration. Dossiers of the ICC Institute of World Business Law, vol 13, ICC Publication No. 768E

Fitzmaurice G (1957) The general principles of international law. Recueil des Cours 92:119

Idumosu I (2011) International investment arbitration and corruption claims: an analysis of World Duty Free v. Kenya. Law Dev Rev 4

Kulick A, Wendler C (2010) A corrupt way to handle corruption? Thoughts on the recent ICISD case law on corruption. In: Legal Issues of Economic Integration. Kluwer Law International, vol 37(1), p 78

Litwin D (2013) On the divide between investor-state arbitration and the global fight against corruption. Transnatl Dispute Manag 3(1)

Llamzon AP (2013) State responsibility for corruption: the attribution asymmetry in international investment arbitration. Transnatl Dispute Manag 3, available at www.transnational-dispute-management.com/article.asp?key=1958

Lotz RA, Busch M (2015) Investment in accordance with the law – specifically corruption. In: Bungenberg M et al (eds) A handbook: international investment law

Meshel T (2013) The use and misuse of the corruption defence in international investment arbitration. J Int Arbitr 30

Raouf M (2009) How should international arbitrators tackle corruption issues? ICSID Rev: Foreign Invest Law J 24(1):116 and 135

Shaw MN (2008) International law, 6th edn. Cambridge University Press, p 786

Wilske S (2010) Sanctions for unethical and illegal behavior in international arbitration: a double-edged sword. Contemp Asia Arbitr J 3

Chapter 11
Multilateral Investment Court?

The analysis and findings made in the chapters above clearly indicate that while there is a strong legal framework, track-record and academic support in combating corruption and fraud in international investment law and arbitration, the efforts are not united and the practice is not uniformed.

It is accepted that, just as any other system of law, international investment law would need time and practice to find its own natural way towards effectively addressing the allegations of illegality. This is in particular true due to the very nature of investor-state disputes that includes public elements and that "requires resources beyond those of a single world court, the expertise of quite a different kind."[1] This is one of the reasons of putting forward a proposition that certain evidentiary issues (i.e. the treatment of *red flags—supra,* Sect. 9.1 of Part III) have to be dealt with differently than they would have been dealt with in the setting of international commercial arbitration.

Having said this, it appears to be obvious that the nature of the ISDS system does call for an expedited, but yet detailed, assessment of the need to have a single international dispute resolution institution. Having such an institution would certainly provide a solid platform for uniting efforts in forming '*appropriate*' legal practices and for adopting consistent approaches to certain legal questions, such as examination of corruption and fraud allegations.

Detailed suggestions on such multilateral dispute resolution institutions, or simply an international investment court, have been elaborated by *Kaufmann-Kohler* and *Potestà* in their study of 2017,[2] and by *Bungenberg* and *Reinisch* in more recent

[1] Llamzon (2014), p. 211 with reference to Paulsson (2007), pp. 879 and 887.

[2] Kaufmann-Kohler and Potestà (2017).

A. Tussupov, *Corruption and Fraud in Investment Arbitration*, EYIEL Monographs - Studies in European and International Economic Law 22,
https://doi.org/10.1007/978-3-030-90606-1_11

studies dating 2019[3] and 2021,[4] while the idea itself has been expressed as early as in 2015 by the then EU Commissioner for Trade *Cecilia Malmström.*[5]

Indeed, having such a single multilateral investment court, as it is being referred to by *Bungenberg* and *Reinisch,*[6] could address "the increased public criticism towards traditional investor-state arbitration – be it ad hoc or institutional,"[7] which would necessarily include the issues of consistency with respect of questions of corruption and fraud. The logic behind such a conclusion is straightforward—having a single institution with permanent judges and a two-tiered system[8] would allow for less voluntarism and more uniformity in deciding investor-state disputes.

Moreover, because the suggested draft charter of such a multilateral investment court includes a provision that declares international legal personality, this could provide additional benefits that go far beyond the issues of consistency and uniformity of legal practice.[9] A court in the form of an intergovernmental organisation in the understanding of public international law would make the doctrine *functus officio,* at least to a certain respect, obsolete. In other words, if now, according to this doctrine, arbitral tribunals cease to exist in law after rendering a final award,[10] then with creation of a single investment court, the relevant dispute resolution body would continue to exist.

The practical relevance of this is multi-headed. However, for the purposes of this monograph, one feature is of particular interest and relevance, namely—being an independent international organisation, the court "with its own organs and with separate legal personality"[11] could enter into legal relationships with other entities, including with anti-money laundering and anti-corruption agencies. This could enable the investment court to have more solid *investigative* powers and resources when being met with the task of examining a multi-million or multi-billion corruption or money-laundering schemes. This could be a *win-win* situation for both the

---

[3] Bungenberg and Reinisch (2019).

[4] Bungenberg and Reinisch (2021).

[5] *Id.,* p. 12 with reference to Malmström (2015) Speech: remarks at the European Parliament on Investment in TTIP of 18 March 2015, available at http://trade.ec.europa.eu/doclib/press/index.cfm?id=1279&title=Speech-Remarks-at-the-European-Parliament-on-Investment-in-TTIP:
"However, I believe that we should aim for a court that goes beyond TTIP. A multilateral court would be a more efficient use of resources and have more legitimacy. That makes it a medium-term objective to be achieved in parallel to our negotiations with the United States. I hope for Parliament's support and advice as we try to achieve it."

[6] Bungenberg and Reinisch (2019).

[7] Bungenberg and Reinisch (2021), p. 8.

[8] Bungenberg and Reinisch (2019), para. 8.

[9] Article 5 of the Draft Statute of the Multilateral Investment Court, in Bungenberg and Reinisch (2021), p. 50.

[10] Berkoff, L.A. (2019), Clarifying an Otherwise Final Award: An Exception to the Functus Officio Doctrine, available at https://businesslawtoday.org/2019/06/clarifying-otherwise-final-award-exception-functus-officio-doctrine/.

[11] Bungenberg and Reinisch (2019), para. 9.

ISDS system and the international efforts in combating crime, corruption and money laundering. This will surely be welcomed by the European financial intelligence units and by other similar entities.[12] In this regard, we could recall the dissenting opinion of *Vicuna* in the Siag v. Egypt case, in which the arbitrator opined that the arbitral tribunal should have sought assistance of the Interpol when examining the allegations of fraud.[13] Clearly, this would have been possible in the case of a multilateral investment court under the *Bungenberg/Reinisch* model.[14]

Besides, having a court in the form of an international organisation would also make it possible for the court to issue practice guidelines and directions that could be binding not only for judges/arbitrators, but also for parties. The reason for this would be the very nature of the court and its constituting instrument, i.e. an international treaty. This could be in particular important and timely for what concerns the rules on taking of evidence, disclosure and cooperation.

With the technological progress, rules and practices have to be constantly updated so as to meet the current realities. The status quo is that the change of the legal framework of the ISDS mechanism is usually affected by the States, who in their own capacity "meet and greet" these issues through participation in various working groups, conventions and conferences. This is in contrast with, for example, the international legal protection of human rights system, where States effectively delegate certain policy matters, let alone procedural questions, to intergovernmental organizations. Having a single multilateral investment court could make the whole system more flexible for necessary change, thereby making it less vulnerable towards rapid socio-economic developments.

For the reasons set out above, the final proposal of this monograph is to expedite and set in motion an active discussion around the creation of a single multilateral investment court with permanent judges and in the form of an international organisation.

References

Bungenberg M, Reinisch A (2019) From bilateral arbitral tribunals and investment courts to a multilateral investment court - options regarding the institutionalization of investor-state dispute settlement, 2nd edn. Springer Open, available at https://link.springer.com/book/10.1007/978-3-662-59732-3

[12] Committee of Experts on the Evaluation of Anti-Money Laundering Measures and the Financing of Terrorism, Financial Intelligence Units, available at https://www.coe.int/en/web/moneyval/implementation/fiu.

[13] Waguih Elie George Siag and Clorinda Vecchi v. the Arab Republic of Egypt, ICSID Case No ARB/05/15, Dissenting Opinion of Professor Francisco Orrego Vicuña to the Final Award, 11 May 2009, p. 4.

[14] Bungenberg and Reinisch (2021), p. 8.

Bungenberg M, Reinisch A (2021) Draft statute of the multilateral investment court, 1st edn. Nomos, available at https://www.nomos-elibrary.de/10.5771/9783748924739/draft-statute-of-the-multilateral-investment-court

Kaufmann-Kohler G, Potestà M (2017) The composition of a multilateral investment court and of an appeal mechanism for investment awards CIDS supplemental report. Geneva Center for International Dispute Settlement, available at https://www.uncitral.org/pdf/english/workinggroups/wg_3/CIDS_Supplemental_Report.pdf

Llamzon A (2014) Corruption in international investment arbitration. Oxford University Press, p 211

Paulsson J (2007) International arbitration and the generation of legal norms: treaty arbitration and international law. In: van den Berg AJ (ed) International Arbitration 2006: 'back to basics?', ICCA International Arbitration Congress Series No. 13, pp 879 and 887

Chapter 12
Conclusions

As was discussed in the introductory chapters of this textbook, international investment law undergoes constant development and changes. Being an integral (and unique) part of public international law, it would be fair to say that it is currently its biggest and fastest engine when it comes to re-shaping and re-formulating certain approaches and legal principles. In light of this and other characteristics, such as its completeness as a system of law with its own dispute settlement and enforcement mechanisms, international investment law is presently in the most convenient position for fighting illicit elements in international legal affairs,[1] irrespective of the fact whether it was originally designed[2] and/or expected to assume such a role.[3]

It is clear now that international investment law is unexpectedly (and hopefully) about to become an "upper dog" in public international law when it comes to combatting corruption and fraud in international economic relations. While it might sound odd for a moment, the truth is that there are no current (international law) alternatives that would be capable of effectively dealing with the "cancer of corruption"[4] with binding legal force. As *Reisman* was arguing, arbitration shall be able to adopt and/or invent its own control mechanisms.[5] Some other authors believe that international arbitration is already "playing a greater role in the global fight

[1] *Llamzon* opined that generally only "few mechanisms under international law have the potential to play a direct role in controlling corruption", Llamzon (2008), pp. 208–212.

[2] *See,* the opinion expressed by Odumosu saying that "[t]he arbitral system is not designed to comprehensively assess the relevant issues that need to be addressed in order to make a robust determination of alleged corruption." in Odumosu (2011), pp. 88–129.

[3] *See generally*, Clouet (2018).

[4] Annual Meetings Speech of the President of the World Bank Group, Mr. James D. Wolfensohn, Coalitions for Change, 28 September 1999, available at https://www.imf.org/external/am/1999/speeches/pr02e.pdf, p. 1.

[5] Reisman (1992).

A. Tussupov, *Corruption and Fraud in Investment Arbitration*, EYIEL Monographs - Studies in European and International Economic Law 22,
https://doi.org/10.1007/978-3-030-90606-1_12

against corruption"[6] and that those who are sceptical about its role "should think twice"[7] before making conclusions in this regard. This leads to a logical and pressing question as to what other theoretical and practical tools would ISDS need for it to be ready for the upcoming and present challenges in its fight against illicit business conduct.

The need for further developing and strengthening of international investment law and its dispute settlement mechanism would be in the best interests of both States and investors. More importantly, this would also be in the interests of the rule of law, justice, integrity and international public policy.

The immediate interest of States in tribunals that are capable of dealing with investments that are tainted by illicit conduct is quite clear—States would not be held entirely accountable for possible wrongdoings because illicit investments should have no place in international investment law and ISDS. However, there is another collateral positive effect of "capable tribunals" for States (or rather for their civil societies), which is the possibility of re-shaping national public policy of host States in a way that would ensure zero tolerance towards corruption. A rare example of an effective act in incentivising a host State to deal with its internal anti-corruption policy and investment climate can be witnessed in the Spentex case.[8]

This collateral positive effect would also be beneficial for foreign *bona fide* investors, as they would receive more assurances that host States follow the rule of law and do not tolerate fraud and corruption. They would also enjoy from better competition without fear of being punished if they do not follow the "rules of the game" of corrupt regimes.[9] Quite generally, the elimination or significant decrease of illicit schemes (including corruption) could have a positive effect on the growth of foreign direct investments.[10]

It has been observed that there is sufficient legal framework in international investment law that can be used for addressing corruption and fraud. It has also been seen that arbitral tribunals are generally capable of dealing with allegations of corruption and fraud. Arbitrators possess all the necessary tools for such types of cases and there is already a solid record of arbitral decisions addressing fraud and corruption. From the chronological analysis of case law, it has become obvious that there is a positive trend of arbitral tribunals becoming more powerful and confident with illegality cases than just a decade ago. The same trend is evident among academic circles in the field of international investment law and arbitration.

[6] Fathallah (2010), p. 90.

[7] Rose (2014), p. 183.

[8] *See,* Spentex v. Uzbekistan discussed in Sect. 6.4 of Part II.

[9] Partasides (2010), p. 48: "Let us also recognise that it must also be opposed for the way in which – for investors – it distorts competition: improperly menacing investors to incur concealed investment costs, and improperly punishing those investors that do not succumb to those menaces."

[10] *Id.* "Evidently, illicit commissions (i.e. bribery) distorts capital markets and negatively affects foreign direct investments."

At the same time and despite the above, there is still a number of outstanding issues that create a situation of uncertainty in international investment arbitration. This uncertainty appears to be primarily based on the lack of consistency in arbitral tribunals' approaches to certain questions, such as proving and substantiating allegations of illicit conduct. This inconsistency in approach becomes even more topical, relevant and obvious when looking at it in light of the statement made sixteen years ago by *Paulson* who observed that "[b]ased on the experience of the last decade, it is hardly an understatement that major disputes between investors and states are being resolved by adjudication every month."[11] The present reality in investment arbitration is even sharper and more intense, which is why the question of consistency of approaches to such important topics as corruption and fraud shall be highly prioritized.

In the frames of this textbook, a number of propositions have been made that could potentially address the outstanding issues and challenges of the ISDS tribunals' combat against corruption and fraud. It was suggested to reconsider the evidentiary standards through, e.g. (i) the use of ordinary (non-heightened) standards of proof, (ii) possibility of sharing or shifting the burden of proof, (iii) admitting and recognizing *red flags* as evidence of illicit misconduct. On a more substantive level, it was suggested to re-examine the current approach to the determination of responsibility for illicit wrongdoing, especially in cases of corruption, where "it takes two to tango". Last, but certainly not least, the monograph touched upon the live topic of creation of a single multilateral investment court with international legal personality. It is strongly believed that such an entity, in the suggested form,[12] could breathe in new life into the system of international legal protection of foreign investments.

Conclusively, the main statement of this monograph is that the ISDS is capable and potentially more powerful than any other system in combating corruption and fraud on international level.

References

Bungenberg M, Reinisch A (2021) Draft statute of the multilateral investment court, 1st edn. Nomos, available at https://www.nomos-elibrary.de/10.5771/9783748924739/draft-statute-of-the-multilateral-investment-court

Clouet LM (2018) Arbitrating under the table: the effect of allegations of corruption in relation to the jurisdiction of the arbitral tribunal and the enforcement of foreign arbitral awards, available at https://nyu.academia.edu/LuisMar%C3%ADaClouet

Fathallah R (2010) Corruption in international commercial and investment arbitration: recent trends and prospects for Arab countries. Int J Arab Arbitr 2(3):90

Llamzon A (2008) The control of corruption through international investment arbitration: potential and limitations. In: Proceedings of the American Society of International Law on 9–12 April, 2008, vol 102, pp 208–212

[11] Llamzon (2014), p. 211 with reference to Paulsson (2007), pp. 879 and 887.

[12] Bungenberg and Reinisch (2021).

Llamzon A (2014) Corruption in international investment arbitration. Oxford University Press, p 211

Odumosu I (2011) International investment arbitration and corruption claims: an analysis of World Duty Free v. Kenya. Law Dev Rev 4(3):88–129

Partasides C (2010) Proving corruption in international arbitration: a balanced standard for the real world. ICSID Rev: Foreign Invest Law J 25(1):48

Paulsson J (2007) International arbitration and the generation of legal norms: treaty arbitration and international law. In: van den Berg AJ (ed) International Arbitration 2006: 'Back to Basics?', ICCA International Arbitration Congress Series No. 13, pp 879 and 887

Reisman WM (1992) Systems of control in international adjudication and arbitration. Duke University Press

Rose C (2014) Questioning the role of international arbitration in the fight against corruption. J Int Arbitr 31:183

Documents

Agreement between the Federative Republic of Brazil and the Federal Democratic Republic of Ethiopia on Investment Cooperation and Facilitation dated 11 April 2018.

Agreement between the Government of the Australia and the Government of the Republic of Indonesia for the Promotion and Protection of Investments dated 17 November 1992.

Agreement between the Government of the People's Republic of China and the Government of Lao People's Democratic Republic concerning the Encouragement and Reciprocal Protection of Investments dated 31 January 1993.

Agreement between the Government of the Republic of Kazakhstan and the Government of the Republic of Uzbekistan on Promotion and Reciprocal Protection of Investments dated 2 June 1997.

Agreement between the Government of the State of Israel and the Government of the Republic of Uzbekistan for the Reciprocal Promotion and Protection of Investments dated 4 July 1994.

Agreement between the Government of the United Kingdom of Great Britain and Northern Ireland and the Government of Romania for the Promotion and Reciprocal Protection of Investments dated 13 July 1995.

Agreement between the Government of the United Kingdom of Great Britain and Northern Ireland and the Government of the Republic of Indonesia for the Promotion and Protection of Investments dated 27 April 1976.

Agreement Between the Islamic Republic of Pakistan and the Republic of Turkey concerning the Reciprocal Promotion and Protection of Investments dated 22 May 2012.

Agreement between the Republic of Kyrgyzstan and the Republic of Turkey concerning the reciprocal promotion and protection of investments dated 28 April 1992.

Agreement for the Promotion and Protection of Investments between the Republic of Italy and the Arab Republic of Egypt dated 2 March 1989.

A. Tussupov, *Corruption and Fraud in Investment Arbitration*, EYIEL Monographs - Studies in European and International Economic Law 22,
https://doi.org/10.1007/978-3-030-90606-1

Agreement on encouragement and reciprocal protection of investments between the Kingdom of the Netherlands and the Republic of Uzbekistan dated 14 March 1996.

Annual Meetings Speech of the President of the World Bank Group, Mr. James D. Wolfensohn, Coalitions for Change, 28 September 1999, available at https://www.imf.org/external/am/1999/speeches/pr02e.pdf.

Articles on Responsibility of States for Internationally Wrongful Acts, Yearbook of the International Law Commission, 2001, Volume II, Part Two.

Code of Laws of the United States of America, Title 18.

Committee of Experts on the Evaluation of Anti-Money Laundering Measures and the Financing of Terrorism, Financial Intelligence Units, available at https://www.coe.int/en/web/moneyval/implementation/fiu.

Competence Center on Arbitration and Crime, Basel Institute on Governance (2019), Corruption and Money Laundering in International Arbitration: A Toolkit for Arbitrators, available at https://www.baselgovernance.org/sites/default/files/2019-05/a_toolkit_for_arbitrators_29_05_2019_single_pages.pdf.

Convention on the Settlement of Investment Disputes between States and Nationals of Other States dated 18 March 1965.

Cooperation and Facilitation Investment Agreement between the Federative Republic of Brazil and the Republic of Suriname dated 2 May 2018.

Criminal Code of the Republic of Kazakhstan dated 16 July 1997, No. 167.

Criminal Division of the U.S. Department of Justice and the Enforcement Division of the U.S. Securities and Exchange Commission (2012), A Resource Guide to the U.S. Foreign Corrupt Practices Act, available at https://www.justice.gov/sites/default/files/criminal-fraud/legacy/2015/01/16/guide.pdf.

Draft articles on Responsibility of States for Internationally Wrongful Acts, with commentaries, adopted by the International Law Commission at its fifty-third session, and submitted to the General Assembly as a part of the Commission's report covering the work of that session (A/56/10), 2001.

Ernst and Young (2013), Navigating today's complex resources-business risks, in Europe Middle East, India and Africa Fraud Survey 2013, available at https://www.ey.com/Publication/vwLUAssets/Navigating_todays_complex_business_risks/$FILE/Navigating_todays_complex_business_risks.pdf.

Free Trade Agreement concluded between the Government of the Argentine Republic and the Government of the Republic of Chile dated 2 November 2017.

Free Trade Agreement concluded between the Government of the United States of America and the Government of the Kingdom of Morocco, entered into force on 1 January 2006.

ICC Commission on Corporate Responsibility and Anti-corruption, ICC Guidelines on Agents, Intermediaries, and Third Parties dated 19 November 2010.

Indicators of Commercial Fraud Prepared by the UNCITRAL Secretariat, United Nations, 2013, available at https://www.uncitral.org/pdf/english/texts/fraud/Recognizing-and-preventing-commercial-fraud-e.pdf.

International Arbitration Rules of the American Arbitration Association (2001).

International Bar Association Rules on the Taking of Evidence in International Arbitration, adopted by a resolution of the IBA Council on 29 May 2010.

International Criminal Court, Finalized Draft Rules of Procedure and Evidence, available at https://undocs.org/pdf?symbol=en/PCNICC/2000/1.

Law of the Republic of Kazakhstan No 410-V dated 18 November 2015 on Combating Corruption (Закон Республики Казахстан от 18 ноября 2015 года № 410-V "О противодействии коррупции").

OECD Convention on Combating Bribery of Foreign Public Officials in International Business Transactions dated 17 December 1997.

Reciprocal Investment Promotion and Protection Agreement between the Government of the Kingdom of Morocco and the government of the Federal Republic of Nigeria dated 3 December 2016.

The UNCITRAL Model Law on International Commercial Arbitration, adopted by the United Nations Commission on International Trade Law on 21 June 1985.

The United Kingdom Arbitration Act (1996).

The United Kingdom Fraud Act (2006).

Transparency International (2018), Corruption Perceptions Index, available at https://www.transparency.org/files/content/pages/CPI_2018_Executive_Summary_EN.pdf.

Transparency International UK, Corruption Statistics, available at https://www.transparency.org.uk/corruption/corruption-statistics/.

UK Government (2017), 'Flag It Up', available at https://flagitup.campaign.gov.uk/.

UNCITRAL Arbitration Rules adopted by the General Assembly Resolution No 31/98.

UNCITRAL Secretariat (2013), Recognizing and Preventing Commercial Fraud, Indicators of Commercial Fraud, United Nations, available at https://www.uncitral.org/pdf/english/texts/fraud/Recognizing-and-preventing-commercial-fraud-e.pdf.

United Nations Convention Against Corruption adopted by the General Assembly resolution No 58/4 of 31 October 2003, available at https://www.justice.gov/sites/default/files/criminal-fraud/legacy/2012/12/06/united-nations-convention-against-corruption.pdf.

United States Foreign Corrupt Practices Act (1977).

Woolf Committee Report on Business Ethics, Global Companies and the Defence Industry: Ethical Business Conduct in Bae Systems Plc 25-26 (2008), prepared at the request of the Board of Directors of Bae Systems Plc.

Cases

Administration of the Prince Von Pless (Germany v. Poland), 1933 P.C.I.J., Series A/B, No. 52.
Alasdair Ross Anderson and others v. Costa Rica, ICSID Case No. ARB(AF)/07/3, Award, 19 May 2010.
Alpha Projektholding GmbH v. Ukraine, ICSID Case No. ARB/07/16, Award, 8 November 2010.
Aquas del Tunari S.A. v. Bolivia, ICSID Case No. ARB/02/3, Decision on Respondent's Objections to Jurisdiction, 21 October 2005.
Armed Activities on the Territory of the Congo (Congo v. Rwanda), Decision on the Jurisdiction of the Court and Admissibility of the Application, 3 February 2006, ICJ Reports 2006.
Asian Agricultural Products Ltd. v. Republic of Sri Lanka, ICSID Case No. ARB/87/3, Final Award, 27 June 1990.
Ayodele v. Citylink Ltd & Anor [2017] EWCA Civ 1913.
Azurix Corp. v. The Argentine Republic, ICSID Case No. ARB/01/12, Decision on the Application for Annulment of the Argentine Republic, 1 September 2009.
Biwater Gauff (Tanzania) Ltd. v. United Republic of Tanzania, ICSID Case No. ARB/05/22, Award, 24 July 2008.
Bloomberry Resorts and Hotels Inc. and Sureste Properties, Inc against Global Gaming Philippines LLC and GGAM Netherlands B.V., Judgement of the High Court of the Republic of Singapore, 3 January 2020.
Case concerning Ahmadou Sadio Diallo (Republic of Guinea v. Democratic Republic of the Congo), Judgment, 30 November 2010, ICJ Reports 2010, p. 639.
Case concerning the factory at Chorzow (Germany v. Poland), Claim for Indemnity (Jurisdiction), 1927, Permanent Court of International Justice, Series A, No 9.
Cementownia "Nowa Huta" S.A. v. Republic of Turkey, ICSID Case No. ARB(AF)/06/2, Award, 17 September 2009.
Churchill Mining PLC and Planet Mining Pty Ltd v. Republic of Indonesia, ICSID Case No. ARB/12/14 and 12/40, Award, 6 December 2016.

A. Tussupov, *Corruption and Fraud in Investment Arbitration*, EYIEL Monographs - Studies in European and International Economic Law 22,
https://doi.org/10.1007/978-3-030-90606-1

CME Czech Republic B.V. (The Netherlands) v. The Czech Republic, UNCITRAL Arbitration Proceedings, Final Award, 14 March 2003.

CME Czech Republic B.V. (The Netherlands) v. The Czech Republic, UNCITRAL Arbitration Proceedings, Separate Opinion of Ian Brownlie, C.B.E., Q.C., 14 March 2003.

CME Czech Republic B.V. (The Netherlands) v. The Czech Republic, UNCITRAL Arbitration Proceedings, Dissenting Opinion of JUDr Jaroslav Handl, 11 September 2001.

Corfu Channel case (United Kingdom of Great Britain and Northern Ireland v. Albania), Preliminary Objections, ICJ Reports 1948, p. 15.

Cortec Mining Kenya Limited, Cortec (Pty) Limited and Stirling Capital Limited v. Republic of Kenya, ICSID Case No. ARB/15/29, Award, 22 October 2018.

Decision taken by the Governing Council of the UN Compensation Commission, 27th meeting, 6th session, UN Doc. S/AC.26/1992/10, 1992.

Desert Line Projects LLC v. The Republic of Yemen, ICSID Case No. ARB/05/17, Award, 6 February 2008.

EDF Services Limited v. Romania, ICSID Case No ARB/05/13, Award, 8 October 2009.

Egerton v. Lord Brownlow, [1853] 4 H.L. 1.

Enron Creditors Recovery Corp. Ponderosa Assets, L.P. v. The Argentine Republic, ICSID Case No. ARB/01/3, Decision on the Application for Annulment of the Argentine Republic, 30 July 2010.

Europe Cement Investment & Trade S.A. v. the Republic of Turkey, ICSID Case No. ARB(AF)/07/2, Award, 13 August 2009.

Feldman v. Mexico, NAFTA, Award, 16 December 2002.

Fisheries Jurisdiction (Spain v. Canada), Decision on Preliminary Objection, ICJ Reports 1998.

Francisco Mallén (United Mexican States) v. U.S.A., Mexico-US General Claims Commission, 1927.

Fraport AG Frankfurt Airport Services Worldwide v. The Republic of the Philippines, ICSID Case No. ARB/11/12, Award, 10 December 2014.

Fraport AG Frankfurt Airport Services Worldwide v. The Republic of the Philippines, ICSID Case No. ARB/03/25, Award, 16 August 2007.

Fraport AG Frankfurt Airport Services Worldwide v. The Republic of the Philippines, ICSID Case No. ARB/03/25, Dissenting Opinion of Mr. Bernardo M. Cremades.

Gabčikovo-Nagymaros Project (Hungary v. Slovakia), ICJ Reports 1997, pp. 7, 76.

German Settlers in Poland, Advisory Opinion, 1923, Permanent Court of International Justice, Ser. B, No. 6.

Glencore International A.G. and C.I. Prodeco S.A. v. Republic of Colombia, ICSID Case No. ARB/16/6, Award, 27 August 2019.

GMS Gas Transmission Company v. The Republic of Argentina, ICSID Case No ARB/01/8, Award, 12 May 2005.

Gustav F W Hamester GmbH & Co KG v. Republic of Ghana, ICSID Case No. ARB/07/24, Award, 18 June 2010.

Gustave Caire (France) v. United Mexican States, French-Mexican Claims Commission, 1929.
Holiday Inns S.A. and others v. Morocco, ICSID Case No ARB/72/1, Decision on Jurisdiction, 2 July 1972.
Hulley Enterprises (Cyprus) Limited v. Russia, UNCITRAL, PCA Case No AA 226, Final Award, 18 July 2014.
ICC Award No. 4145, Second Interim Award, Yearbook of Commercial Arbitration 1987, p. 97.
Inceysa Vallisoletana S.L. v. The Republic of El Salvador, ICSID Case No. ARB/03/26, Award, 2 August 2006.
Inmaris Perestroika Sailing Maritime Services GmbH and others v. Ukraine ICSID Case No ARB/08/8, Decision on Jurisdiction, 8 March 2010.
International Thunderbird Gaming Corporation v. Mexico, UNCITRAL (NAFTA), Award, 26 January 2006.
Ioannis Kardassopoulos v. Georgia, ICSID Case No. ARB/05/18, Decision on Jurisdiction, 6 July 2007.
Italian Republic v. Republic of Cuba, Ad hoc Arbitration, Final Award, 1 November 2008.
Jan Oostergetel and Theodora Laurentius v. Slovak Republic, UNCITRAL, Final Award, 23 April 2012.
Karkey Karadeniz Elektrik Uretim A.S. v. The Islamic Republic of Pakistan, ICSID Case No. ARB/13/1, Award, 22 August 2017.
Kenneth P. Yeager v. The Islamic Republic of Iran, Iran – United States of America Claims Tribunal, Case No. 10199, 1987.
Legal Consequences for States of the Continued Presence of South Africa in Namibia (South West Africa) notwithstanding Security Council Resolution 276 (1970), Advisory Opinion, ICJ Reports 1971, p. 16.
Liman Caspian Oil BV and NCL Dutch Investment BV v. The Republic of Kazakhstan, ICSID Case No ARB/07/14, Award, 22 June 2010.
Malicorp Limited v. The Arab Republic of Egypt, ICSID Case No. ARB/08/18, Award, 7 February 2011.
Maritime International Nominees Establishment v. the Government of Guinea, ICSID Case No. ARB/84/4, Decision on the Application by Guinea for Partial Annulment of the Arbitral Award dated 6 January 1988 Ad Hoc Committee, 14 December 1989.
Metalpar S.A. and Buen Aire S.A. v. Argentine, ICSID Case No. ARB/03/5, Decision on Jurisdiction, 21 April 2006.
Metal-Tech Ltd. v. Republic of Uzbekistan, ICSID Case No. ARB/10/3, Award, 4 October 2013.
Methanex Corporation v. United States of America, NAFTA, Partial Award on Jurisdiction and Admissibility, 7 August 2002.
Methanex Corporation v. United States of America, NAFTA, Final Award, 3 August 2005.
Mexico v. United States (US Trucking Case), Ad hoc Arbitration, Final Report, 6 February 2001.

Middle East Cement Shipping and Handling Co. S.A. v. the Arab Republic of Egypt, ICSID Case No ARB/99/6, Decision on Jurisdiction, 28 November 2000.
Military and Paramilitary Activities in and against Nicaragua (Nicaragua v. United States of America) (Merits), Dissenting Opinion of Judge Schwebel, ICJ Reports 1986, pp. 259, 391.
Mytilineos Holdings SA v. Serbia & Montenegro, UNCITRAL, Partial Award, 8 September 2006.
Niko Resources (Bangladesh) Ltd. v. Bangladesh Petroleum Exploration & Production Company Limited and Bangladesh Oil Gas and Mineral Corporation, ICSID Case No. ARB/10/18, Decision on Jurisdiction, 19 August 2013.
Niko Resources (Bangladesh) Ltd. v. Bangladesh Petroleum Exploration & Production Company Limited and Bangladesh Oil Gas and Mineral Corporation, ICSID Case No. ARB/10/18, Decision on Corruption Claim, 25 February 2019.
Oil Platforms (Iran v. USA), Judgment, ICJ Reports 2003, p. 161.
Philip Morris Asia Limited v. Commonwealth of Australia, PCA Case No. 2012-12, Award on Jurisdiction and Admissibility, 17 December 2015.
Phoenix Action, Ltd. v. The Czech Republic, ICSID Case No. ARB/06/5, Award, 15 April 2009.
Plama Consortium Limited v. Republic of Bulgaria, ICSID Case No. ARB/03/24, Decision on Jurisdiction, 8 February 2005.
Plama Consortium Limited v. Republic of Bulgaria, ICSID Case No. ARB/03/24, Award, 27 August 2008.
Quiborax S.A., Non Metallic Minerals S.A. and Allan Fosk Kaplún v. Plurinational State of Bolivia, ICSID Case No. ARB/06/2, Decision on Jurisdiction, 27 September 2012.
Renée Rose Levy and Gremcitel S.A. v. Republic of Peru, ICSID Case No. ARB/11/17, Award, 9 January 2015.
RSM Production Corporation v. Grenada, ICSID Case No. ARB/05/14, Final Award, 13 March 2009.
Rumeli Telekom A.S. and Telsim Mobil Telekomunikasyon Hizmetleri A.S. v. The Republic of Kazakhstan, ICSID Case No. ARB/05/16, Award, 29 July 2008.
Saba Fakes v. Turkey, ICSID Case No. ARB/07/20, Award, 14 July 2010.
Salini Costruttori S.p.A. and Italstrade S.p.A. v. The Kingdom of Morocco [I], ICSID Case No. ARB/00/4, Decision on Jurisdiction, 31 July 2001.
Salini Costruttori S.p.A. and Italstrade S.p.A. v. The Hashemite Kingdom of Jordan, ICSID Case No. ARB/02/13, Award, 31 January 2006.
Saluka Investments BV v. The Czech Republic, UNCITRAL, Partial Award, 17 March 2006.
Sanum Investments Limited v. The Lao People's Democratic Republic, PCA Case No. 2013-13, Award of Jurisdiction, 13 December 2013.
Sanum Investments Limited v. The Lao People's Democratic Republic, PCA Case No. 2013-13, Award, 6 August 2019.
Sistem Mühendislik Insaat Sanayi ve Ticaret A.S. v. the Kyrgyz Republic, ICSID Case No. ARB(AF)/06/1, Award, 9 September 2009.

South West Africa Cases (Ethiopia v. South Africa; Liberia v. South Africa), First Phase, ICJ Reports 1962, p. 319.
South West Africa Cases (Ethiopia v. South Africa; Liberia v. South Africa), Second Phase, ICJ Reports 1966, p. 6.
Southern Pacific Properties (Middle East) Limited v. Egypt, ICSID Case No. ARB/84/3, Award, 20 May 1992.
Suez, Sociedad General de Aguas de Barcelona, S.A.and Vivendi Universal, S.A. v. Argentine Republic, ICSID Case No. ARB/03/19, Decision on Liability, 30 July 2010.
Swembalt AB, Sweden v. Latvia, UNCITRAL, Award, 23 October 2000.
Technical Medioambientales Tecmed, S.A. v. Mexico, ICSID Case No. ARB(AF)/00/2, Award, 29 May 2003.
Tokios Tokeles v. Ukraine, ICSID Case No. ARB/02/18, Decision on Jurisdiction, 29 April 2004.
Tokios Tokeles v. Ukraine, ICSID Case No. ARB/02/18, Award, 26 July 2007.
TSA Spectrum de Argentina S.A. v. The Argentine Republic, ICSID Case No. ARB/05/5, Award, 19 December 2008.
United States Diplomatic and Consular Staff in Tehran (United States of America v. Iran), ICJ Judgement, ICJ Reports, 1980.
Venezuela Holdings B.V. and others v. The Bolivarian Republic of Venezuela, ICSID Case No. ARB/07/27, Decision on Jurisdiction, 10 June 2010.
Vladislav Kim and others v. The Republic of Uzbekistan, ICSID Case No. ARB/13/6, Decision on Jurisdiction, 8 March 2017.
Waguih Elie George Siag and Clorinda Vecchi v. The Arab Republic of Egypt, ICSID Case No ARB/05/15, Dissenting Opinion of Professor Francisco Orrego Vicuña to the Final Award, 11 May 2009.
Waguih Elie George Siag and Clorinda Vecchi v. The Arab Republic of Egypt, ICSID Case No ARB/05/15, Award, 1 June 2009.
Waste Management, Inc v. Mexico, ICSID Case No ARB(AF)/00/3, Dissenting opinion of Ms Keith Highet, 30 April 2004.
Wena Hotels Limited v. The Arab Republic of Egypt, ICSID Case No ARB/98/4, Award, 8 December 2000.
Wena Hotels Limited v. The Arab Republic of Egypt, ICSID Case No ARB/98/4, Decision on the Application by the Arab Republic of Egypt for Annulment of the Arbitral Award, 28 January 2002.
Westacre Investments Inc. v. Jugoimport-SDRP Holding Co. Ltd and Beogradska Banka, ICC Case No. 7047.
Westinghouse International Projects Company, Westinghouse Elec. S.A. and Barns & Roe Enterprise, Inc. v. National Power Corporation and the Republic of the Philippines, ICC Case No 6401, Preliminary Award.
World Duty Free Company Limited v. The Republic of Kenya, ICSID Case No. ARB/00/7, Award, 4 October 2006.
Yukos Universal Limited (Isle of Man) v. The Russian Federation, PCA Case No. 2005-04/AA227.

The manufacturer's authorised representative in the EU is Springer Nature Customer Service Centre GmbH, Europaplatz 3, 69115 Heidelberg, Germany. If you have any concerns regarding our products, please contact ProductSafety@springernature.com

Printed and bound by CPI Group (UK) Ltd, Croydon, CR0 4YY
28/09/2026
02224088-0005